Community of Strangers

Community of Strangers

A Journal of Discovery in Uganda

A. F. Robertson

LONDON
Scolar Press

SCOLAR PRESS
James Price Publishing Limited
13 Brunswick Centre London WC1N 1AF

2430 Bancroft Way
Berkeley California 94704

First published 1978
This revised edition published 1986
ISBN 0 86967 715 X

Printed in Great Britain by
Whitstable Litho, Whitstable, Kent

Acknowledgements

A book of this kind involves so many debts that it seems almost invidious to single out a few names for thanks.

From the beginning I have been influenced profoundly by the work of Audrey Richards, and much of what may strike the reader as original may be attributed directly or indirectly to her. Detailed acknowledgement in the text would become monotonous, and the best I can do is express my sincere gratitude at the outset.

In the original research I received invaluable help from my Edinburgh supervisors, Malcolm Ruel, Kenneth Little and John Pilgrim. I was also greatly assisted by conversation and correspondence with David McMaster, Martin Southwold, Henry West, Brian Langlands, H. B. Thomas, Michael Twaddle and Jean La Fontaine.

Of many friends at Makerere University I am particularly grateful to Caroline Hutton, Raymond Apthorpe, Simon Charsley, Martin Doornbos, Rainier Arnhold and George Mukulu. My association with the East African Institute of Social Research was of inestimable value.

The style of this book owes a great deal to discussion in a Cambridge seminar which I shared for several years with Esther Goody and a changing group of very able anthropology graduate students.

Many friends have advised and encouraged me while I tried to knock my tale into shape. I am particularly grateful to my wife Francesca, to Barbara Bray, John Dunn, Graham Hough and Lucy Mair.

The enormous debt I owe to the people of Bugerere, and the officials and chiefs who gave me so much help and advice, is self-evident. Sometime I hope to find a more direct way of expressing my gratitude, but in the meantime—thank you Amos, Joseph and Bonny Moses Sekasi.

I have written about the Uganda of the mid-sixties, and it must be apparent that the opinions and actions of the people referred to in this book have no bearing on present circumstances in Uganda. Lest there be any doubt, may I assert that responsibility for what I have written and the way I have written it is mine, and mine alone.

A.F.R. June 1977

A year after this book was first published, Idi Amin was ousted by Tanzanian troops and a small force of Ugandan exiles. Shortly afterwards I renewed contact with Amos Natyera and Bonny Moses Sekasi. Happily, they and other friends were indeed 'still there', but their letters made Bugerere seem small and distant, as though viewed through the wrong end of a telescope. Copies of *Community of Strangers* were received with some excitement, but also with regret that there was no Luganda edition. Bugerere had escaped the worst of the violence which had afflicted Uganda, and Bonny Moses, now 'a father of four handsome sons' declared confidently that 'We are working hand to hand with the new elite Govt. and we expect fruitful future'. He had found employment as a local government health officer and small businessman, and had plans to sell this book locally.

The successive governments of Dr Yosef Lule (a former Vice-Chancellor of Makerere University) and Godfrey Binaisa struggled with the political and economic wreckage of Uganda but eventually, as most people expected or feared, Milton Obote returned to power in 1980. Although he was evidently an older and wiser man, he could do little to re-establish civil order: army atrocities continued with renewed vigour, and civil war became widespread in Uganda. In July 1985 rebel troops under Brigadier General Basilio Olara Okello moved into Kampala, and Obote took refuge in Zambia. Since then the new military regime has sought to make peace with the National Resistance Army, which is still entrenched in the countryside under the leadership of Yoweri Museveni, a veteran of the opposition to Amin.

Once again, as communications degenerate I have lost touch with my friends in Bugerere. I hope most fervently that they have escaped the appalling massacres which have afflicted the region since 1982.

But I also hope that before we are all much older we may be able to meet in tranquility, repair the breach, and resume the process of discovery.

A.F.R. January 1986

For my parents
with gratitude
and affection

Contents

Figures

Maps

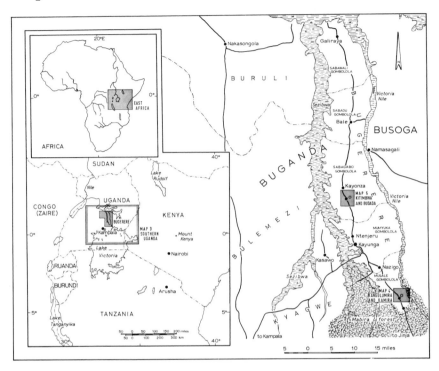

Map 1.   Bugerere, and key to maps 3–5

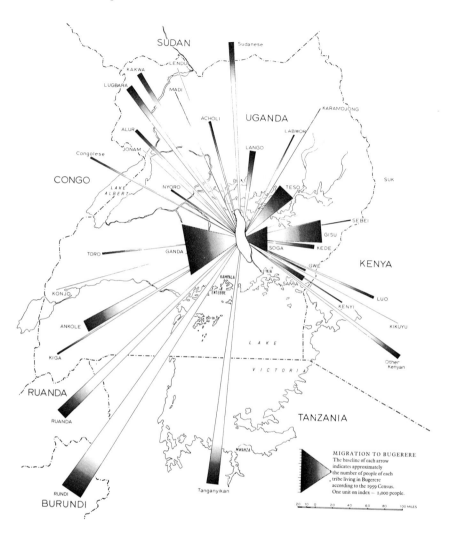

Map 2.   Migration to Bugerere

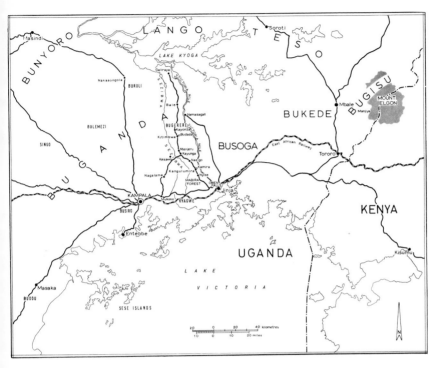

Map 3.   Southern Uganda

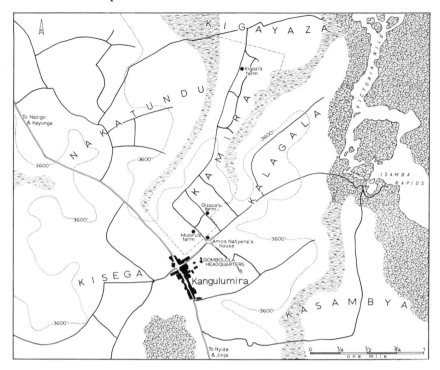

Map 4.   Kangulumira and Kamira

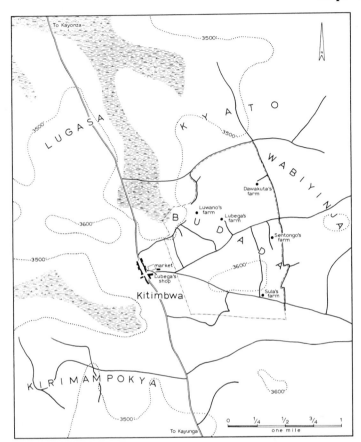

Map 5.   Kitimbwa and Budada

'I marched up the left bank of the Nile at a considerable distance from the water, to the Isamba Rapids, passing through rich jungle and plantain-gardens . . . A small black fly, with thick shoulders and bullet head, infests the place, and torments the naked arms and legs of the people with its sharp stings to an extent that must render life miserable to them. . . . Nango, an old friend, and district officer of the place, first refreshed us with a dish of plantain-squash and dried fish, with pombé. He told us he is often threatened by elephants, but he sedulously keeps them off with charms; for if they ever tasted a plantain they would never leave the garden until they had cleared it out. He then took us to see the nearest falls of the Nile—extremely beautiful, but very confined. The water ran deep between its banks, which were covered with fine grass, soft cloudy acacias, and festoons of lilac convolvuli; whilst here and there, where the land had slipped above the rapids, bared pieces of red earth could be seen, like that of Devonshire; there, too, the waters, impeded by a natural dam, looked like a huge mill-pond, sullen and dark, in which two crocodiles, laving about, were looking out for prey. From the high banks we looked down upon a line of sloping wooded islets lying across the stream, which divide its waters, and, by interrupting them, cause at once both dam and rapids. The whole was more fairylike, wild, and romantic than—I must confess my thoughts took that shape—anything I ever saw outside of a theatre. It was exactly the sort of place, in fact, where, bridged across from one side-slip to the other, on a moonlight night, brigands would assemble to enact some dreadful tragedy.'

John Hanning Speke, *Journal of the Discovery of the Source of the Nile*, London 1863; Everyman Edition, pp. 367–8.

Introduction

After the soldiers' second vengeful visit to Kangulumira the storm broke. Curtains of rain swept through the coffee and banana groves, and the water coursing down the hill towards the Nile cut gullies in the red earth. The roaring of the downpour on the tin roof made it difficult to think, so I settled down in a chair by the doorway and dozed.

When the pale evening sunlight finally broke through, I stepped outside to breathe the cool, fresh air. After any other storm Amos's house would have been alive with voices, the women making hurried preparations for supper and the naked children splashing in the water which still trickled from the eaves. This evening a deathly silence hung over Kangulumira. The town was empty, the houses locked and shuttered. I wondered if I was the only person who had not raced, like the rainwater, down the hill towards the river.

After four days of excitement, defiance and mounting apprehension among the townspeople, the army's assault and the drenching rain seemed to provide the hiatus for which I had been waiting. I opened the metal box in which I had packed the things which were most important to me, and checked through its contents. Here were the notebooks, file cards and interview records, the maps, photographs and official documents which I had collected painstakingly during the past fifteen months. I dreaded that all this might be lost, stolen or confiscated before I left Uganda.

The box was as much as I could carry on the motor cycle, and I had given much thought to what I should pack into the limited space. I found room in one corner for the little barkcloth packet of protection magic which I had bought at Kitimbwa. Now seemed as good a time as any to test its efficacy. I pulled out a large bundle of papers and debated whether or not I should burn them. They were carbon copies of the voluminous correspondence in which I had indulged during my stay in Uganda. I had found the discipline of a fieldwork diary very irksome and had taken to filling out its pages by putting a piece of carbon paper under each letter I wrote.

'Mr Sunday, you are still there!'

The voice at the door startled me. It was Amos, drenched and muddy. He was plainly as relieved to see me as I was to see him, and we grasped each other as if to confirm that we were both, indeed, still there.

I pushed the letters back into the metal box and they remained there, virtually untouched, for ten years. They turned up again while I was moving house in Cambridge, and reading through them for the first time was a strange and enlightening experience. The candour of this correspondence brought to mind people, places and events which I had almost forgotten, and contrasted sharply with the sober and dispassionate data from which I had constructed my doctoral thesis. I saw for the first time with any degree of objectivity my own involvement in the circumstances I had been trying to describe. The letters to my family and friends, to supervisors and fellow students, made it evident that I was more closely involved with the people of Bugerere and their problems than I had previously supposed. At times I seemed almost indistinguishable from the people I had set out to study, a young immigrant attempting to make my way in a strange new society. These letters, which had seemed irrelevant when I was writing my thesis, now seemed to provide the starting point for a book about Bugerere.

The present unhappy plight of the people of Uganda suggests a further reason for writing this book. From the perspective of the outside world, darkness is descending once again on this part of Africa. The Englishman of the 1970s, informed by newspapers and films, may be forgiven for feeling that there is no longer any very clear distinction between the Uganda of today and the Uganda described by Speke more than a century ago:

Reports came today of new cruelties at the palace. Kasoro improved on their off-hand manslaughter by saying that two Kamravionas and two Sakibobos, as well as the Wakungu of Sunna's time, had been executed by the orders of king Mtesa. He told us, moreover, that if Mtesa ever has a dream that his father directs him to kill anybody as being dangerous to his person, the order is religiously kept. . . .*

* John Hanning Speke, *Journal of the Discovery of the Source of the Nile*, 1863; Everyman edition, p. 367.

In drawing attention to ordinary people in the extraordinary circumstances of Bugerere I have tried to present, on balance, an optimistic
picture of how strangers have come together to build new communities and to reconcile the great differences of language, culture and
physical appearance among themselves. I do not believe that the
collapse of the Uganda state has reduced the people of this beautiful
country to despair or depravity. However, it seems that increasingly
they will have been obliged to look inwards to the moral order of
their own villages rather than outwards to their national political
leaders.

I have not attempted to disguise the schisms and hardships, for
these are an inevitable part of all social life. What the people of
Bugerere have achieved is really no more and no less remarkable than
what ordinary people have been achieving all over the world for
millennia: a practical adjustment to one another and to an environment
which is often capricious. There is nothing allegorical about the
growth of Kamira and Budada villages, but there is perhaps something of more general concern to be learned from intimate observation of their progress.

This book records my own efforts to observe and understand.

1 Edinburgh

In 1964 I was twenty-two years old and living as a fractious student with my parents in the southern suburbs of Edinburgh. I had just completed four years of an honours course in Social Anthropology at Edinburgh University and, being otherwise unemployable, had registered as a doctoral candidate. The Edinburgh Anthropology department was a small and friendly place and the prospect of a year's research in Africa seemed a pleasant and exciting way of taking flight from the parental nest.

My decision to make a career in Social Anthropology was probably the first completely independent choice I had ever made. After a dreary school curriculum the prospectus for the Anthropology degree course seemed, to my Scottish Presbyterian mind, wickedly wonderful. The reading list in the University Calendar included White's *Street Corner Society* and Malinowski's *Sexual Life of Savages*. My mind was immediately made up, although my parents had some understandable misgivings; in those days the word 'social' had a certain ideological chilliness about it, and the subject did not seem to carry with it any very clear prospects of being able to earn an honest living.

The undergraduate course in Social Anthropology was an attractive one, allowing us to study psychology, economics, linguistics and, if we wished, such distinctively Scots subjects as Logic-and-Metaphysics and Political Economy. I chose to study phonetics for a year, having been greatly impressed by a famous film of Mrs Uldal's glottis, which was kept in a permanent display unit in the phonetics department. Between classes one might press a button and watch this extraordinary spectacle, opening and closing like a strange sea-creature. As honours students we were also obliged to prepare a short dissertation for our final examination, and were encouraged to base this on original research. I spent an idyllic summer on the small

Spanish Mediterranean island of Formentera, ostensibly studying the initial impact of the tourist boom on the peasant population. The experience was salutary in many respects, not the least of which was a discovery of the difficulty of extracting information about and constructing explanations of social phenomena. I had prepared quite carefully, studying Catalan from a small text book; this turned out to be Classical Catalan, and my limited efforts to use it were convulsingly funny to the Formentereño peasants. I was taken aback to discover that the changing social structure of the island was not immediately obvious. I made some progress by pestering the proprietors of the small inns and hotels, but the farmers themselves proved taciturn. I tried to bribe them with cognac, but they were usually able to outdrink me before I could persuade them to admit that there *was* a social structure and that it might be changing.

In the summer of 1964, after I had graduated, I had some further experience of research, this time working as a sociological interviewer in Sheffield. In a sense this brought me into territory and society even more alien than Formentera. The project was concerned with people about my own age and their experiences in work since leaving school five years previously. In the back-to-back streets of Attercliffe I learned how exacting three hours of conversation with another human being can be, and how each session is a unique drama, even though for the interviewer it may be the hundredth. I made many mistakes; there was nothing in my experience to tell me, as I raised my hand with trepidation to knock on the first door, that only policemen and undertakers use the front door of a Sheffield working-class house.

That autumn my preparations for research in Uganda began in earnest. I considered doing research in India, where I was born, but eventually decided in favour of East Africa, which I had studied for a year as an undergraduate. My research interests reflected my own restless frame of mind, as well as changing approaches in Social Anthropology. Previously anthropologists had tended to concentrate on societies which were both unfamiliar and relatively self-contained; to understand the workings of society they had visited isolated and apparently stable communities on distant Pacific islands and in lonely mountain valleys. Now we were encouraged to think of all societies as continually changing, and to accept that a respectable anthropologist could study urban industrial communities as well as faraway villages. While it was certainly important to understand how a society maintains continuity from generation to generation, it was increasingly important to know more about how it changes. I decided that I wanted to work in a place where there was no reason to suppose that a stable, long-established social order prevailed. More particularly, I wanted to find out how *new* communities established themselves. I wondered if I might find this kind of situation in a squatter community on the margins of one of Africa's rapidly expanding cities. I raked through the monographs, maps and population censuses in the Edinburgh libraries but could see nothing which very clearly fitted my intentions.

For advice I sought out a geographer, Dr David McMaster, who knew East Africa well. Without hesitation he drew out the new atlas of Uganda and opened it at a tribal map. It was covered with 'piegraphs' showing how big a slice of the population of each District was accounted for by people from each East African tribe. He put his finger on one 'pie' which had by far the largest number of different tribal segments. This particular District lay on a narrow strip of land along the west bank of the Victoria Nile, between its Lake Victoria source and where it drains into the marshes of Lake Kyoga some seventy miles further north (see Map 1). 'I would suggest,' he said, 'that you work in Bugerere.' Hearing the name for the first time I noted that the accent was on the second syllable. I must confess that I found both the name and the location unexciting. I suppose I still had vague fantasies about anthropological research in what I assumed to be the style of Malinowski: blue seas and silver sands, with dusky maidens casting leis around my neck. However there was little doubt that, for my declared purposes, Bugerere looked ideal.

I set out at once to discover more about the place. There was a surprising amount of information available, beginning with the observations of Speke on his journey to discover the Lake Victoria source of the Nile. I even spoke to several people who had visited Bugerere, and began to draw together some ideas about the particular theme of my own research.

Although situated at the heart of one of the most fertile and populous parts of Africa it is clear that up to 1952 Bugerere was a very uncongenial place to live. The northern part was infested with Tsetse and the southern part with an even greater pest, aptly named *Simulium damnosum*. 'This little fly', wrote the missionary G. R.

Blackledge in 1902, 'is the means of driving away large numbers of Baganda [from Bugerere] and of course prevents the influx of others.' Locally called the *mbwa* or dog fly, it transmits the parasitic filarial worm *Onchocerca volvulus*, which causes symptoms akin to elephantiasis and may eventually blind its hosts. At best, the fly's irritating bite causes severe local irritation and ulcers. The larvae thrived on weeds trailing in the fast-flowing water of the Victoria Nile, and the forest nearby provided an ideal habitat for the adults. Compared with this pest the mosquitoes, which still abound in the swampy areas around Bugerere, pale into insignificance.

However, the agricultural potential of the area was obvious and in 1952 the construction of the Owen Falls hydro-electric dam near the source of the Nile provided an opportunity to eradicate the *mbwa* fly and open up the countryside around the river for settlement. Using the sluices, DDT was administered to the river water to exterminate the larvae along the banks. Within a matter of weeks, *mbwa* had been effectively wiped out. About the same time a causeway was built across the swamp along the west of Bugerere, and part of an old wartime Bailey bridge from the Thames was erected over the Sezibwa river. The opportunities for growing and selling cash crops were now greatly increased, and settlers came flooding into the untenanted lands from all over East Africa (see Map 2). I recognised many of the names on the atlas map from my reading of the ethnography: there were Basoga from the eastern bank of the Nile, Bagisu from the hills around Mount Elgon, numerous immigrants from the densely populated kingdoms of Ruanda and Burundi, Nilotic people from the Southern Sudan, Alur and Lugbara from the eastern Congo. There were so many people, as different as Japanese are from English, all gathered together into such a confined space within such a short period of time. The censuses told me that where, in 1950, there had been uninhabited forest, settlement ten years later had reached densities greater than one thousand people to the square mile.

Here, with a vengeance, was the sociological problem for which I had been looking. What kind of social order could possibly be emerging in such circumstances? I had seven months in which to contemplate this question, to read everything I could find which seemed remotely relevant, to decide how I was going to organise my research, and to plan for the trip. My Edinburgh supervisors insisted that before I left I should have a clear idea not only about how I should set about my research, but also about the kind of things I would be likely to discover and even the sorts of conclusion I might eventually draw. By the time I had prepared three seminar papers, the project was beginning to feel as if it was all in the bag. I found the large-scale, 1:50,000 topographical maps of the area particularly helpful, and studied them with such care that when I eventually got to Bugerere I had strong feelings of *déjà vu*. They were maps on the human scale, with individual huts marked as pinpoints. I knew that although the maps were not very old they were already very much out of date as far as settlement in Bugerere was concerned, but from them I began to form ideas about where I should live and how I might make my surveys. Another mine of information was a set of documents quaintly entitled *Memoirs of the Research Division of the Uganda Protectorate Department of Agriculture*. These provided special maps of Bugerere showing rainfall, soils, temperature variation, density of settlement and agriculture, the crops grown and even things I had never heard of, such as 'Physiological Potential' and 'Assessments of Land Productivity'. From these I learned that Bugerere contained striking ecological variations along its north-south axis, with 'dark red plastic clays' in the heavily settled southern part, and 'fine yellow sand' a mere seventy miles away in the thinly populated north. Every discovery raised more questions: for example, did particular immigrant tribes prefer particular environments along this ecological spectrum?

In terms of public support for higher education we certainly live in privileged times. Nevertheless it is interesting to reflect that the year I applied to the Scottish Education Department for a research grant, one third of their studentships remained unclaimed. I was awarded a total of £450 per year for three years and, after some negotiation, my fare to and from Uganda 'by the cheapest possible means'. I was not prepared to take the SED too literally on this point and booked a passage on the Braemar Castle to Mombasa, paying myself the premium for a place in a four-berth cabin with a porthole as I thought it unlikely that I could survive in the bowels of the ship. The SED appeared never to have had an anthropologist on its books before, and this made for some difficulties in communication. Laboratory expenses for science students had become an acceptable charge on their well-husbanded funds, but it would have been outrageous to suggest to them that a second-hand motor cycle might be an essential research tool in the African bush. In due course, when the sponsorship of research was reorganised nationally on a disciplinary basis, communications became much easier. At a later date when I was preparing for a year of research in Ghana, my request for funds for 'conventional payments to informants' (i.e. gin) raised no eyebrows.

In the months before my departure I elicited and received a great deal of advice from the cognoscenti about how to survive in Uganda. My mother, with a long experience of rough living as a planter's wife in India, put several items into my trunk with the plea that I should not gruffly turn them out. Each of these, from the pieces of butter muslin to the three large polythene bags, proved invaluable at some later stage. My cousin, who had spent many years in Malawi, exhorted me not to wear shorts as the risk of being confused for an American Peace Corps man was too great. Shortly before I left, the Professor summoned me into his inner sanctum, observed with faint surprise that I was leaving the departmental nest, and offered three further pieces of counsel: remember the old maxim 'take me to your leader'; lay off the local girls, it usually causes bad feeling; and don't be a Boy Scout—above all be sure to have a comfortable bed.

There are many of us who regret that air travel has now virtually replaced slow, leisurely travel across the surface of the earth. Between the departure from home and the impending new life in Uganda, the voyage on the Braemar Castle was a very pleasant hiatus. There was the nostalgic experience of sailing past Formentera one morning, three unexpected days ashore in strike-bound Genoa, sailing through the leeward smoke of Stromboli, and the progress through the Suez canal which evoked childhood memories of passages to and from India. Jet travel is quick and now so very much cheaper but this is poor compensation for the amusing eccentricities and relaxation of ship-board life. Parting company with the Braemar Castle was almost as great a rupture as leaving Edinburgh; the crowds of black faces on the quay at Mombasa and the intense heat came as stern reminders that I was about to set foot on a very different continent.

In the evening as the train wound its way up out of Mombasa the view from my compartment window seemed too unreal to be related to the textbook Africa with which I felt familiar. The single track seemed to pass right through family compounds full of waving children and smells of woodsmoke and supper. With so much to see I regretted the twelve hours of equatorial darkness; next morning the spectacle had changed to racing herds of game and the vast depression of the Rift Valley. As we threaded back and forth over the equator I thought enviously of Winston Churchill who had made the same journey many years before, sitting on a couch strapped to the cowcatcher on the front of the train. At one point we crossed a ravine at the bottom of which ran the slender lines of our own track.

Early next morning I woke to the clatter and spicy smells of Jinja, near Speke's source of the Nile on Lake Victoria. I sat attentively at the window, for we would shortly pass within a few miles to the south of Bugerere. The early morning was misty and overcast; I could see chilly figures in long white garments moving about coughing, or urinating with a curious lack of concern about the passing train. Everywhere there was lush green vegetation, predominantly the broad leaves of banana plants and the darker colour of what I later discovered to be coffee. Here and there I could see mean little houses sitting in patches of bare red earth, square boxes of mud with tin roofs and shuttered windows.

As we wound our way through the low hills towards Kampala the sun brightened the landscape, but as feelings of apprehension and nostalgia gripped me, my eyes seemed unable to absorb very much of the busy and colourful world passing by.

2 Kampala

In April 1965 Kampala was, for some, the Paris of Africa, a small cosmopolitan city set in a summer garden. Scattered around its periphery were a number of African clubs and bars—'Satellite', 'Susannah', 'High Life' and 'Stratocruise'—each full of cold beer, electric guitars and coloured lights. Congolese and Kenyan musicians in cotton suits and winkle-picker shoes played bounding East African music and reproduced international hit records with almost phonographic precision. In the commerce, cuisine and architecture of Kampala the Asian presence was unmistakable, and it is hard to imagine the city now that this vital part of its population has been evicted. For some, Kampala was also the Rome of Africa, built on seven hills, maybe more, each of them dominated by an important building—the Anglican and Catholic cathedrals, the Kibuli mosque, the palace of the Kabaka of Buganda, the army barracks, the radio station.

From these hills one might catch a glimpse of Lake Victoria, that shallow inland sea which helped to give Kampala the lush, temperate climate which British expatriates liked to call 'perpetual English summer'. At nearby Entebbe, on the lake shore, three generations of officials had sailed, fished, golfed and administered the Protectorate of Uganda, and since Independence in 1963 successive heads of state have continued to make it their home.

In 1965, Kampala was the capital of two African countries: the newly independent state of Uganda, and the long-established Kingdom of Buganda. The latter was ruled by its urbane, Cambridge-educated Kabaka, Sir Edward Mutesa, whose green and pleasant realm extended around the northern shores of the lake. His two million subjects regarded themselves as politically and culturally quite distinct from the remaining two-thirds of the population of Uganda, and had struggled to secure for themselves a special, quasi-federal status in the Independence constitution. Kampala boasted two legislative assembly buildings, the *Bulange* of the Kabaka's government, and the Uganda Parliament, a parting gift of the British. Apolo Milton Obote, the Prime Minister of Uganda, was a man whose origins, education, experience and aspirations were quite different from those of the Kabaka, Sir Edward Mutesa. He came from a chiefly family in Lango, a northern district as different from the Kingdom of Buganda as Turkey might be from England. Obote's mission was to unite a new nation whose regional and cultural components were extremely varied; in the northeast, tall naked men herded cattle on the dusty plains of Karamoja, and in the southwest, stocky Bantu-speaking people farmed the crowded hill-terraces of Kigezi. The dominant position of Buganda posed the greatest single obstacle to national unity and inevitably the years following Independence brought a trial of strength between Obote and the Kabaka.

Near the end of my stay in Uganda I was to see Obote's triumph, the Kabaka's flight to exile in London, and the abolition of the Kingdom of Buganda. In Kampala the rising fortunes of Apolo Milton Obote were much in evidence, for example in the new Apollo Hotel, which Kampala wags referred to as the Milton Hilton. As the new President of Uganda, Obote was confronted with a problem very similar to the one I had chosen to study in the villages of Bugerere: how can order and prosperity be established in a population which is so very diverse in almost every respect? Dr Obote's failure to solve this and other problems brought his own exile to neighbouring Tanzania in 1971, but changing the regime and the name of the Apollo hotel (now the International) has in no way relieved the deepening schisms within the Republic of Uganda.

After its majestic journey through East Africa the railway creeps into Kampala along a valley filled with shacks and sidings (see Map 3). Waiting to meet me at the station was Caroline Hutton, a sociologist whom I had met at home the previous summer. With practised efficiency she extricated my baggage and superintended the loading of it into her car. We drove along the main street, crowded with Asian shops, and down the broad avenue at the foot of Makerere hill where fruit bats hung in clusters from the tall barkcloth trees.

The askari on duty at the main gate of Makerere University hovered suspiciously at the car window and then waved us through into the compound of the East African Institute of Social Research nearby. Caroline was a Research Fellow of the Institute and I had arranged a more humble Associateship there during my stay in Uganda. I was given the key to a small Institute flat with the warning that newcomers were easy prey for the ever-vigilant burglars. From the discreetly barred windows I could look down to the red tiled roofs of the library and offices, the flame trees and frangipani and the hills of the city. The attentive Caroline, without whom I should have been quite lost, directed me to Bhimji's grocery store at the foot of Makerere hill. There I found everything I might expect in a well-stocked Edinburgh shop and much else besides. There were cardboard cushions of fresh milk, packets of cornflakes, Courvoisier brandy, needles for Primus stoves and coriander seeds.

During my first week at EAISR I met my local supervisor, Raymond Apthorpe, and the community of researchers on whom my work and welfare came to depend so much. To start with, their experience and confidence made me feel very green and slightly resentful. On the second day I put on a tie and went for lunch with Ralph Tanner, the Institute's Director. He agreed soberly that my funds were perilously low and said that he would write some appeals to Edinburgh on my behalf. He pointed out that I was more likely to survive financially out in the field than in Kampala. The fact that I was in Bugerere ten days later was more a tribute to the Institute and its Administrator Simon Musoke, than my own will or skill.

The first task was to get official permission to undertake research, a process which involved a slow, downward penetration of the government hierarchy, starting with the Ugandan Ministry of Education. For two days Simon Musoke led me from desk to desk, picking up letters of authorisation and introduction. In the offices of the Buganda Kingdom Government he was greeted with warmth and respect and as we stepped over other supplicants in the crowded corridors I knew that I was getting privileged treatment; it was only after struggling with the bureaucracy myself in other countries that I came to recognise just how expeditiously my credentials were established in Buganda.

My next task was to present my letters at the East Mengo District Office, and at the headquarters of the Bugerere Saza (county) itself. On my third or fourth day in Kampala I was introduced to George Mukulu, a mature sociology student at the University who had family connections in Bugerere. Thin, bespectacled George kindly agreed to escort me on my first sortie, and I prevailed on the complaisant Caroline to drive us the 150-mile round trip. The fact that it was Easter weekend did nothing to allay my impatience, and as we set out both of them expressed some doubts that Good Friday was a suitable day to transact official business.

The East Mengo District Office was closed, so we proceeded from Mukono up the new Italian-built highway towards the Sezibwa river (see Map 3). The transition from Kyaggwe county into Bugerere was unremarkable. As we drove into the trading township of Kayunga I looked for the exciting, heterogeneous new world I had come to anticipate, but I could not find it. Kayunga was like any of the other predominantly Asian *duka* trading centres we had sailed through on the main road, full of open-fronted shops, Pepsi-Cola and Mobil signs, litter and strutting chickens. Two miles away at Ntenjeru the Saza headquarters was deserted. Back in Kayunga George set about finding somewhere for me to live. He introduced me to a friend-of-a-friend, and over glasses of beer in one of the local 'hotels' we debated how much I should pay for the rent of a room in a newly-built house. The proprietor extolled its amenities and the price crept up and up until we came to the roof. There wasn't one, not yet. It was getting late, and I gloomily agreed with George and Caroline that I should have to return to Kayunga on a more propitious day.

I was now recognised at the Institute as something of a charitable cause, and Simon Musoke raided the store for field equipment for me. Some means of transport was my most pressing need. The news that I was to be paid £80 for an article on Formentera prompted me to go out in search of a secondhand motor cycle. At one of the main dealers I bought a 350cc BSA for £150. It had been rebuilt after a road accident and its owner had proved either unable or unwilling to reclaim it. As I wobbled off in search of licence and insurance the disadvantages of knowing nothing whatever about motor cycles began to dawn on me. The frame had apparently not recovered from the collision, and at certain speeds the wheels would struggle to bring themselves into alignment, thumping dangerously. It needed constant attention; I still have bad dreams about some of my longer rides, and about cack-handed village mechanics enthusiastically tearing the engine to pieces, cold-chiselling the bolts loose and stepping back onto small vital parts spread over the earth around them. By the time I sold it I knew each pin, cog and nut by everything but its proper name, and eventually I could put my fingers into the hot, silent metal with the familiarity of a soldier who is made monotonously to strip and reassemble his gun.

For my second visit to Bugerere George Mukulu took me firmly in hand. He arranged the hire of the Institute's van and drove me briskly to Kayunga. First he introduced me to a respectable but unemployed schoolteacher who he felt might become my assistant and interpreter while I settled down in Bugerere. We then set out to inspect other lodgings, this time a room at the back of a bar. We stepped off the cracking crust of tarmac which ran through the town, over a ditch full of green slime, and up a bank of red earth to a small grubby building plastered with drink advertisements. At thirty shillings a month I was assured that I had a bargain, but I said rather sourly that I would have to think about it.

We then drove to the county headquarters, and once again found it deserted. Eventually we raised a clerk, with whom I left my letters. He said that he would try to arrange for me to stay for a few days in the small rest house in the Saza compound. He pointed out that there I would have an askari to protect me from the *kondos*. George informed me mildly that *kondos* were armed brigands.

I was finding my introduction to Bugerere discouraging, and as the shillings clocked up on the milometer of the Institute's van, my malaise deepened. The empty government compound at Ntenjeru seemed as inhospitable as the black crowds in Kayunga. To cheer me up, George said that he would take me into the *real* Bugerere to visit his uncle. As we bounced on and on through the banana and coffee trees I could discern neither social order nor social disorder, and began to wonder how much I really cared.

At length we pulled up in front of a large square tin-roofed house made of mud and reeds, faced with cement. I sat glaring at the circle of snotty-nosed children which quickly formed around the van, while George discovered that his uncle was not at home. I opened the van door and the children fled, screaming '*muzungu*'—'white man'. George's aunt did not need to be told what a visitor from the city really wanted, and they set off with several of the larger children into the banana plantation. They re-emerged some time later laden with stems of *matoke*, the green banana, staple food of Buganda. With the Institute's van set low on its springs, and part of our mission at least accomplished, we crept cautiously back towards the main road to Kampala. George told me, unnecessarily, that Bugerere had become the principal supplier of this commodity to the city. I could already see that survival would depend on my accustoming myself to it. George gave me a hand of matoke for my supper and without much enthusiasm I chopped off the tarry skins and boiled the fruit to a flavourless pulp. I concluded that there must be more to preparing matoke than was immediately obvious.

Next day Simon Musoke presented me with my bill for hiring the van. My despondency over this was to some extent balanced by an unexpected windfall: on opening a wardrobe in my Institute flat I found it full of empty beer bottles. Gleefully I took them down to Bhimji's and claimed the cash deposit. That evening I was accosted by an outraged steward with extravagant ideas about the value of his plundered cache. Although I received much kind hospitality, life in Kampala was indeed proving expensive. I tried to resist the attraction of the nightclubs and the menus of Christo's Three Star Restaurant, and concentrated my time and my resources on collecting maps, equipment and provisions.

In the early afternoon of Sunday 25 April the exploited Caroline drove my possessions to Ntenjeru, and I followed on my motor cycle. Leaving the Institute at Kampala was very like leaving the ship at Mombasa, cutting another link with home and things familiar. About thirty-five miles from the city the heavens opened and my red shirt bled into my white trousers. The motor cycle coughed to a standstill and I shoved it into a small, muddy village. The amateur mechanics clustered round it attentively.

3 Ntenjeru

The county headquarters at Ntenjeru sat in a meadow of scythed grass in one shady corner of which stood the rest house. It was a small concrete cube with a tin roof, and beside it stood a latrine, a water tank and a smaller concrete box in which Sam Kasajja was billeted. Shortly after my arrival he presented himself to me with much stamping and saluting. He wore a red fez, well-starched khaki shirt and shorts, puttees wound round and round his thin legs, and big red boots. Explaining that he was my guardian angel he plunged into his hut and reappeared waving a farmer's machete. He told me graphically how he proposed to despatch the kondos. During the next few weeks kondos were not much on my mind but it was reassuring to have him at hand, singing, starching and polishing all day long. The only other sounds of life were the cooing of pigeons and the persistent chiming of a tiny blue bird in the trees around us. The rest house was completely bare apart from a large cabinet with wire mesh doors; a variety of insects seemed to have taken possession of it so I chose not to investigate too closely. Having practised at Makerere I set up my own possessions speedily: the camp bed and mosquito net, collapsible washstand, stove, table and folding chairs, the oil lamp and my books and papers. I boiled some matoke and spooned it down with some vegetable soup out of a packet. The mosquitoes then drove me to bed, where I lay listening to the news from the General Overseas Service of the BBC on a tiny transistor radio which I had bought on the ship.

I rose at one o'clock next morning, opened the shutters and let the bright sunlight stream in. One o'clock in the Ganda timetable is, quite sensibly, sunrise, translating to approximately 7.00 a.m. East African Standard Time. The morning was fresh and invigorating; as I breakfasted on sweet green oranges, bread and coffee, I began to feel marvellously optimistic.

With my Professor's advice about seeking out the chief very much

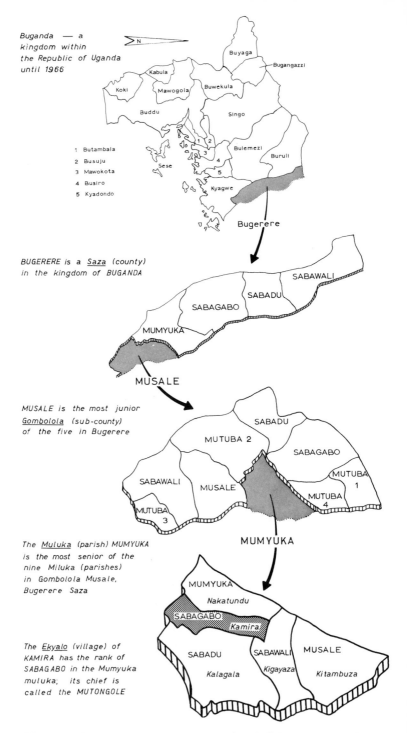

Buganda — a kingdom within the Republic of Uganda until 1966

1 Butambala
2 Busuju
3 Mawokota
4 Busiro
5 Kyadondo

BUGERERE is a <u>Saza</u> (county) in the kingdom of BUGANDA

MUSALE is the most junior <u>Gombolola</u> (sub-county) of the five in Bugerere

The <u>Muluka</u> (parish) MUMYUKA is the most senior of the nine Miluka (parishes) in Gombolola Musale, Bugerere Saza

The <u>Ekyalo</u> (village) of KAMIRA has the rank of SABAGABO in the Mumyuka muluka; its chief is called the MUTONGOLE

Figure 1.   The political hierarchy and territorial divisions in Buganda

in mind, I strode out across the grass to pay my respects at the Saza headquarters. The Saza chief's office was already crowded, but as usual I was ushered to the head of the queue. The young clerk who escorted me opened the door and dropped to his knees. With what I thought were swift anthropological reflexes I did likewise. The chief waved me to a chair with an embarrassed smile. His figure, built to heroic proportions, was packed into a dark suit. He sat behind a desk cluttered with files, dockets, penstands, a telephone, and a large bell for summoning his staff. He welcomed me with great charm and, pointing to the kneeling clerk, explained: 'This is our custom, when I sit here I am the Kabaka.' As I later discovered, even the lowliest village chief in Buganda should be accorded the respect due to the king himself when he acts in an official capacity. There is the intriguing corollary that the Kabaka should never enter one of his courts when it is sitting, for to do so would produce the untenable situation of a king coming into his own presence.

Waving my letter of introduction, the Saza chief declared: 'We are ready for your work.' He explained how information about my presence was already filtering down through the hierarchy of chiefs in Bugerere. I have tried to show on the accompanying diagram (Figure 1) how this long-established pattern of political divisions and subdivisions works in Buganda. At each level one finds the same titles, in order: Mumyuka, Sabaddu, Sabagabo, Sabawali, Musale and then Mutuba I, II, III and so on. In the past these divisions had military as well as administrative implications, and the maxim that a chief rules people rather than land still persists.

The Saza chief had already informed his five *gombolola*, or subcounty chiefs, of my plans. Mumyuka, the most senior of these, had his offices in Kayunga, and the newest and most junior *gombolola* was Musale, in the extreme south. The creation of Musale out of part of Mumyuka in 1953 illustrates the flexibility of the Ganda political divisions. As population increases and spreads outwards into new territory, so new village, parish, gombolola and even Saza units are created. Each of the five gombolola chiefs was supposed to tell his subordinate parish, *Muluka*, chiefs about me. These chiefs constituted the lowest level of the salaried, civil servant pyramid, but below them were the *batongole* (*mutongole* in the singular), the village chiefs on whom the whole system ultimately depended. Although they did not receive salaries they were obliged to act as fiscal agents, electoral officers, health, social welfare and soil conservation officials, and so on; indeed, anything which involved the relationship between the people and the government concerned the village chiefs. It was sobering to reflect that, if other more pressing interests did not interrupt the flow of communication, the entire Bugerere population of a little over one hundred thousand might eventually be prepared to meet me.

By the time the chief had explained this intricate political structure to me, the questions I proposed to ask him about order and disorder all seemed a little superfluous. He agreed that the growth of a society consisting of so many different kinds of people was a matter of great interest, and encouraged me to return to discuss matters with him when I had made some progress. He then waved at the young clerk who was shifting from knee to knee on the hard concrete floor: 'This is Godfrey, he will assist you while you settle in Bugerere.' Happy to have the problem of an assistant so swiftly resolved, I took Godfrey back to the rest house to explain to him what I proposed to do during the next few weeks, and how I hoped he would help me.

Godfrey was a round-faced eighteen-year-old, very respectful and anxious to please. He had had a patchy secondary school education, and seemed to find my frenetic plans to impose conceptual order on Bugerere a little bewildering. I told him that I wanted to go out and interview my first victim that very afternoon. We discussed the way I should be introduced and the list of questions I proposed to use, painstakingly prepared in Kampala with the assistance of George Mukulu. I explained to Godfrey that my knowledge of the Luganda language was still negligible, and that I should depend on him not only as an interpreter but as a tutor. I then pulled out my large-scale map of the Kayunga area and spread it on the table. I explained that since the map had been drawn many more villages and homesteads than were marked must have been established. My purpose was to find out who these people were and what experiences they had had. I proposed to spread my enquiries over an area of about sixteen square miles. I pointed out that the settlement pattern was not nucleated into compact villages, but that the houses were scattered all over the landscape. I had to find a scientific way of picking a representative sample of households, and I explained to Godfrey the ingenious method I had devised: around each intersection of the horizontal and lateral gridlines on the map I had drawn a small circle.

We would proceed by motor cycle to each of these points, about half a mile apart, and interview the head of the nearest homestead. I put my finger on a circle near Ntenjeru and declared: 'this is where we shall go this afternoon'.

Godfrey was despatched to a quiet corner to commit my introduction to memory. He was still mumbling it as he climbed onto the back of the motor cycle at 5.00 p.m. (eleven o'clock Ganda time), by which time we hoped that our victim would have finished his day's work. Our trajectory took us near to Kayunga and there, virtually on the gridline intersection as near as we could judge, stood the familiar square tin-roofed house. Under a low thatched shelter to one side a woman was sitting by a charcoal stove preparing matoke. I encouraged Godfrey to make the running, and he slowly advanced towards her. She came over and sat at his feet, and a long exchange commenced. Ganda greetings are formal and copious, and like English greetings have the great virtue of conveying no hard information. However they must be allowed to run their full course before conversation proper may begin. Eventually she called the master of the house and produced tiny folding chairs for us to sit on. He emerged, wearing the white, nightshirt-like *kanzu* favoured by the Ganda, and a threadbare grey sports jacket. He was tall, middle-aged, and looked formidably dour. He held my fingertips briefly between his, and the greetings began again: 'Is the Lake calm?'; 'Thank you for your endeavours'; and so on, until they tapered off into a series of *eh* sounds. He then eyed Godfrey sceptically as he launched into his introduction.

Parts of it I recognised: I had come from Scotland and was now working through Makerere University, I hoped to discover enough about Bugerere to be able to write a book. Other bits sounded less familiar, and when I recognised the ominous word 'secret' I chipped in and asked Godfrey to translate a few simple sentences, one by one. Our victim's bloodshot eyes were still fastened on Godfrey's damp face, then with a small gesture he called for silence.

He then embarked on a long interrogation of his own, the questions and answers going slowly round and round the triangle. The anthropologist Margaret Mead once observed that a warm smile is the most useful fieldwork tool. I gave him a warm smile. The bloodshot eyes fixed on it expressionlessly.

After explaining in many different ways precisely who I was and what practical use my research might be to *him*, I felt the ball was slowly returning to my court. I edged my way cautiously into what I hoped were some of the more bland questions on my list. Gradually I extracted from him that he was a Ganda and that he had come to Bugerere from neighbouring Kyaggwe in 1950 to work as a clinic orderly at Ntenjeru. He was now retired on a small pension and rented about four acres of land. Surreptitiously I drew a small note-pad from my shirt pocket and scribbled in it as he spoke. He was married and had six children, and he hired two Ruandan labourers for a few hours each day to look after his four cows and weed his cotton. He warmed to my questions about how much he spent on his children's education, but when I asked him how much he earned, his gaze hardened again. I felt the time had come to call it a day. As we took our leave he asked me if he could come and see me at the rest house. He wanted to prepare a list of questions like mine and buy a little notebook to jot down my answers. Godfrey and I took refuge in a bar in Kayunga to recover from what we felt had been a baptism of fire.

When I woke next morning to Sam Kasajja's singing I decided that our interviews needed more careful rehearsal and stage-management. During that day I worked back and forth over the routine with Godfrey. I made him translate his own Luganda transla-tions back into English to discover mistakes and unsuspected nuances of meaning. I pretended to be a hostile informant and barked awk-ward questions at him. We reduced the introduction to bare essen-tials and rearranged the order of the questions. At 4.00 p.m. we set out grimly on the motor cycle for our next gridline intersection. After some discussion we settled on a small, decrepit house with shuttered windows. An old woman was sitting under the eaves on a raffia mat, occasionally hissing at the chickens which were scratching among a few handfuls of coffee beans drying in the sun. She went through the greetings with us in a quavering voice. Godfrey asked where the master of the house was and she said that he was in Paradise. She then said that she was poor and destitute and that it was a happy chance that God had sent someone to talk to her. She nodded vaguely as Godfrey parroted our introduction, and replied with a catalogue of her afflictions. Adopting a bedside manner I asked her about her former home in the north of Bugerere, her family and her small farm. In her answers she expatiated on her illnesses, demanding remedies

An interview in Bugerere. Joseph is sitting on my right

and advice. Abruptly, she declared she was tired, but before dismissing us she asked querulously why we had not brought an old woman some sugar for her tea. Thereafter I took to carrying bags of sugar and tea, strictly for distribution to the elderly.

Next morning I wrote out an account of interview number two, and the spring snapping it into my neat black file was the music of progress and order. I made a few additional comments in volume one of my field notebook, and in my diary brooded over what I had achieved. So far it seemed doubtful who was interviewing whom. Other researchers had warned me that the Ganda were hard work, at least until one got to know them well. What, I wondered, was the most efficient way of making their close acquaintance?

To our delight, the next two gridline intersections yielded young and enthusiastic householders who answered all our questions clearly and frankly, took us on tours of their farms, asked questions about life in Britain, and gave us cups of sweet milky tea. Greedily I collected from them their motives for coming to Bugerere and their attitudes to life there. I even asked them for advice about how I might proceed, advice which then and thereafter was of the greatest importance to my research tactics. To add to the feast of information they pressed on us gifts of eggs and sweet bananas, and asked if they might come and visit me at the rest house. Although gratified I felt just a little uneasy about my capacity to cope with the reciprocal flow of attention and hospitality which I was initiating.

Several days later, looking back over nine interviews, I was concerned to discover an apparent flaw in my scientific selection procedure: all of them were Ganda, although the census told me that Ganda constituted barely a third of the Bugerere population. It occurred to me that so far I had concentrated on the area around Kayunga, and the time had come to switch to a more recently-settled area. A mile or two further north and east I began to meet people from Ruanda, Burundi and from Busoga on the opposite bank of the Nile, but in the lottery of the gridline intersections the Ganda still predominated. This affected my strategy, for I was still unsure which language I should invest precious time and limited talent in learning. I wondered whether, in such a diverse East African population, Swahili would prove to be the *lingua franca*, but it became apparent that so strong was the political and administrative presence of the Ganda that theirs was the language of the new community. I had started learning Luganda in Edinburgh from a small primer and a Linguaphone record, and at Ntenjeru I practised in the mornings with Godfrey. Afterwards, while I busied myself with my reports, Godfrey wrote exercises in English on a number of useful topics: 'The typical Ganda house', 'Marriage in Buganda' and so on. He was unenthusiastic about domestic architecture ('I can't convice you about the chichen [kitchen] because I am no longer a woman') but warmed to his own biography ('My family was too poor and unhappy at first because of my father's love of intoxicating drink'). On these efforts, which I snapped into another file, I wreaked my revenge for his mirth over my Luganda. A small difference of stress in the word *amazi* was the difference between water and shit, and Godfrey would wait with his face contorted for me to fall into the trap.

My limited ability to communicate exacerbated the lonely seclusion of the rest house, and I came to look forward to the afternoon excursions into people's homes. I also became obsessive about international news, constructing my day around morning and evening bulletins on the radio. I suppose it is a natural response for people who feel isolated to reach out into the world in this way. On the occasions I felt particularly gloomy I would look up at the sky; it seemed so much more massive in Africa than in Britain, with its deep blue and mountainous clouds. I was intrigued to discover that newcomers to Bugerere other than myself could find it a source of consolation; the new alien surroundings to which one was tied, and home, out of sight over the horizon, were both embraced by this same immense vault.

One afternoon about a week after my arrival, when Godfrey and I were setting out for another gridline intersection, I was surprised to see a white man bounding past on the pillion of a motor scooter. Although all white men begin to look alike in these circumstances I was sure I had recognised Professor Raymond Apthorpe, my Makerere supervisor. We raced off in pursuit. He dismounted, thanked the scooterist for the lift, and said brightly that he had come to visit me. Godfrey was astonished that so lofty a figure should choose to travel in this mundane way, but it transpired that his car, full of Institute people, had lost its way and Raymond had thumbed a lift to the Saza headquarters to sort things out. It was very gratifying to see them and we had a jolly party, drinking tea out of a strange collection of receptacles.

Every day brought at least one visitor to the rest house. There was Issa Kiwanuka, an Afro-Asian youth who gave me an intriguing picture of the social isolation of the Asian trading community at Kayunga and the periodic outbursts of African hostility to their infamous commercial zeal. Issa Kiwanuka represented an incongruous unison of the two groups and accordingly suffered acutely from identity problems. Throughout my stay in Bugerere misfits of all kinds would gravitate to my door, a source of instruction in such cases as Issa, but more often an embarrassment. Issa Kiwanuka introduced me to Popatlal Savina, a patriarch of the Indian community in Kayunga. He came to Kampala from Bombay in 1928, via a network of family connections which had been laid down since labour was imported from India to build the East African Railway at the turn of the century. Scraping together capital, Popatlal moved out to the trading posts of Kasawo and Nagalama in Kyaggwe, and from there to Kayunga in 1931. First he rented a small shop, selling and repairing bicycles, and his business slowly expanded into his present general wholesaling enterprise. This assured him a position of power and patronage within the Asian community and in Kayunga at large. A rather incongruous figure, squatting in his dhoti amid stacks of transistor radios and sacks of grain, receipt books and tinkling tills, he described the privations of the early days. Stock had to be brought across the Sezibwa by canoe; he had to suffer the plague of insects, family tragedies and fluctuations in commodity prices. Although the veteran of several trade boycotts, he still sold with a smile and bought with a sneer.

Another visitor to the rest house announced himself by letter in somewhat florid French: 'I have the honour to request you to permit me to ask you to give me work in your establishment. My problem is that I am poor and that I cannot work for the Baganda who don't pay up, and so I remain poor. I beg you to take my poverty into your charge and to see if you can redeem me from my misery. I am sure and certain that I will work in whatever way you wish. Be assured of the blessing of your poor orphan Claudien Kabuguma.' On my request he came to see me, a tall thin-faced boy dressed in drainpipe trousers, winkle-picker shoes and Robin Hood hat. I offered him a cigarette which he accepted and smoked inexpertly. I explained to him that although I was the only European resident in Bugerere I was not, as he thought, an estate owner. He explained that he came from a noble tutsi family in Ruanda and was a refugee from the bloody revolution which had swept his country three years previously. He had escaped to Buganda, but was soon lost in an ocean of low-caste Hutu immigrant labourers from Ruanda. Many hundreds of thousands of them had been working for Ganda farmers for decades, returning home each year to their poor and overcrowded country with their tiny wages. Nothing Claudien could tell the Ganda about his education and background could persuade them that he was in any way exceptional to the common run of Ruandan labourers. I told him that I was a student, and that in my way I was also hard-up. Asphyxiated by his cigarette he staggered outside for some fresh air. When he had recovered I told him that in the meantime I would pay him five shillings each for as many letters as he cared to write me, describing his experiences both in the past and the present. During the next two weeks I collected a short but vivid account of his experiences:

Since my birth until the destruction of our Kingdom I did not know the meaning of poverty and misfortune; but here I am now, miserable on account of our cursed country and our deposed race. My father was of the princely race (Tutsi), and during our happy days we were rich. There were four children in my father's house. My father was a sub-chief and we had four herds of cattle each with its herdsmen. O Ruanda, happy country, noble country, hopeful country before the revolution! With the winding rivers and the beautiful mountain ranges, volcanoes, fertile valleys—I cannot think of it without weeping. I shall never be able to forget Ruanda.

Before the death of our King, Charles Rudahigiru, the Belgians were telling the Bahutu people that the Kingdom is not as good as the Republic, and that they wanted eventually to turn Ruanda into a Republic. The Bahutu and the Belgians decided together on the Republic. They signed to the effect that when the Ruandan King died no one should rule in his place. Two months later the Ruandan King died of poison; the princes and all the Royal Family acknowledged his little brother Kigeli V as King. The war began that very day. Guns fired day and night; a vast number died and others were scattered to other countries. Most were trapped and were put to death with swords or bullets. Then they set up the Republic.

At that time I was at school. I heard it said that my father was dead and that my family had been killed in the battle. That day the blood flowed like the waters of a river. I was at school in Burundi, and the government there ordered everyone to go back to their own country. The Congolese went to their country, and the Bahutu Ruandans to Ruanda, but all the Batutsi Ruandan children were afraid to return to Ruanda as the revolution was not yet over. One of my teachers gave me 500 francs and I went down to the south of Burundi and into Tanganyika where I found work with the Catholic Fathers. When I got my hands on my wages I went off to a refugee camp to look for my parents. I never found them.

I pressed on into Buganda. I met some people from back home, these were not my relatives but some of our former neighbours. There were a lot of us, some working in Masaka and others at the Mission in Buddu; there were even some who traded in merchandise like tobacco, bananas and so on. All together, there were around eighty Tutsi people but not all living in the one camp. Only the bachelors lived together, two or three in a hut. Eventually I came to Kayunga where I was told there was money.

Kayunga is a small town which has lately grown and progressed on account of agricultural produce, but this is not much of an advantage because the rich blacks and the Indians don't pay as much as they should. It is rare for a worker around here to get his hands on as much as 60 or 70 shillings a month. Walking about in the evening here you find youths, prostitutes and above all the drunks who never let up all night. There are many Ruandans here in Kayunga, although there are more Barundi. We would like to get together on Sunday evenings to discuss our country Ruanda, but we do not have the right to and it is impossible to get permission from the government. The government doesn't like this kind of get-together.

One night I went to visit my Democratic Party politician friend. When I got there he started to chat politics, and eventually asked me why I had not joined the DP. I replied something like this: 'I came here as a refugee and I can not push myself into the politics of a nation which is not my own.' There is no alternative but to say this, but it would be truer to say that there are far too many politicians among us Ruandans.

My dear friend, save me as quickly as possible from the following three things: (1) government tax; (2) rent (lodgings); (3) nakedness (clothes in rags). In any event it is essential that I find work as soon as possible; here at Kayunga the police in the town are working night and day to book those who have not yet paid poll tax. Secondly, I have not yet paid rent for my lodgings; and my clothes are just about worn out.

After five letters I received no more. Thereafter I was frustrated in all my efforts to trace him.

By comparison my only real problem, an attack of toothache, seemed extremely trivial. With a swollen jaw I walked to the Ntenjeru clinic one morning, and as usual I was escorted past the ailing, the lame and the pregnant to the head of the queue. The orderly looked at me doubtfully and produced a large pair of rusty pliers from a drawer. I turned tail and fled to Kampala where, at the splendid Mulago hospital, a charming young lady from Birmingham dug out an abcessed tooth. I had to go back for further treatment, and I wondered vaguely if my problem was a psychosomatic urge to return to the sanctuary of Kampala.

At Ntenjeru I lived frugally, calculating that two shillings' worth of matoke provided staple for nine days. By contrast the motor cycle seemed a wild extravagance. Information about my culinary technique spread quickly from a shocked Sam Kasajja to the Saza headquarters, and I began shamelessly to receive small gifts of food from the staff as well as from my interview informants. Each morning a can of milk from the Saza chief's cows was delivered to my doorstep. One afternoon two maidens with cooking knives appeared shyly at my window. They introduced themselves as Florence and Beatrice and explained that their father, the Saza chief, had sent them to prepare my lunch for me. As it was already 3.00 p.m. and I had not yet accustomed myself to Ganda eating habits, I had to tell them that I had fed. Over a cup of tea we discussed Jim Reeves and Elvis Presley and then they returned to tell their father that my floor needed sweeping. Next morning as I was having breakfast I saw a procession of government prisoners winding across the grass towards me, armed with brushes, mops and shovels. Under the stentorian directions of Sam Kasajja they gave me the most thorough spring-clean.

With Sam Kasajja I developed a friendly rapport, and we even slipped off furtively together to a nearby shebeen on a couple of occasions. As he changed back and forth from his starched uniform to his civvies our relationship vacillated between the formal and the informal. One morning a piece of paper came rustling under my door: 'Sir my brother has come give me ten shillings Sir for repay pay day with respect Sam Kasajja.' While he paced slowly down the path I pushed an envelope under his door: 'Herewith ten shillings, greet your brother, no trouble, Mr Sunday.' Early in my stay Godfrey and the people we met had settled on this pious rendering of my first name, Sandy. I remained Mr Sunday throughout my stay in Bugerere.

My antics gave Sam Kasajja frequent cause for perplexity. Simon Musoke at the Institute had equipped me with a canvas bath which held itself up by the pressure of the water it contained. Experimenting early in my stay, I drew off several buckets from the rainwater tank and poured them in. Anticipating a refreshing and leisurely bath, I stepped in but accidentally trod on the edge; in an instant the entire bath was empty. Sam Kasajja was alarmed to see a sheet of water race out from under my door and over the doorstep. He was moved to scold me for this prodigious waste of our valuable supply of water, telling me that Bugerere had been suffering from drought for several weeks. Thereafter I abandoned the bath and became as fanatical in my conservation of water as anyone. I gave Sam Kasajja greatest cause for concern on my second day at Ntenjeru when I decided to reinforce my rapidly fading suntan. I spread a towel on the grass beside the rest house and stretched out on it. After a few moments I was covered with insects, sweat and the long thin shadow of my guardian angel. No amount of explanation could assure him that I was not very seriously ill. Thereafter I resigned myself to the yellowish pallor of Europeans in this part of Africa.

I had some sympathy from Sam Kasajja over a more unpleasant incident which befell me. One morning Godfrey and I rode on the motor cycle into the market place at Kayunga to buy a piece of goat meat for my supper. As we were leaving, a man with a very unfriendly face stopped us and remonstrated vigorously. A crowd of fifty or sixty people quickly gathered and as the man, who turned out to be an official in charge of the market place, became more and more excited Godfrey and I were pinned down. Although I found the close proximity of so many black hands and faces very disturbing I kept quiet while Godfrey, with commendable calm, tried to deal with the situation. Eventually my attention was directed to a tiny, illegible, ankle-high notice at the entrance to the market place declaring that all manner of vehicles were prohibited there. The debate about how I should be punished raged around me for half an hour. As Godfrey fed in small fragments of information about who I was and what I was doing in Bugerere, a body of opinion began to develop that perhaps mine was a case for lenient treatment. As the market official saw the handsome fine he proposed to exact being whittled down, his behaviour became more extravagant: what hope was there for an independent Uganda in which white men could continue to behave as they pleased? But the tide turned steadily in my favour, and with the payment of two shillings and much finger-wagging we were released. Two days later Sam Kasajja's brother, visiting from distant Ankole country, pedalled his bicycle across the market place to the same butcher's stall. The official descended on him in wrath and made of him a dramatic and more profitable public example.

By now I could sympathise with Claudien Kabuguma's picture of Kayunga as an aggressive honky-tonk town. The same was true to a lesser extent of all the trading centres strung out along the main road running north and south through Bugerere. In due course I came to appreciate the contrast between village Bugerere and these centres, the latter tending to draw out from the surrounding community the malaise and insecurity in this heterogeneous and shifting population. Political party enthusiasm which was by and large mute in the villages became boisterously overt in the townships. Although con-stituency and parliamentary representation were matters of small in-terest, the party branches thrived, recruiting support indiscriminately from among the young and rootless. Passers-by were challenged with party slogans and salutes in the streets; there was UPC, the ruling Uganda People's Congress and their national rival the Democratic Party. The potent third force was the Ganda nationalist party *Kabaka Yekka*, 'the Kabaka, He Alone'. In the late afternoons politicking was a frenetic form of recreation, party loyalties being traded without demur for a Pepsi or a beer and a little bonhomie. As I passed through Kayunga and the other towns I responded like most other newcomers uncertain of the way the political winds were blowing: I returned each challenge and each salute exactly as it was given.

As I explored Bugerere from my base at Ntenjeru my topographical knowledge improved and my sense of what 'a community' in Bugerere might look like became clearer. The landscape consisted of rounded ridges, higher in the south of the Saza and flattening out towards the north. These ridges were separated by patches of swamp which helped to demarcate village boundaries. Everywhere the roads rose and fell, bisecting the ridges and dropping into the mushy valleys between them. Homesteads were strung out along the roads, set back twenty or thirty yards in their banana and coffee groves. I was told that an ideal holding ran from the crest of the ridge down into the swamp, providing a range of well-drained and moist soil for a variety of crops. The enormous expanse of Lake Victoria to the south exerted a pronounced influence on the climate and ecology of Bugerere. Dark rain clouds overhung the extreme south each afternoon, but a perceptible change came with every mile one proceeded northwards. A difficult and often impassable road threaded its way south out of the county through the dense Mabira forest towards Jinja. The Sezibwa bridge had always been the principal exit from Bugerere, even for its southernmost inhabitants. There the rich mud and green foliage was in sharp contrast to the dry north at Galiraya, where the land sank into the reed beds of Lake Kyoga. The *murram* road of compacted earth and stones gave way to soft drifting sand, and for long stretches there were no dwellings to be seen, only occasional herds of cattle, monkeys, and brightly coloured birds and butterflies. South of Kayunga there was scarcely a patch of uncultivated land.

With each intrusion into the small and distinct world of the homesteads I visited I pieced together a little more information about the old and the new residents of Bugerere and their way of life. It seemed that the more recent immigrants, and those from further afield, were more ready to discuss their experiences with me. The one Ganda farmer who refused point-blank to have anything to do with me contrasted sharply with the several newcomers nearer my own age with whom I conversed avidly for many hours. In these encounters I began to discover better ways of communicating and expressing myself. I had to remind myself continually that the self-revelation I was demanding was a strange experience for the people I visited—usually unannounced. Several were discomfited to find themselves the focus of this curiosity: 'why have you come so far to find me? Here I simply cultivate the soil . . .' However, for many of the people I met the experience of migration and settlement was momentous enough, and the new life in Bugerere sufficiently perplexing, for my questions to engage their interest. For all of them I was undoubtedly an oddity, but it seemed that the business of trying to understand what was going on in Bugerere made a good deal of sense to them. Occasionally I was suspected of being a government tax agent or a white land-grabber, but in general I both presented myself and was apparently accepted for what I was: a poor scholar. On one occasion when a drunken intruder interrupted an interview, I was amused to hear my host defend my credentials: 'Don't be afraid of him, he is only a schoolboy who has come to learn our history.'

The more I conversed with the people of Bugerere, the more I seemed to lose sight of the grand anthropological vista which I had prepared so carefully in Edinburgh. My awareness of the problem and its wider context seemed to shatter into innumerable fragments of vivid personal experience. From time to time I was reminded of my original objective overview of the situation, particularly when I met visiting government officials at Ntenjeru. I had one brief conversation with the Kabaka's dapper, diminutive Prime Minister, sitting in the back of his sleek black Mercedes. To him, Bugerere was essentially a soaring cash-crop statistic, the fruits of a successful marriage of Ganda entrepreneur and immigrant labour force. The Buganda government had no plans to control immigration or settlement in the area, but the Prime Minister would be pleased to hear my views on 'the labour supply situation' if I cared to call on him in Kampala in due course.

After four weeks I felt very keenly the need to move out of the seclusion of the rest house and into an ordinary community. I had visited fifty-two homesteads in the Ntenjeru area and felt that the time had come to find a village in which I could live and work for the next few months. I decided to look for one in the crowded south, some twenty-five miles away in the vicinity of the new township of Kangulumira. Later I proposed to pick a second village in the north, around Kayonza. As I felt I had learned so much from my Kayunga area sample, I decided that while I worked in these two villages I would carry out similar surveys in the area round about them. This would give me some idea of how representative the two villages were, and help to familiarise me with the wider environment.

Godfrey, who had served me patiently and faithfully, was to be posted as a clerk to Galiraya, a prospect he viewed with dismay. The Saza headquarters staff had been more than kind, and towards the end of my stay at Ntenjeru I was an honoured guest at the wedding of one of them. This was a grand affair in the local Anglican church, with the Saza chief himself acting as master of ceremonies. The parson exhorted the groom to be content with a single wife, and the bride to be faithful and subservient. Much of the time was devoted to the taking of a series of formal photographs, for which the Ganda have a particular penchant. In the evening we joined the married couple for a noisy party at their new home. The newlyweds sat side by side in the lamplight while specially commissioned drummers and musicians sang their praises; a few flattering verses were devoted to me. The mosquitoes made me their favoured guest as well, so I settled down in a comfortable armchair, smiled benignly, and anaesthetised myself with drink.

4 Kangulumira

The prospect of a move to Kangulumira (see Map 4) was invigorating. The town was much more picturesque than Kayunga, its height giving it fine vistas over rolling countryside and putting it mercifully beyond the reach of most of the mosquitoes. To the south there was a patch of uncleared forest belonging to one of the missions, where vines trailed and monkeys swung in the tall trees. Two miles away to the east the Nile plunged through a series of rapids and falls which had impressed the explorer Speke more than a century before.

Apart from being a pleasant place to live, it was clear that the Kangulumira area posed a rich variety of sociological questions. The censuses told me that between 1948 and 1959 the population had increased by more than 1,000 per cent, that little more than a quarter of the people were Ganda, and that the rest consisted of a very diverse collection of East African tribes. Although the influx was so recent, there were interesting indications that the bulk of the population consisted of settlers and not just migrant labourers: the proportions of men and women were nearly equal, and the number of children in the area suggested that a new generation was rising rapidly. Examination of more recent local records indicated that the tidal wave of immigrants was abating; given the high population density over most of the area, this was understandable. My surveys showed a steady drop in the amount of land newcomers had been able to acquire in recent years, and a correspondingly steep rise in the price they had to pay for it. In this southernmost *gombolola*, Musale, the pioneers of the late 1940s still had forty or fifty acres, while a new arrival could only expect to find a couple.

The censuses also told me that over the previous twenty years there had been some shift in the population of Bugerere itself towards the fertile south. Population growth in the Sabuddu area had been slight, and in my area surveys I picked up a number of householders

Bugerere landscape, looking south towards Kangulumira, showing density of cultivation and settlement

who had moved south in pursuit of greater economic opportunities. They were apparently being replaced by other poorer immigrants for whom the drier north was still relatively attractive.

My choice of a village which I could study in detail was mainly contingent on where I could find somewhere to stay. In such situations the visiting investigator is faced with three broad alternatives: he can live at some population centre in an hotel or official rest house; he can lodge with a family which is prepared to put up with him; or he can pitch camp or build a hut wherever he can find the space. At Ntenjeru I had found that for an anthropologist the first of these alternatives is not very satisfactory, and outside the government compound at Kangulumira there was hardly a scrap of unused land on which I might have pitched a tent; so I set out to find lodgings. Most other young immigrants could depend on relatives or friends in the vicinity, but I had to depend on my own initiative. The people who might have given floorspace to a young Ruandan labourer were obviously diffident about offering a white man hospitality. My first offer of a room came, improbably, from the Kangulumira midwife. Although quite recently built it lacked certain necessities, such as a door. This I could have remedied, but the prospect of living in such close proximity to the traumas of childbirth was off-putting. Eventually my accommodation problem, like so many others, was solved by the gombolola chief of Musale.

I presented myself and my credentials at the gombolola office on my first visit to Kangulumira. In appearance the government compound was a suitably reduced version of the Saza headquarters. At one side of the chief's house was a tall fence of interwoven reeds and a grove of barkcloth trees, symbols of chiefly office. I reflected that this was similar to the custom of planting a special green and gilt lamp-post by the front door of a civic dignitary in Edinburgh. Another official perquisite he enjoyed was an allotment of forty-nine acres of farmland, which he and his predecessors had chosen to sublet. The chief was a relative newcomer to the area, having been posted to Kangulumira only the previous year. In the Ganda bureaucratic hierarchy chiefs are moved around a good deal; the chief explained that each posting was graded according to the number of resident taxpayers and that in this respect Musale constituted promotion to the top of the list. In round figures he was responsible for sixty square miles containing forty thousand people from thirty different tribes, ten thousand of them taxpayers. As dealings with all federal and national government departments were channelled through his office, he was always busy. All disputes and breaches of the peace were brought to him and he could fine up to fifty shillings or imprison for thirty days; more serious cases were heard by a visiting magistrate twice a week. To assist him in his multifarious duties he had a deputy, eight parish chiefs and their subsidiary village chiefs, three clerks, two cashiers and five Askaris. On my second visit he sent me to see Amos Natyera, a farmer and merchant who lived near Kangulumira in a house which seemed to the chief sufficiently capacious to accommodate vagrant scholars.

I was directed to a substantial building made of cement blocks under a long sloping roof of corrugated iron sheets. Across the front was a row of tall doors, indicating a shop or store. On a beam in front of them hung a scale, and from the scale hung a cloth full of freshly picked coffee cherries. A small group of people stood around it arguing loudly. When I appeared a wiry man of about thirty detached himself from the group and pumped my hand vigorously. He had wild eyes and wore a shirt quartered in the green and white of the Democratic Party. In a husky voice he introduced himself as Amos Natyera. He pulled open one of the large doors and led me into a room furnished with sofa, easy chairs, occasional tables with dainty cloths on them, and a hefty wooden radiogram. A child was sent scurrying off to town for bottles of beer while I explained myself to him. He declared that my work was important and that, as a progressive man, he would do all he could to assist me. The room in which we were sitting was his best but it was mine if I wanted it. I said that I doubted I could afford such gracious accommodation, and he declared that rent did not matter to him. I accepted his offer with shameless alacrity, for it was more than I could have hoped for. I could live with an immigrant family but could also have a measure of privacy. Around the store there would be a lot of interesting activity, and Kangulumira was to hand. A nearby track sloped down towards the Nile, providing an incline on which I could start my capricious motor cycle. With these advantages I felt I could dismiss the possible risk of being too closely associated with a merchant and a man whose party loyalties were so overt.

In our colonial heritage there is a stereotype of the African which sees him as lazy and unambitious, subservient but good-humoured.

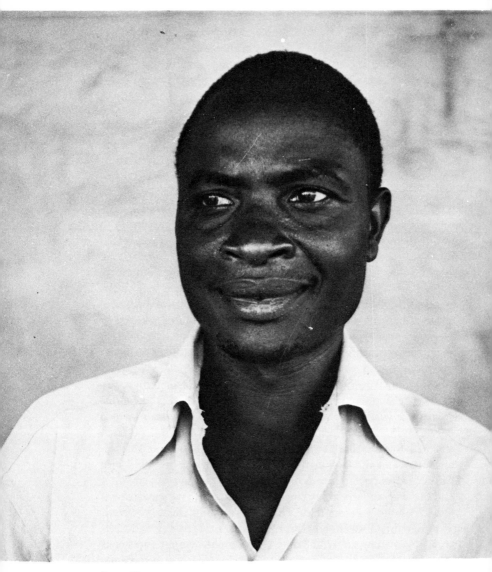

Amos Natyera

During the few years I have spent in Africa I have met too many men like Amos Natyera to attach any credence to this view. He lived at a killing pace, seeming rarely to pause to eat or sleep. Although he enjoyed *marwa* (millet beer), work, argument and planning were more intoxicating to him. Commercially there were many opportunities for men like him as there were no Asian traders in the area; Kangulumira was very assertively an African town as the result of a policy of exclusion rigorously applied by the early settlers.

'Listen,' Amos said to me one day, gripping my arm as if he felt one or other of us might suddenly take off, 'this is really important—write it down in your book.'

He then described how, when he was a small boy in the hills of his native Bugisu, he had a vivid dream about coming to a new land full of tall green trees. About this time his father died, and his uncle did not prove very willing to take care of his mother and brothers and sisters. Amos was particularly distressed because there was no-one to pay for his education. Impetuous as ever, he ran away from home and found a miserable job as a clothes-washer for an Asian shop-keeper in Teso District. He went back home, but ran away again to Jinja to enlist as a trainee bus conductor. In 1949 Amos's mother Asinasi despaired of making ends meet at home and decided to strike out on her own with her children. Fellow countrymen who had been to Buganda told her that some people were cutting farms out of the pestilential forest of Bugerere and so, fortified by her intense Christian faith, she became one of the pioneering settlers of Kamira village. Amos came from Jinja to see her, and as he walked through the Mabira forest he recognised the landscape of his childhood dream. Shortly after, he quit Jinja with his day's takings in his pocket and came to join Asinasi in the promised land. He started a farm of his own in 1954, but now his energies were devoted to expanding his coffee and maize buying business. On my first visit I was astonished to see electric light bulbs in the house. There was a power line from his house to Kangulumira and from thence to the Owen Falls hydro-electric dam at Jinja. During my stay he took delivery of a magnificent red maize mill, which he ran day and night grinding meal for people from miles around.

Two days later Amos moved his furniture and radiogram to the small living room at the back of the house, and I took possession of the front room. Although we became good friends I am still unsure why he inconvenienced himself in this way. I suppose he regarded me as some kind of link with the outside world; I served to expand his horizons. His approach to life was roundly pragmatic and although he had a taste for the exotic, like many scholars I have known his enquiries were mainly concerned to interpret his own position in the world and to make it more responsive to his will. In the evenings he would drop in for a rapid-fire discussion of the day's news, or he would burst in during the day waving a newspaper or a political tract and demanding explanations or opinions. What was the difference between communism and apartheid? Was the fact that immigrants could not rise very high in the Ganda political hierarchy or get access to freehold land a matter of apartheid? How could *he* get access to freehold land? My answers were often inadequate, but his proprietary interest in me did not extend much further than my role as a human encyclopedia. Once or twice I heard his voice raised in argument at the back of the house: 'as my European was telling me only the other day . . .' To my great relief he never pried or questioned me about my own researches among his neighbours and friends, although it might well have been to his advantage to do so. I must have offended or perturbed him on many occasions but he tolerated me with remarkable forbearance and good humour.

For eight months I lived under Amos's roof, with Amos's three wives and six children, and a good many other creatures besides. A colony of two or three dozen bats lived in the timberwork above my door and swirled round the room at night. Some of the less pleasant denizens inhabited a couple of tons of *robusta* coffee in the storeroom adjacent to mine. Amos's house and Amos's roof did not quite connect; the walls rose to about seven feet and there was a large gap between them and the long sloping roof. This kept the front of the house pleasantly cool but meant that conversations could easily be overheard in any part of the building. I never learned the guttural Lugisu language well enough to eavesdrop effectively on the family, but heard enough to warn me of the need to be discreet in my own discussions. My room was a refuge, and at times I found the procession of callers at the store more irksome than instructive. I soon became the local freak show, and silent groups would form in my doorway blotting out the light. The women were particularly inquisitive, watching in fascination as I wrote, washed or boiled a kettle. A sudden movement would evoke a burst of chatter. The bolder women would crane their necks in and make an inventory of my possessions: 'papers, table, typewriter, mosquito net, more papers. . . .' I had ruses to deal with this when it became a nuisance; if I moved suddenly as if to take off my trousers they would flee squealing. Children were more omnipresent but more manageable, and I became very fond of several of them. As there were no windows I hung a sheet of translucent plastic, which my mother had thoughtfully provided, over the door, but there was often a row of small black faces peeking up at me from underneath it. Adults were often amused to find me in conversation with them but I found their clear young voices excellent for my halting Luganda, and their indiscretion in certain matters most informative. For them, the threshold of somebody else's house was no obstacle, and there was little that happened in the community which escaped their watchful eyes. Of course I recognised ruefully that the intrusions I suffered were no more than a *quid pro quo* for my daily intrusions into the homes of the people round about me. I noticed, however, that the people I came to know well in the village nearby were very much more circumspect in their visiting than strangers from further afield.

As word went around that I was looking for an assistant, several young men came to call on me. A Mugisu called John seemed to combine a pleasant personality with linguistic talent, so I arranged a day's work with him. On the appointed morning he failed to turn up and I sat at Amos's house all day fretting about the waste of time. In the evening there was a knock on my door and when I opened it I was alarmed to see a tall black police constable standing there. He handed me a scrap of paper with agitated handwriting on it: 'Dear Mr Sunday, my Father, yesterday I was caught as to the traffic condition. Please come at once with 500 shillings to Luzira prison, Kampala. Yours faithful friend, John.' The constable explained gruffly that John had prevailed on him to deliver the message, against his better judgement, so I thanked him and tipped him for his pains. Next morning I learned from John's relatives that, unlicensed and uninsured, he had been involved in a minor collision on a motor cycle which he had borrowed without permission. I wrote to him at Luzira prison explaining that I could not raise the necessary £25. John seemed to understand that this was an appeal for patronage which I could hardly be expected to fulfil, and when he was released from gaol some nine months later he did not reproach me. With John incarcerated, I engaged Joseph Kanene, a primary school teacher from Bukede district with an amiable personality and a knowledge of a useful range of languages. He worked with me for the rest of my stay in Bugerere and proved an excellent public relations man as well as a patient and sensitive assistant. He worked with me every afternoon for a paltry £10 a month. With his neatly pressed shirt and trousers and shaved parting he always looked smart, and it undoubtedly pained him to have to work with someone whose appearance was as sloppy as mine. He would sit primly behind me on the motor cycle, navigating to gridline intersections with unerring accuracy and muttering imprecations when my driving became lethal.

In my early weeks at Kangulumira, Joseph and I were directed to meet some of the early settlers of the area. I consistently found the youthfulness of these pioneers surprising, and had to remind myself that the countryside which was now so densely settled was thick forest at the time of my birth. I was also surprised to discover that Bugerere had a history, and that many of these frontiersmen took a keen interest in it. One afternoon Bernardo Gizaza, a near-neighbour of Amos's, came to tell me with excitement that he had just 'dug up history'. He took me to his farm and showed me that where he had been planting banana suckers he had unearthed a bed of hard ferrous clinker and part of an earthenware bellows. He recognised these as traces of important iron smelting work which had taken place in the forest over a century previously. Smiths working for the kings of Buganda had made charcoal in forest clearings, smelted iron and manufactured spears and knives. In those days Bugerere was a troubled frontier zone between Buganda and the rival state of Bunyoro in the north. The fact that Bugerere was for so long a marchland suggests another reason why it remained unattractive for settlers.

It is notoriously difficult to make historical sense of such an area, and both the accounts I collected myself and the documents I studied in the excellent archives at Makerere University were full of conflicting evidence. People told me about strange figures who had dominated the area in the past; one of these was a certain Mr Chorley who arrived late on the scene, a white man with a formidable reputation as a hunter. Perhaps some student in the future will find it as difficult to make sense of Mr Sunday as I did unravelling the adventures of Mr Chorley. Eventually I had sorted out the shifting geographical boundaries and fluid time scales sufficiently to be able to see at least in outline the antecedents of the area.

The people who were regarded as the indigenes of the northern part of Bugerere were called Banyala. In the eighteenth century they had some political coherence under the chiefs of the dominant Mupina clan, and were apparently tenuous vassals of the Bunyoro state. To Bunyoro they were of strategic importance as they could control the Nile waterways, and could thus act as an eastern buffer to the Baganda. Speke was one of the explorers who encountered them in their canoes and found them rude and unfriendly. To the Baganda they have always been frontier riff-raff; they allege that the Banyala earned their name from the shameless behaviour of one of the Mupina chiefs while he was attending a feast at the Ganda court, *okunyala* meaning to urinate. The Banyala in fact seem to have preferred to call their country by another name, Wunga. Towards the end of the eighteenth century Buganda took possession of what is now the south of Bugerere, and a piece of Busoga on the other bank of the Nile besides. This became known as Bulondoganyi, and its main purpose seems to have been to secure the trade route from Buganda across the Nile. The few residents of the area were placed in the charge of an appointed vassal chief with the title Mulondo.

The history of the early part of the nineteenth century is dominated by a freebooting character called Namuyonjo. He was originally a Nyoro prince who, for some unnamed mischief, was driven out of his home land. He sought asylum from the Kabaka of Buganda and he and his retinue were allowed to settle in Kooki Saza. He started to squeeze a little tribute for himself out of the local peasants, so he was flushed out by the Kabaka's men and chased into Bulondoganyi where he was reluctantly spared because of his royal blood. Before long he was interfering with the trade route and was driven north into Bunyala. There he sought asylum with Kojjo Mupina, the Nyala chief, and started to interest himself in the local politics. After some double-dealing he killed Kojjo and seized his insignia of office, setting up his own hereditary chiefship and renaming Bunyala 'Namuyonjo's Country'. He then proceeded to play the gadfly with both Buganda and Bunyoro, making tentative alliances where and when it suited him. The area to the north of what is now Kayunga was almost perpetually embattled, and anyone trying to pass through Namuyonjo's domain was subjected to a good deal of harassment.

General Gordon, Emin Pasha and Speke all had to run the gauntlet of Namuyonjo's canoes as they made their way north along the Nile to Lake Kyoga. This impertinence must have caused the Kabaka of Buganda much vexation. The problem was resolved by a remarkable Ganda general, Semei Kakungulu, whom the historian H. B. Thomas has described as 'perhaps the last of the conquistadors of Central Africa'.*

In 1889 Kakungulu was awarded the Mulondo chiefship for his victories in the Ganda war against the Moslems. He had become a devout Protestant and set up a mission at his headquarters on Magala hill. At this time the Ganda, aided and abetted by the British, were stepping up their campaign against the Nyoro, and Kakungulu's undoubted talents as a general were in much demand. Thomas remarks that Kakungulu obviously enjoyed his role as baron of the marches, and that he gained a reputation for being autocratic but not unduly oppressive. His takeover of Bunyala from Namuyonjo's heir Mutale was apparently quite pacific; the story goes that with an impressive and orderly force behind him, Kakungulu sent, without comment, a cooking knife, a hoe and a spear to Mutale. Mutale prudently chose the symbols of acquiescence and peace, the knife and the hoe, and exiled himself on a small island on Lake Kyoga. Kakungulu proceeded north, establishing a series of fortifications, the largest of which was at Galiraya (Galilee) which he built near the Kyoga shore in 1895.

By the turn of the century Kakungulu had established an administration in the classic Ganda idiom at Bale, and the united Bulondoganyi and Bunyala were designated a Saza of Buganda and renamed Bugerere. Thomas remarks that 'it is a tribute to his leadership that many of his assistants were Banyala. The area was at peace and was beginning to export food for the Bunyoro garrisons'. However, Kakungulu did not rest for long. He embarked on a remarkable campaign in which the territories to the north and east of Buganda, Teso, Bukede, Bugisu, Budama and Busoga, were brought under political control and given the Ganda structure of administration. Kakungulu took with him large numbers of Banyala, who in due course became his chiefs and lieutenants in the pacified areas.

* H. B. Thomas, 'Capax Imperii: the story of Semei Kakunguru', *Uganda Journal*, vol. 6, no. 3, 1939, pp. 125–36.

Among those who lamented his departure was the missionary G. R. Blackledge:

This remarkable man, who is one of the most beloved and capable of Baganda chiefs, was chief of Wunga [Bunyala], and while there was able to gather around him hundreds of Baganda and a great and important work was being done. Churches were being built throughout the district and the chief thrust the weight of his great influence and position on the side of Christianity, encouraging his own young men to go and teach and preach. Then in 1900 everything was upset and disorganised by the departure of Kakungulu for Bukedi simply draining the district of Baganda and in his place we got a chief who not only brought few people, but who holding a form of godliness daily denies the power thereof . . .*

In 1900, the beginning of an important epoch in the history of Buganda, Bugerere was indeed a desolate place; Kakungulu had vacated the north, and tsetse and *mbwa* fly ruled the south. 1900 is the date of the famous Uganda Agreement engineered by Sir Harry Johnston, which sought primarily to bring stability to a politically troubled Buganda. It included a drastic reorganisation of land tenure in the kingdom, by which eight thousand square miles were arbitrarily allocated, virtually in freehold, to a thousand leading chiefs and their retinues. Measured out in square *mile* units, this land has been called *mailo* ever since. Other tracts of land were reserved for government officials, the missions, and other bodies; 1,500 square miles of forest was placed in the care of the Uganda Administration; and the remaining 9,000 square miles of waste and uncultivated land was vested in the British Crown. There were not very many people in Bugerere who could lay claim to *mailo* land there. Initially sixty claimants were allocated a total of 205 square miles; they included various heirs of the Bunyala and Bulondoganyi chiefs, but many were absentee claimants who could not lay their hands on land elsewhere in Buganda. When all the *mailo* allocations had been made, two thirds of Bugerere remained unclaimed, and was duly vested in the Crown. This *govumenti* land was to have important implications in the subsequent development of the Saza.

During the first three decades of this century nothing of much

* G. R. Blackledge, 'Bugerere and the Bukoba mission', *Uganda Notes*, July 1902, pp. 47–49, 52.

importance seems to have happened in Bugerere. Some of the *mailo* allottees allowed Ganda peasants from more populous areas to move in and take up smallholdings on their land. Although hostilities between Bunyoro and Buganda had abated, the sovereignty of Bugerere remained a matter of dispute and it was only during the period of my stay that a government commission finally settled the matter in Buganda's favour. Tsetse control measures meant that in the interest of later development agricultural settlement had to be temporarily restricted in the centre of the Saza. Nevertheless, during the 1940s there was a noticeable movement of people into the Kayunga area, attracted by the availability of land and responding to the boom in cotton which had been building up in previous decades. Probably a greater stimulus was the market for matoke in the expanding urban centres of Kampala and Jinja; Bugerere quickly established itself and has since remained the principal supplier of this commodity. Hitherto the administrative and commercial centre had been at Bale, where there was a large cotton ginnery and a ferry across the Nile to the rail head at Namasagali, but with the development of the trading centre at Kayunga and the opening up of the route west to Kampala, the commercial focus and the seat of administration shifted south.

In 1945 Nakumanyanja was chief of the only parish in what is now Musale gombolola. He told me that there were only thirty-five people in his charge. In the late 1940s the reserves of *govumenti* land in his area were tapped to provide a resettlement area for Baganda ex-servicemen who had fought in the 1939–45 War. Nazigo remains the only official settlement scheme in Bugerere; the major influx which commenced in the 1950s with the elimination of *mbwa* fly has been quite spontaneous and unplanned. For payment of a ten shilling 'Temporary Occupation License' each year any citizen of Uganda could take up a five acre plot of rich forest land. In fact, many took much more than five acres, few people had licences, and official registration of plots was almost unheard of. While the local Ganda administration struggled to keep pace with the situation, news of the bonanza travelled far and wide. Early settlers were co-opted as village chiefs and marked out farms for newcomers as best they could. A maxim which still applies is that if you don't cultivate the plot, it is not yours and can be claimed by another prospective tenant. A ruse adopted by the greedy was to claim forty acres or so and cultivate around the perimeter to give the appearance of full occupancy. A

Joseph standing in a piece of land which has just been cleared from the forest about six miles north-east of Kangulumira. The undergrowth in the background is still smouldering

market in *govumenti* land tenancies soon appeared, the price rising far beyond what was being paid for the freehold land which remained a Ganda prerogative. The rule that any Ugandan can make a bid for any piece of unused *govumenti* land has made cultivation virtually contiguous throughout the area; there is no common land, and the intensity with which the soil is being used does not bode well for the future.

The provision of what planners grandly call 'infrastructure facilities', schools, hospitals, agricultural services, roads and so on, has hardly begun. Efforts at wider community development are characteristically homespun, with appalling private clinics and schools proliferating throughout the area. No cartographer could hope to keep pace with the changes on the map of Bugerere; for anyone who has ever wondered how villages get their names, Bugerere is of almost limitless interest. Some are mundane and rather obvious terms of reference: Kisoga and Kinyaruanda are two of the relatively few examples of villages called after the tribe of the initial group of settlers. One parish chief I met described his efforts to find less prosaic names: Wabiyinja, a rock pool, and Bisakabidugala, a dark forested place. When he ran out of ideas he simply 'took places I knew at home in Bulemezi Saza'. A good many villages bear the name of a prominent original settler; one of these is Kisawula, home of Fesito Musawula, now quite a wealthy farmer.

Musawula was about forty-five when I met him. He was a Mukungulu, the name used to describe the followers of Kakungulu and their descendants. Musawula's father was born near Galiraya in the north of Bugerere and as a young man accompanied Kakungulu to Teso, where he served first as an administrator and then as a teacher. The Bakungulu were never very popular in the pacified areas, and Musawula's father encouraged him to return to his homeland to find a farm. He crossed Lake Kyoga and walked south, and late in 1949 staked his claim to a piece of forested *govumenti* land west of Kangulumira. To start with there were many hardships. Wild animals made it difficult to grow crops, and food had to be bought from Popatlal Savina at Kayunga. He and his wife had to wear garments which must have looked rather like heavy tracksuits to protect themselves from the *mbwa* fly. The extermination of *mbwa* three years later seemed like a miracle, and it was not long before his farm began to prosper. As clearance of the forest around him was to his own advantage he was pleased to direct the settlement of other newcomers, and soon had the gratification of being the Mutongole chief of his own village. At the time I met him he had a large, well-built house and a flourishing forty-acre farm. Like his father, he was a devout Protestant, and declared: 'Work is my way of life'. His faith did not deter him from having three wives, all of whom were Nyala Bakungulu. He had fierce loyalty to his origins which I found striking, although at that time I still had no clear picture of tribal inter-relationships in Bugerere.

Later I learned that the return of the Bakungulu had become an issue of major significance in the life of Bugerere. In the early 1960s a large group of them petitioned the Kabaka of Buganda for a *mailo* grant so that they could resettle in Bugerere. Fifty to sixty families were promised freeholdings drawn from the reserves of *govumenti* land, but it transpired that this land was already occupied by other immigrants. Official records no longer bore any resemblance to the real situation. In 1963 a party of established settlers, fearing eviction, set out in a lorry to make a counter-petition to the Kabaka. The first of the Bakungulu to arrive were fiercely ostracised, and although evictions do not appear to have taken place the matter is still highly contentious. It served to make explicit a number of fundamental questions which must have occurred to many Bugerere immigrants: to whom does the land really belong? Who, if anyone, has a prior claim? How secure and how durable is tenancy on *govumenti* land? Who holds political sway, the Kabaka, the Uganda government, or the people of Bugerere themselves?

On my first morning at Amos's house I woke to the sound of children singing. A large number of them seemed to be marching to and fro outside my door. As I lay listening, a tenor voice began to lead them: '*Amalebe, ho!*' The shrill voices replied: '*Amalebe go munyanja.*'

I got out of bed, and the tenor voice sang out: '*Abaganda, ho!*', and the children chorused: '*Abaganda go munyanja.*' As I put my clothes on each new verse brought another tribe, '*Abagisu, ho! Abasoga, ho! Abatoro, ho!*' Greatly intrigued I opened the door and let the sunlight stream in.

The song had given way to a regular chant. Across the wide laterite square in front of the house was a long line of children. '*Up-ee!*' they shouted, standing on tip-toe and stretching their arms up. Some

The children of Mr Musoke's school doing morning exercises outside
Amos's house, Kangulumira

were tall and some were tiny, and the colour of their bodies ranged from light chocolate to jet black. They were stripped to their drawers, some tight and some sagging, and before them stood a young man with his arms straight up, wearing singlet and trousers. '*Down-ee!*' As they all swept down to touch their toes I was confronted by a row of brightly coloured behinds. After a few more up-ees and down-ees, their master clapped and the children regrouped facing me. After a count of three they chorused: '*Good-ee morning sir!*'

Mr Musoke came forward and shook my hand politely, explaining that he ran the nearby primary school and that his children exercised every morning in front of Amos's house. I requested a reprise of the *Amalebe* song, and he led his motley throng round and round, singing with redoubled enthusiasm.

Later Mr Musoke explained that he had children from fifteen or twenty different tribes in his school, and in the face of a babel of different languages, singing had become an important medium of instruction and discipline. The *Amalebe* song, which he had composed himself, referred to the kerosene cans which the children drummed on their way to fetch water for their families each day. Although they had all come from different places they met by the water; although they had come from all over East Africa they had met in Bugerere by the shores of Lake Victoria. They sang together, and were happy.

I was, of course, impressed by this cheerful enactment of integration, particularly because the distinctive origins of each child were not played down, but were celebrated noisily in the song. Before very long a new verse had been included for my benefit: '*Abazungu, ho!*' Europeans were, after all, just another kind of tribe. In retrospect, there was some significance in the fact that the chorus-master was a Muganda; not only did he teach the children in his own language, Luganda, he always addressed them collectively as 'Abaganda'. Bugerere was, after all, a Ganda Saza.

I arrived in Buganda armed with preconceptions about the notion of *tribe*. This was a period in which African countries were still gaining and consolidating their independence, and there were strong political interests in asserting national unity rather than diversity. The idea was gaining currency that 'tribe' was a colonial invention, one of the devices by which European governments divided and ruled. As an imperial handmaiden, British Social Anthropology had played an important part in this mischief. It was cynically said that professional success depended on finding a tribe and then explaining over many years how different it was from the tribes of neighbouring anthropologists. In choosing to study the heterogeneous situation in Bugerere I was quite explicitly trying to avoid this kind of indictment. Even so, I still find it something of a disadvantage in seminar or common room that I have never had a tribe which I can flourish authoritatively: 'Of course, among the Bongo-Bongo things are really *quite* different. . . .' I had a conventional liberal concern about interethnic relations, and it is probable that I went to Bugerere with a vague hope that I might discover some formula for racial harmony. In my quest for integration my mistake was to assume that the people of Bugerere would regard tribal identity as something to be suppressed. In my interviews I asked coyly: 'Where were you born?' or 'Where were you living before you came here?' and the answers came back with disconcerting candour: 'I am a Muganda by tribe, I come from Masaka'. Unlike national politicians and academic liberals, the people of Bugerere did not shrink from the notion of tribe. For them, it was a simple and effective framework of identities within which their differences could be discussed, understood and perhaps reconciled.

As such candour as Mr Musoke's song persuaded me to relax my view of tribalism, I began to learn something of how the people themselves construed the social diversity around them. Africans are by no means exempt from that general human proclivity for maintaining and even inventing ethnic boundaries. The assumption that in Africa these boundaries are unimportant or simply a colonial invention is in itself a kind of racist misjudgement. Perhaps if *their* ethnicity differs from *ours* it is only because theirs is freer from intellectual deceit.

One day as we were approaching a group of people sitting under a tree I asked Joseph to indicate discreetly a particular individual whom I had not yet met. Joseph replied 'He is the black man'. When I protested that they were all black men, he was clearly shocked at my insensitivity. He was proud of his own light colour and occasionally expressed dismay that his forearms were being tanned as he rode in the sun on the back of the motor cycle. Fair-skinned women were in high demand and it was generally agreed that in this regard Gisu girls were very desirable. In those days, before the assertion that black is beautiful had gained any currency in Africa, magazines were full of advertisements for patent skin lighteners. These could produce uneven and disfiguring effects, sometimes resembling the greyish-pink scar-tissue which develops on black skin. Young women with modern pretensions also spent a great deal of time trying to straighten their hair, combing it out and tying it until their heads looked like pincushions. The women seemed to care more about these things than their husbands or suitors, for when I asked men to define for me the ideal wife, physical appearance was rarely mentioned.

Light skin and white skin seemed to be regarded as two quite different things. My own skin was an object of fascination; a child touching my arm would express surprise that it was not hard and cold. For my part I must confess to feeling some surprise that a black child felt as warm and soft as any white child. Eventually, as my complexion darkened and my beard took hold I was often mistaken for an Arab, a bemusing and not always advantageous identity. Unpleasant stereotypes of the white men greatly affected my rapport with children. White flesh was considered morbid and in childhood lore Europeans were bogey-men and cannibals. Occasionally mothers would bring errant children to my door, volunteering to sell me them for supper. Needless to say, this distressed me almost as much as the children. All white men look alike, and people who did not know me well would tell me that they had seen me, or my 'brother', if another European ventured into Bugerere. With my camera I developed an appreciation for African faces, the blacker the better, for they picked up lights and reflections in ways which fair complexions cannot. However, as I got to know my neighbours their colour ceased to be the most significant distinguishing feature; the tall Moslem, Wamubireggwe, looked just like my cousin. When I saw a picture of myself taken with a group of village friends I found my pallor shocking. I was even more disturbed on the couple of occasions when I encountered an African albino.

As I ingratiated myself with the local community I had to suffer some trials of my European identity. With some liquor inside him, anyone who had been treated badly by a white man could become acrimonious; this was particularly true of older men who had served with the British army. I was once involved in a scuffle with two or three of them, well soused with marwa beer and bent on discovering whether I had a hairy chest. Real animosity was reserved for the Asians, but I found my view of the Europeans in East Africa changing markedly from the perspective of Bugerere. Both the older colonial flotsam and the new species of expatriate businessman seemed very distant and dissociated from me, and on the few occasions I met them the feeling seemed to be reciprocated. The washed-out and disaffected appearance of white women in Kampala and Jinja had not escaped the attention of my new friends. One afternoon while eating and drinking with some young men I was treated to a free impression of two European ladies window-shopping in Kampala. It was devastatingly funny, a superb piece of observation and mimicry.

Local officials rarely expressed any misgivings about the heterogeneity of the Bugerere population. They never translated their worries about kondos and crime into tribal terms, nor, to my surprise, did they seem disposed to account for political disaffection in terms of ethnic inter-relationships. The fact that they were nearly all from the Ganda minority only made their attitude more perplexing; were they really so sure that they had the upper hand? A sample of parishes in each of the Gombololas showed that already 35 per cent of the village chiefs were neither Ganda nor Nyala, although there appeared to be no foreigners in the hierarchy above this level. I began to wonder whether officials were, like me, trying to 'disinvent' tribal differences to preserve a myth of political stability. In centres like Kayunga disaffection was expressed mainly in the idiom of party political rivalry and only rarely in terms of open ethnic conflict; even then the main schism was between Africans and Asians. Although I did not study the matter very closely, tribal affiliation was apparently quite important in building up party loyalties, but even the Ganda national party *Kabaka Yekka* included many immigrants and it did not seem sufficient to say that they were just trying to pass themselves off as Baganda.

I conversed in some detail about tribal differences with Israeli Bune, a well-established settler in Kamira village. He was a member of the Kuku tribe from the distant Southern Sudan, a people who were very different in language, culture and physical appearance from the Ganda or Gisu. Bune had great experience of the problems of immigration and settlement and spoke about them candidly and perceptively. He told me that Kuku newcomers were usually impressed by three particular things when they first arrived; one was the *gomasi*, the long gown with tufted sleeves worn by the Ganda

women. Another was the consumption of matoke; it was interesting
that this was also central to the European stereotype of the Ganda
way of life. A third surprising feature was the southerners' predilec-
tion for banana beer, which to the Kuku was a sweet, sticky and
nauseous concoction. Bune described the progress of the Kuku newcomer as follows:

When you come first you go slowly until you know what to do. The
few who never understand go back north to their homes. To start with
you have no fear, no fear at all. If you want to stay you will find no
problem in getting land, you will only have to find the money. The
private landowners will pester you about rent, but here in Bugerere
there is plenty of *govumenti* land. That is good, and if you are Kuku
you can get some and make your own farm. We cannot buy *mailo* land,
that is for the Baganda alone, for they know each other. The Baganda
blame us for being foreign—they say we are lucky to get farms on their
land. They call us foreigners but if they came to our country we would
welcome them and give them a [tribal] name. Now at home people are
fleeing because of the war, the place is like a desert. But no matter how
long we stay here we shall always be Kuku. You cannot forget your
tribe, even if you came here as a baby you cannot forget your tribe.

In the villages the heterogeneity of Bugerere was readily apparent.
Newcomers built houses in the styles to which they were accustomed,
only later following the bungalow pattern which prevailed in the
more affluent south of Uganda. Side by side in a village one might
see the cluster of conical thatched huts of a settler from the Southern
Sudan and the mud-and-reed box of a Soga family. Now and then
people from the more distant tribes would gather at the home of an
established settler for drink, talk and their own kind of music and
dancing. Once every two years the Gisu held large *imbalu* ceremonies
at which their boys were circumcised; unfortunately I missed this,
but was assured that neighbours and friends from other tribes were
invited to join in the parties. To many of them circumcision was an
outlandish business, but the offer of a free drink could hardly be
refused. The Bagisu could be very chauvinistic about *Masaba*, their
Mount Elgon home, but this did not diminish their enthusiasm for
the peace (*mirembe*) and freedom (*ddembe*) of Bugerere. I heard a good
deal of the tensions of life in the crowded villages of kinsmen at home
in Masaba. 'It is brothers who fight,' I was told. 'Here we do not fear
our neighbours.' At Kangulumira there was a primary marketing
co-operative called the Masaba Growers Co-operative Society, of

The homestead of a Southern Sudanese immigrant in Kamira. Although thatched and built of rather poor materials, the shape of the house on the left conforms roughly to the contemporary Ganda norm, but the conical granaries for millet and maize in the background are quite foreign to Ganda architecture. Note the cassava drying in the courtyard, and the banana plants which indicate that this Kuku family now includes the southern Ugandan staple *matoke* in their diet

which Amos Natyera was secretary. It was a branch not of the Ganda, but of the powerful Bugisu Co-operative Union, and looked at first sight like an exclusive tribal affair. Again there was a surprise: several of the members, including the chairman, were Baganda.

As I observed them, tribal inter-relationships were careful and discreet rather than free and easy. Obviously the attitudes of the Baganda were very important, and it was some time before I began to understand how they as a group reacted to their diverse neighbours. I concluded that although they were a minority they could afford to be complacent, as the political hierarchy, the *lingua franca* and the privileges of freehold land tenure were at least nominally theirs. Moreover, Buganda had been one of the most cosmopolitan parts of East Africa for a very long time. I had learned a number of words for 'foreigner', pejorative and polite, but very rarely heard them used in Bugerere; the Baganda and others usually referred explicitly to tribes or regions. Because of the history of conflict, 'Nyoro' appeared to be the most slighting term for a foreigner in Luganda, but as relatively few Banyoro had migrated to Bugerere there was little cause for embarrassment. As I progressed with my surveys I found some statistical evidence of the advantages of being Ganda. For example, 62 per cent of the Baganda householders had five or more acres of land, compared with 38 per cent of the Basoga, 32 per cent of the Bagisu, and just 9 per cent of the Northerners.* 68 per cent of the Baganda hired labourers, compared with 36 per cent of the Bagisu, 33 per cent of the Basoga and just 5 per cent of the Northerners. These advantages meant that the Baganda had more money: 58 per cent of them earned £30 or more a year, compared with 49 per cent of the industrious Bagisu, 35 per cent of the Basoga and 27 per cent of the Northerners.

The Baganda are well known in East Africa for their haughty demeanour. I was warned of this by others who had worked in Buganda, and in my own dealings with them I found them proud, correct and rather pompous—in other words, quite like the English. However, many of my kindest friends and most helpful informants were Baganda. True, the three people who refused to have anything to do with me in my investigations were all Baganda, and even my

---

* I have grouped together as 'Northerners' those in my surveys from the Lugbara, Alur, Kakwa and Kuku tribes (see Map 2).

Ganda friends did not hesitate to tell me if they felt that my questions were impertinent. I knew that *en masse* their pride and prejudice could infuriate a man like Amos Natyera but, like me, he was always quick to point out that some of his best friends were Baganda. Their barbed charm could sometimes catch one off one's guard: a farmer I visited greeted me politely and explained that he would not call me 'sir' because during his career as a railways clerk he had suffered too many indignities at the hands of my white 'brothers'. Some of the stiffness of Ganda politeness had been carrie dinto community relationships; the Bagisu saluted one another briskly, and it was quaint to hear one of them greet a Ruandan neighbour with such stylised Ganda queries as 'Is the lake calm?'

It was generally recognised that Bugerere was, after all, part of the Ganda kingdom, and most of the immigrants would be prepared to concede the prior claim of the Baganda. In the villages the Baganda did not seem anxious to alienate their neighbours, perhaps because they did not regard themselves as in any real sense the sons of the Bugerere soil. The Baganda are unusual in that loyalty to a particular piece of territory has never meant very much to them. Martin Southwold, one of the most prominent students of the Baganda, has remarked that not many of them remain in the village of their birth throughout their lives. *Okusenguka*, transferring allegiance, was an important Ganda tradition, and commoners would attach themselves to a chief where and when it seemed to their advantage to do so. In modern usage *okusenguka* means to go out and find a piece of land, which was what so many Baganda were doing in Bugerere. If the majority of them had no inclination to lord it over their new and diverse neighbours it may have been partly because they felt themselves to be as much immigrants as any, subject to much the same problems and experiences. However, in most respects the Banyala, the natives of the north of Bugerere, were rather different, and I shall describe them and their attitudes more fully later. I have already mentioned the passions which were aroused by the return of the Bakungulu and their assertion of territorial rights.

An interesting index of Ganda involvement in community life was their intermarriage with the other people of Bugerere. Official records and my own surveys both indicated the surprising fact that they, more than any other tribe, were prepared to marry outside their own group: 21 per cent of all Ganda marriages were cross-tribal, compared with 14 per cent of Gisu marriages. The Baganda were also the least inclined to 'import' a spouse from their own home areas, depending in their choice of a partner much more on new friends and contacts in Bugerere. Only 31 per cent of the Baganda I interviewed had brought a wife from home, compared with 57 per cent of the Bagisu and 55 per cent of the Northerners. I was able to debate with Amos whether this was valid evidence that the Baganda were not pursuing a policy of *apartheid*.

As I settled down to work in the Kangulumira area I found the ambivalence about tribal identities perplexing. Did they or did they not matter? People were candid about their tribal origins, but they were also concerned that they should not become contentious. Tribal solidarity seemed to be primarily an emotional affair and was much more obvious in a recreational context than in local politics or economics. A good deal of enthusiasm was channelled into political party activities, but it was very difficult to see what local interests and issues were being transacted in that arena. Did individuals have no other generalised perceptions of themselves and their interests within the wider Bugerere population? I felt sure they must, for if there was anything like 'a society' in Bugerere there must be divisions and oppositions within it, however rudimentary, of which the people themselves were aware and which they might be persuaded to discuss with me.

Before I arrived in Bugerere I knew I could expect to find large numbers of immigrant labourers working for settled farmers. In my preliminary study I had formed an opinion about these labourers which, had it not been more subconscious than conscious, I might have termed grandly a hypothesis. I suppose I found it satisfying to think of Bugerere as a land of open opportunity where a little pioneering spirit could act as a great leveller. The censuses told me that the people from the north and west who had habitually laboured for the Baganda had become landholders and farmers in Bugerere. I saw labouring and settlement as a continuum, the opportunities for wage-earning providing a means for the landless people of East Africa to invest in farms of their own. In planning my research there seemed no point in making a blunt distinction betewen labourer and farmer, as so many people seemed to be in transition between the two categories. Many of the farmers I met who hired labourers on a more or less permanent basis housed them on their own compounds.

Labourers working on a monthly or piecework basis lived in over-crowded, ramshackle huts scattered about the villages. They were predominantly young bachelors, and when I met them I tended to think of them as prospective settlers. I was not unduly perturbed to discover that they viewed their employers with a good deal of cynicism: they were unsympathetic, hectoring, suspicious, and expected too much work for far too little money. Few labourers seemed very optimistic about their prospects for finding land and settling in Bugerere.

It gradually became apparent that, from the perspective of the established immigrant, labourers were a class apart. Dependence on such a cheap and abundant supply of labour did not prevent the settler from displacing his feelings of insecurity and distrust onto these *bapakasi*, 'porters' in East African English. The 'porters' were seen as a fifth column moving continually through the fragile social order of Bugerere. Who were the kondos, of whose nocturnal predations I was always being warned and against whom honest citizens barred their doors at night? They were porters turned desperados. Who was blamed for the disappearance of a chicken, or an unexpected pregnancy? The hungry and footloose young men, strolling around waiting for last month's wages. The prison at Kangulumira was full of porters, and sitting roped together on the floor of the magistrate's court they presented a scruffy, disrespectful and uncontrite appearance. They hooted with mirth as each successful complainant prostrated himself in gratitude before the magistrate, and they were led back to the rickety prison hut. My own insensitivity to the category of *bapakasi* landed me in trouble more than once. Mosa Ngobi, an immigrant to Kamira village from Busoga, had a young distant relative living with him, to whom he paid wages for helping with the farm work. My casual reference to the young man as a 'porter' produced much consternation, and a stern rebuke from Mosa: how could I confuse his 'brother' with a mere labourer? Although clearly very sensitive, the distinction between who was and was not a porter seemed to me far from absolute.

In daily life the relationship between labourer and immigrant was often strained but seldom overtly hostile. I met some farmers who appeared to treat their labourers virtually as members of the family. If they were within earshot the householder would usually refer to them as 'lodgers' or by some other circumlocution. It was well known that widows or divorced women often formed close and more or less permanent relationships with labourers, but local gossip of course tended to see this as indiscretion and opportunism.

As usual, I looked to my surveys and my slowly accumulating statistics for elucidation about this apparent class distinction. One fact was immediately clear: the Baganda virtually never worked as agricultural labourers. Twelve per cent of them had worked for wages, but in shops or in the factories at Kampala and Jinja. By comparison, 31 per cent of the Basoga I interviewed had at some stage worked for another farmer in Bugerere, as had 21 per cent of the Bagisu. Three quarters of the Northerners had been 'porters', as had nearly all the Banyaruanda and Barundi and other western people; many of them were still doing occasional wage labour at the time I met them. An interesting statistic was how long each householder had to wait in Bugerere before acquiring a piece of land: 70 per cent of the Baganda did not have to wait at all, compared with only 18 per cent of the Northerners, most of whom had to work for more than five years to raise sufficient capital to buy rights to land. Although these figures suggested that there were strong tribal undertones to the 'porter' identity, it was rather disconcerting that the settlers themselves did not seem anxious to see it as such. There seemed to be some 'doublethink' going on, for tribal identities could be used to distinguish *among* settlers, or *among* porters, but only rarely *between* the two. For example, a farmer would readily use tribal stereotypes in discussing his labourers: Banyaruanda were scruffy and light-fingered, but were very good at looking after coffee, while the northern Lugbara were fractious but adept at cotton cultivation.

After much consideration I arrived at what may seem a banal conclusion: acquisition of rights in a piece of land marked the most significant shift in social status in Bugerere, and the most substantive distinction in the eyes of the people themselves. A seasonal rent which prohibited building and restricted cultivation to annual crops like cotton was not good enough, although as a way of raising capital it was a means to the desired end. It is not difficult to understand why enduring rights in land were of such importance in the process of settlement. To be able to build a house, to be independent and self-sufficient and to have the resources to raise a family are all matters of fundamental human concern. Although I myself had no experience of the process, I could understand that 'settling down' is a momentous stage in the life of any individual. The migrant is presented with a particular dilemma: where shall he put down roots—at home or abroad? In the immigrant society this choice, multiplied so many times, assumes great significance, and it is not difficult to understand why the settlers should see the commitment of their own lives as in sharp contrast to those who, as yet, are uncommitted. For the settler the security of household and homestead is a matter of supreme importance which, in an uncertain world, puts him at the mercy of his neighbours. The need for social order becomes imperative, and as the immigrant acquires a grip on Bugerere, so Bugerere acquires a grip on him.

Although many immigrants might have found this formulation agreeably neat and exact, I could be less confident that it accounted for the wide variety of experience which I observed day by day. The individual's view of reality may divide up into black and white, but efforts to observe reality more objectively usually show that it has a disconcerting habit of spreading out into shades of grey. I was discovering in Bugerere that the notions of 'commitment' and 'permanence' are extremely mercurial in an immigrant society, and that even the most thoroughly established settler could pull up his roots and depart home if the balance of opportunity and responsibility suddenly shifted in that direction. The individual life stories I was collecting made it clear that the decision to settle was seldom an immediate and irrevocable one; visions of the 'promised land' such as Amos had experienced were uncommon, and newcomers were usually cagey about their prospects in Bugerere. Settlement, it seemed, was less a matter of conscious choice than a slow process of fulfilment in which the acquisition of land was an important early step.

As I grappled with these problems I had to acknowledge that I had got all the sociological problems I had asked for. Bugerere society was not made, it was in the making. There was no complete overview to be had, either from my own supposedly objective stance or from the perspective of the settlers themselves. Although there were people who could tell me the history of the area, and felt this to be important, there was no aged guru who could encapsulate for me the social ethos in a few well-turned sentences. I was always impressed how my task as I presented it—'discovering how people live in Bugerere'—seemed to be accepted as a plausible one. In an important way, life itself was a process of discovery in Bugerere, and Bugerere society not much more than the sum total of these individual quests. When I placed my own experiences beside those of the people I talked to I began to feel that all I had done was to professionalise the task of discovery in an eccentric way.

As I rushed between gridline intersections, intruded into people's homes and sat at my table in Amos's house counting heads and shuffling papers, I began to abstract from the colourful individual accounts of migration a list of reasons why people had chosen to come to Bugerere. Each region exerted its own distinctive kinds of 'push', and Bugerere held correspondingly different attractions for members of different tribes. My money and time were so limited that I could only manage brief visits to the homelands of a few of the Bugerere immigrants, but I found all of these excursions illuminating. The most common answer to my blunt question: 'Why did you come to Bugerere?' was 'To find money'. None was available at home, and it was needed to pay tax, for marriage and for the education of children. Liability for tax is a modern, state-imposed initiation into manhood; suddenly there comes a time when every young man is under pressure to find money, in Uganda a minimum of sixty-five shillings to be paid all at once. A home which could sustain the needs of a child can no longer meet such demands, and the youth has to quit in pursuit of opportunities elsewhere. Again, if he wishes to marry and have children the young man may discover that the family farm is unable to provide the necessary resources. In the many overcrowded areas of East Africa the only alternative to hunger and deprivation is migration.

I found the hills of south-west Uganda and Ruanda (see Map 2) as beautiful as Claudien Kabuguma had nostalgically described them. The hillsides were scored into terraces, and the tiny fields dotted with clusters of round thatched huts. Farming was a struggle for subsistence and a struggle against depletion of the soil; cash cropping was a luxury few could afford, and although insistent in its demands for tax the government had done very little to develop local opportunities. Instead, the authorities preferred to encourage the movement of labour to regions like Buganda where economic growth seemed more propitious. In places like Kigezi and Bugisu land had been divided into plots which were hardly viable, and as resources seemed to shrink, family quarrels became endemic and tensions spilled over into accusations of sorcery, witchcraft and other mis-

Mosa Ngobi and family, Kamira. The picture, posed by Ngobi, is a classic presentation of the established immigrant family to the world at large: in the arrangement of this close family group the distinctions of age and sex are clearly evident

chief. In Busoga and in the crowded areas of Buganda itself soils were becoming impoverished, and farms which once grew heavy stems of matoke were now only fit for the cultivation of cassava and sweet potatoes. The Luganda word *nnaku*, bringing together notions of sadness, tiredness and trouble, was often used to describe circumstances at home. There is a graphic expression: '*ennaku zinzimbyeko akayu*', 'trouble has built a little house on me'. When I asked them why they had left home, many of the immigrants would sigh and simply say '*nnaku*'.

As a young man Mosa Ngobi lived in Busoga on his father's land, with two full brothers and two brothers by another of his father's wives. The farm was neither large nor very fertile, and when Mosa and his elder brother married their father marked out for them small subsistence plots, but the family continued to grow cotton as a joint enterprise. Ngobi had married when he was seventeen and for some time the arrangement was quite agreeable, but by the time four of the brothers were married competition over resources, particularly shares of the cotton crop, was becoming acute. One day in 1952 the five sons were taking the cotton in a hired truck to the ginnery when it crashed, injuring the youngest, unmarried brother. Their father detailed one brother to collect the boy from hospital next day; Mosa was to go and fetch the boy's mother, who now lived elsewhere; the rest were to see about the cotton. As he was about to set out next morning, Mosa noticed that there were no men about the farm, so he waited for three hours until his father came back home. The situation was ripe for a quarrel. The father's first charge was of disobedience, and as the argument became more heated Mosa was accused of jealousy of the youngest brother. Wounded, Mosa withdrew to his own plot and for the next few days ignored his father. Still very vexed, his father then instructed the rest of the family to have nothing to do with Mosa. As this had no effect, he began to put it about that he wanted to sell Mosa's plot.

Mosa went to his father in a fury. The old man tore off his kanzu and waved his genitals at Mosa, declaring histrionically that he was no son of his.

Mosa had no choice but to depart rapidly from this awful scene. He was honest enough to appreciate that there were other tensions underlying the immediate dispute. 'I knew I could never be a real man if I stayed at home,' he told me, 'I wanted many things, money, another wife . . .'. His first urge was to go to Nairobi, which he had for long harboured a desire to see, but as his wife had a brother in Bugerere they went to stay with him. A few months later he had established his family on their present two-acre farm in Kamira village. I asked him about his father: 'He was our first visitor', Mosa replied. Although he told his story not entirely without rancour, it was clear that family tensions had been relieved.

Although my longer motor–cycle journeys continued to be traumatic, travel in East Africa was not as difficult as I have probably made it appear. Buses ran regularly and few of the Bugerere immigrants were more than a couple of days' journey from home. There were also numerous taxis; for six shillings I could travel in a smart new Peugeot estate car with eight other people from Kangulumira to Kampala. Many ramshackle vehicles plied the byways where police patrols rarely ventured to enforce licensing and other regulations. I once travelled to Kayunga in a Vauxhall family saloon car of the type my father had owned in the 1950s. Inside it there were sixteen adults and four children, and as a privileged passenger I sat on the third layer of laps in the back, with my torso thrust sideways out of the window. Once while Joseph and I were riding along on the motor cycle, one of these taxis burst in front of us, hurling bodies out in all directions. I ran forward expecting the worst, but the passengers dusted themselves down resignedly, packed themselves back into the car while the driver hooted impatiently, and continued on their way. Such delights were beyond the reach of the poorest migrants, for whom 'footing' was the only practicable means of travel. Driving to the west one could see groups of young men on the long journey from Ruanda into Buganda. This was the way a good many of them had made their first trip to Bugerere, walking alone or with small groups of friends.

I learned a good deal about these newcomers from the writings of anthropologists who had studied the various communities in East Africa from which they came. John Middleton has described how emigration has become a routine part of life for the Lugbara of northern Uganda (see Map 2). Although the departure of so many young men to work in the south was causing important changes in the economy and family life, ties with home remained very strong. Anyone who remained away for too long or who settled abroad was deemed to be 'lost'. Middleton explained:

By migrating outside their own country Lugbara are able to borrow and use the soil fertility and land of southern Uganda, and also lessen the land pressure in their own areas. By migrating temporarily the migrants do not break their ties with family and community, but get over the immediate problem of land scarcity; as they grow more senior in the lineage they can acquire land and send their juniors in their turn.*

For many of the young men, migration has all the excitement of getting out and seeing the world. Aidan Southall has described how the Alur youth returns to his northern Uganda home with a sense of worldly-wisdom: 'This is exemplified clearly by the tremendous swagger of bearing adopted by returned migrant youths in front of girls at home.'† The young ladies in question might have wondered about this display of urbanity had they seen the unglamorous circumstances in which most of the Alur labourers were obliged to live in the south.

A man would only take his wife and children to Bugerere if he had some foothold there—usually a piece of land. The people I met made it clear that such a move was seldom undertaken lightly, as it amounted to a much more serious detachment from the home community than the departure of a young bachelor. The newcomers who arrived as complete families were usually refugees or exiles, and as such suffered particular hardship in making a new home for themselves in Bugerere. In the 1960s Uganda was a haven for displaced people from neighbouring countries, from civil war in the Congo and Sudan and from genocide in Ruanda and Urundi. In Bugerere I met many victims of the long and debilitating struggle between the Southern Sudanese and their northern rulers. Some of them were not only supporting their own families, they were sending small sums of money to the *Anyanya* guerillas in their homeland.

In her classic study of migrant labour in Buganda, Audrey Richards noted that there was a 'network of kinship connexions spread wide over Uganda by which they [the migrants] pass news and get help in difficulties, secure jobs and land and get information

---

* John Middleton, *The Lugbara of Uganda*, Holt, Rinehart and Winston, Chicago 1965, p. 13.
† Aidan Southall, 'Alur migrants' in Audrey Richards (ed.), *Economic Development and Tribal Change*, Heffer and Sons, Cambridge 1954, p. 150.

from their home country.'* One of the penalties of making good in Bugerere was that success brought a procession of 'brothers' and friends-of-friends in pursuit of money and an economic niche. Although settlers often complained that people at home had an exaggerated idea of Bugerere as a land flowing with milk and honey, most of them had to admit that not so long ago they were themselves dependent on the support and advice of an established relative. Family interconnections ramified throughout Bugerere, providing a valuable economic intelligence network. The newcomer would put this to work particularly if he was looking for a piece of land. He had a broad choice between a small piece of expensive but fertile land in Musale, with family and friends never very far away, or a larger piece of poorer but cheap land further north, where the secure feeling of close settlement was lacking. In the Kangulumira area, opportunities presented themselves sporadically here and there, and anyone with a piece of land to spare could expect stiff competition for it. In selling, material interests usually outweighed family sentiments, and this had had the effect of undermining the formation of tribal enclaves; one is more likely to extract a higher price from a stranger than a brother. For people with land to spare, selling small parcels of land was an important way of raising funds, and in the crowded areas there was an increasing tendency towards the fragmentation of holdings.

As the mutongole chief of Kangulumira told me, a prospective buyer may have to spend several months 'footing' around Bugerere: 'everywhere he goes he asks, until the price, the chicken and the land suit him'. The *price* was demanded by the existing tenant, and the *chicken* went to the parish chief, with a quarter share to the mutongole chief and something for the two or three established villagers who helped to witness the boundaries. As the chicken was now reckoned to be proportional to the price, it was almost invariably rendered in cash. This could amount to as much as five hundred shillings in the south—a veritable poultry farm. However, it was the principal means of securing tenure, and everyone attached much importance to these formalities. The transaction would involve several visits to the mutongole chief who, with one or two of the other established villagers, would vet the newcomer and explain to him his rights and obligations. Locally, all this was considered much

* Audrey Richards (ed.), *Economic Development and Tribal Change*, Heffer and Sons, Cambridge 1954, p. 185.

more important than the ten shilling Temporary Occupation Licence which *govumenti* land tenants were supposed to buy. Little effort was made to collect this fee and in 1968 the Uganda Government abandoned its attempts to license public land, assigning to tenants the proprietary rights which most of them assumed they already had. Although there were many foreign tenants on the Ganda-owned *mailo* land, and their rights were well protected legally, most immigrants preferred the relative freedom of *govumenti* land to dependence on a private landowner. Many of the *mailo* owners were, in their turn, waking up to the fact that extensive farming of their own estates was much more profitable than collecting the small annual rents due from tenants.

However important finding and securing rights to a piece of land might be, the establishment of the immigrant ultimately depended on the elaboration of other, more complex bonds between himself and the community around him. As time passed he became less dependent on ties with home and slowly he and his growing family built up new relationships within the village in Bugerere. He would notice with mixed feelings that his visits home were becoming less regular and meant less than they used to. To understand how a newcomer could be drawn into a local network of dependence, and how the focus of his affections could shift towards his new home and the people around him, I had to re-orient my own research. So far I had been concerned with the individuals whom I had met at gridline intersections, their experiences and problems, and their perceptions of the world. By looking closely at the immigrant household in its community setting I hoped to find out more about the kind of commitment people had to their new society, and the way in which the emerging social order was impressing itself on their lives.

5 Kamira

Amos Natyera's house stood on a crossroads about a quarter of a mile out of Kangulumira town (see Map 4). One road ran up to the simple but attractive Anglican church on the hill overlooking Kangulumira, another ran downhill towards the Nile, and a third road ran along the L-shaped ridge of Kamira village and down to more recent areas of settlement along the banks of the river. When I arrived I thought that Amos's house was in Kamira, as it stood on the village side of the junction, but I was shown a narrow path about twenty yards away between Mr Musoke's schoolhouse and a farm, which marked the boundary with Kangulumira. Amos's mother and a couple of in-laws lived in Kamira and he had his own three-acre farm there, so he felt very much part of the village. All the people of Kamira had to pass my door on their visits to Kangulumira, and I was able to greet them and chat with them regularly. Although I did not live within the boundaries of the village I felt that I was well placed to get to know it and its people.

A few days after I moved my belongings into Amos's front room I entertained the village chief, Erika Musoke, to beer and biscuits. He was an elderly Muganda with large, anxious eyes, heavy lips and a rather vague manner. It must have been unsettling for him to hear a stranger declare that he proposed to get to know all the subjects of this little realm, and to try to unravel its secrets. He took this stoically, as one of the many burdens which a servant of the Kabaka must bear. As the first and most distinguished victim of my questioning, he told me that he was a native of Bukoba in adjacent Kyaggwe county and had come to Bugerere in 1942. He settled first near the Nile to the south of Kayunga, but wild animals and the *mbwa* fly made life too miserable. He was a distant relative of Martin Luther Nsibiirwa, a former Prime Minister of Buganda who had been allocated a *mailo* estate at Kangulumira. As this higher gound was less pestilential,

Musoke was glad to accept the offer of a tenancy. Later in the 1940s he was followed by other immigrants who also took tenancies on Nsibiirwa's land, and then started to clear farms on the forested *govumenti* land on the north-eastern side of the estate. Musoke had been appointed one of Nsibiirwa's stewards, and had gradually assumed responsibility for settling newcomers on the adjacent *govumenti* land as well. In 1950 the extension of settlement along the Kamira ridge warranted the official recognition of a new village, and Musoke was duly appointed its mutongole chief. This had produced the rather odd situation of a village which consisted of a mixture of freehold and public land, and a chief who was not actually resident. Musoke lived on the other side of the main road into Kangulumira in Nakatundu village, and depended heavily on his Gisu deputy, Wasozi, who was a full resident of Kamira.

Musoke told me that Kamira ranked Sabagabo in the Mumyuka parish of Musale gombolola. This description of its position within the political hierarchy (see Figure 1, page 18) served as a useful historical guide: Kamira must have been the third village in the first parish to be formally recognised, making it an 'old' village by Bugerere standards. Now, Musoke told me, it was 'full up'. Later I counted 83 homesteads within the village boundaries, and a resident population of 490 people. Including the 62 labourers who were working in the village while I was there, the inhabitants were packed in at a density of a little over 1,000 to the square mile. At our first meeting I told the chief that I had had difficulty trying to sort out the boundaries of Kamira, and with a sigh he agreed that we should take a walk the following morning. Circumambulation was not strictly possible, as on each side the ridge ran down into black, sludgy swamp. Instead, we walked the mile-and-a-half from Amos's house to the north-eastern end of the village where there was a brief argument about which of two tiny, straggling paths marked the boundary with Kigayaza. As we moved through the village, periodically squeezing our way down narrow pathways for a sight of the swamp, our little procession grew in size and our beating of the bounds became an itinerant discussion of my purposes in Kamira. Information was passed back over one person's shoulder to the man behind, the 'oh' with which each explanation was received indicating diminishing credulity the longer the queue tailed back. Confusion was doubtless compounded the following day when I set out on my own to make a rough map of the village; I could see people watching me anxiously out of the corners of their eyes as I paced solemnly hither and thither, mumbling numbers and scratching lines on sheets of graph paper.

This map, which went through numerous slowly-elaborating editions, became very important to me. It was not simply a practical guide to my research, it circumscribed in a satisfying way the community which I had adopted. It was also a record of what I had accomplished, for as the weeks passed I was able to tick off the households whose heads I had interviewed in detail. Before I left Kamira I had paced out the dimensions of each farm, and the sum of all these fragments came to 351 acres, a little over half a square mile. When I later calculated the area of the village from air photographs I was relieved to discover that my measurements were in quite close agreement. Kamira was indeed 'full up' in the sense that all the land was under cultivation, including the swampy margins, where vegetables were grown. As a longer-established and more densely settled village, farms in Kamira were on average two-thirds the size of those I sampled by the gridline technique in the surrounding area. With few exceptions each house was set in its own property, close to the roadway through the village which in some stretches looked as crowded as a suburban street. Here and there tracks led down to shallow wells in the swamp, which provided a murky and intermittent supply of water. Mercifully, Amos had a concrete rainwater tank which I was able to use, sparingly, for most of my stay. Other people collected rainwater off their roofs in old oil drums, or simply by putting a pot against the stem of a banana plant.

Houses were sited as high as possible on the ridge, for such practical reasons as good drainage and relative freedom from mosquitoes. The Kangulumira end formed a small plateau fifty to a hundred feet higher than the rest of the village and had for this reason been favoured by the earlier settlers. As I got to know each household I was able to reconstruct the history of settlement; I have shown the various stages of this on the accompanying maps (Figure 2), as they had important implications for the life of the village as I came to know it. Luka Manyala was the first of the present inhabitants to arrive. In 1946 he rented five acres of Nsibiirwa's *mailo* land, but a year later he moved across the path to add a further eight acres of *govumenti* land to his holding. A fellow Mugisu, Wanyela, moved onto the piece of land now occupied by Amos Natyera's house and

sheds, but when he was later offered a good price for this he shifted
further along the ridge to a new farm. About the same time Esimafesi
Salongo arrived from Busoga and took up the *mailo* tenancy next to
Manyala. Bernardo Gizaza was the first of a series of Gisu immigrants who came to Kamira in 1949. He took about nine acres of
govumenti land in a superb position in the heart of the 'plateau'; when
he was clearing the forest and bush he left one massive tree at the
entrance to his home, which now towers over the intense cultivation
of the village as a prominent landmark and a symbol of the seniority
of this important villager. Another Mugisu, Simewo Mazaki, was
next to arrive, and he was followed by his neighbour Israeli Bune, a
Southern Sudanese of the Kuku tribe who had worked for several
years as a labourer in the Kayunga area. The 1949 newcomers, who
included Amos's mother Asinasi, spread themselves out along the
ridge; although Bagisu preponderated there were also two Baganda
and a Murundi who, like Bune, had served time as a labourer in
Buganda.

Figure 2 shows how these earlier settlers still have the largest
holdings, even though many of them have sold off pieces of their
land. Between 1950 and 1954 the population of the village doubled
and the third map indicates the very wide range of tribes involved.
This group of settlers are scattered throughout the village, filling up
the north-eastern end and the gaps between their predecessors'

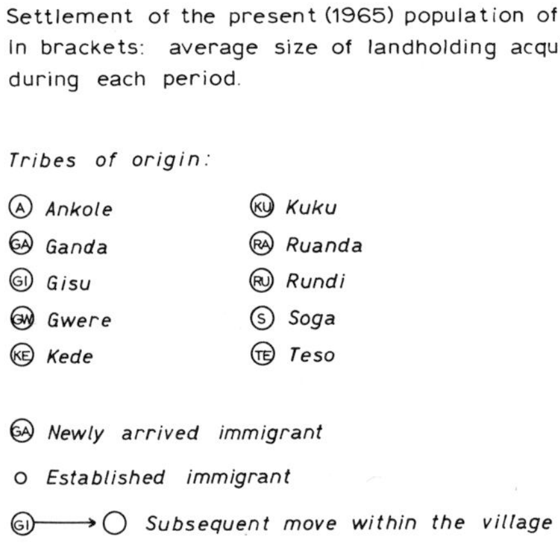

Settlement of the present (1965) population of Kamira.
In brackets: average size of landholding acquired
during each period.

Tribes of origin:

Ⓐ *Ankole*   ⓀⓊ *Kuku*

ⒼⒶ *Ganda*   ⓇⒶ *Ruanda*

Ⓖⓘ *Gisu*   ⓇⓊ *Rundi*

ⒼⓌ *Gwere*   Ⓢ *Soga*

ⓀⒺ *Kede*   ⓉⒺ *Teso*

ⒼⒶ *Newly arrived immigrant*

○ *Established immigrant*

Ⓖⓘ——▸○ *Subsequent move within the village*

Figure 2.   The settlement history of Kamira

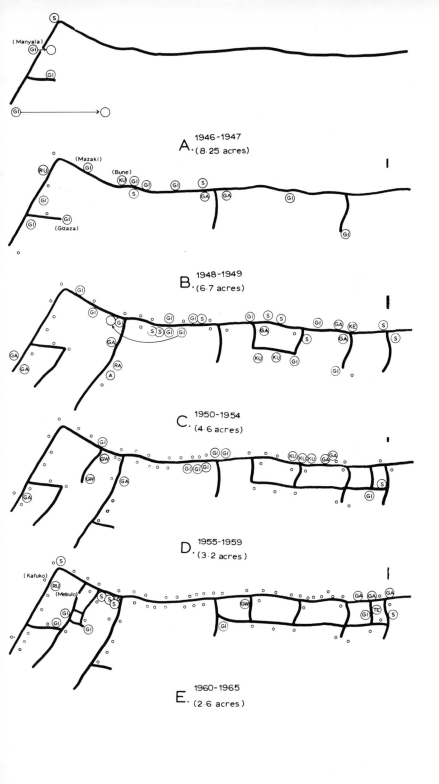

A. 1946-1947
(8.25 acres)

B. 1948-1949
(6.7 acres)

C. 1950-1954
(4.6 acres)

D. 1955-1959
(3.2 acres)

E. 1960-1965
(2.6 acres)

farms. The established settlers often assisted them: Bune found modest plots on the eastern slopes of Kamira for two distant kinsmen, and after living with his elder brother Nalyanyi for seven years, the young Mugisu Wamembi was able to buy two acres of the land held by his Ganda neighbour Mukasa. A few of the settlers who arrived between 1955 and 1959 took over farms from the handful of people who had decided to quit the village. Since then newcomers have had to buy pieces of land from established villagers, moving into spaces here and there along the main road and secondary pathways. Some, like the most recent arrival Kafifi (a Musoga), have compromised by renting a small house plot on the main road from another villager, while farming less desirable half-acre fragments of land down by the swamp. Settlers looking for additional pieces of land have found that since they first arrived prices have rocketed; even a wealthy newcomer could not hope to buy a farm a quarter of the size of the one staked out by Luka Manyala.

The map of Kamira which I finally produced made it evident that the social ingredients of the village had been mixed together very thoroughly. Newcomers and veteran settlers lived side-by-side, larger and smaller farms were intermingled, and members of each of the ten tribes represented in the village were distributed very evenly. Although a majority of thirty-five of the householders came from Bugisu, and half of these from the same clan area (Lucheke), they did not cluster together nor did they dominate particular sections of Kamira. It was strange to reflect that what had been a forested ridge only sixteen years previously was now a crowded, thriving community. The newness of Kamira and the variety of its people presented all the questions of adjustment and integration for which I hoped to find answers. Already I had a very strong suspicion that the evident tranquility of village life had been achieved because of, rather than in spite of, the remarkable admixture of its population.

I began my systematic invasion of the homesteads in Kamira by following up one or two of Amos's introductions. These tended to be men with much the same businesslike approach to life as Amos himself. There was Lameka Kigozi, 'the most progressive farmer' of the village, and his friendly rival Lameka Mubiru, both Baganda. Kigozi could speak to me in English, which I found an enormous relief; Mubiru, alive to its commercial advantages, wanted to learn the language, and sought me out as a tutor. He visited me often and became a kind and helpful friend, but I think my Luganda benefited more from our conversations than his English. His favourite expression was '*We learn by our mistakes*', and he had a disconcerting habit of saying this to me brightly, apropos of nothing whatever. I was uncomfortably aware that in intruding myself into the life of the village there were many mistakes to be made, particularly violations of good neighbourly relations. To accomplish my task I had to run against the prevailing feelings of respect for domestic privacy. No ordinary newcomer could have achieved this kind of licence, but clearly I had to avoid, as best I could, giving cause for resentment. The local response to a newly-arrived resident was courteous and rather formal, not unlike my reception many years later in a suburban Cambridge neighbourhood. After a day or two in Kamira some of my new neighbours sought me out, introducing themselves and bringing me small gifts of food which, in my continuing state of penury, I was delighted to accept.

Although neighbourly proprieties were highly valued, each household was nevertheless a distinct social domain. While Luganda was the language of the community, the language of the homestead was, quite naturally, the mother-tongue of each settler. Among the more recent arrivals domestic architecture and organisation bore distinctive tribal imprints, but I was impressed how, among the longer-established residents, many overt expressions of their different origins had disappeared. House design, farming techniques and so on seemed to be settling on a southern Ugandan, Ganda-influenced standard. In particular, the rising generation of children who ranged freely through the homesteads of the village were almost indistinguishable. Even those prominent distinctions which remained seemed to be loosing their tribal specificity. Drink was a good example: *marwa*, the Gisu millet beer, seemed to be enjoyed by everyone (myself included) but few immigrant palates had adapted to *mwenge*, the Ganda banana beer. Communication between households in Luganda was polite and circumspect but still remarkably free and efficient, even among the newcomers. Having chatted with some of my neighbours I felt sure that gossip played an important part in village life. Accordingly, I took every opportunity to explain as fully and honestly as I could what my work and my intentions were. I scattered my visits around the villages in the hope that groups of neighbours could form some reliable and positive ideas about me.

Living with Amos I was a dependent rather than an independent member of the community. I have often wondered how my rapport with the people of Kamira might have been improved if I had lived there with a wife and children; I am sure this would have given me a greater sense of dependence on my neighbours' good will. As it was, I was just another young bachelor away from home, like so many others in Bugerere. Nevertheless, I learned a great deal by being able to share a roof with Amos and his family. From the perspective of this domain I noticed things about Kamira which I would otherwise have missed. The house was a scene of persistent activity; this could be a little wearing if I was trying to work or sleep, but as most of the domestic chores and child-rearing took place in the back yard I did not often have cause for complaint.

My own subsidiary domestic organisation was undoubtedly eccentric and the subject of enduring local curiosity. For example, the rubbish which I produced was investigated with great interest by both children and adults. I soon learned to burn things like discarded field notes which I did not wish to fall into the hands of my neighbours. The way in which bottles and tins were carried off from the rubbish heap behind Amos's house made me reflect on the cash value, in Uganda, of the contents of the average British dustbin. One day Mrs Amos Number One came to me in tears: 'You have destroyed my saucepan!' She waved in front of me an empty two-pound tin of Kenyan marmalade which I had just thrown out. To decant its contents into a plastic ant-free container I had made a small air-hole in the base. Thereafter I had to resort to other messier ways of transferring the marmalade in order to leave Mrs Amos's saucepans inviolate.

I wanted someone to come in for a couple of hours each day to wash and sweep-up and make lunch, and Amos's network of patronage threw up an eighteen-year-old Gisu called Abudu Gidudu. Although his visits coincided with the period I set aside to write up my previous day's interviews, they were usually a source of light relief. He insisted in calling me 'Father', which disconcerted me as I was only four years his senior but which was, as I soon learned, a device to remind me of my responsibility for him, particularly in such matters as advances on wages. He would sit with a large bowl out on the doorstep, washing my underwear and chatting with the callers at Amos's store. His final chore each day was to fill the bowl up with

Abudu Gidudu at work on my underwear

water and scrub his huge feet with Omo. The main attraction of the job was the opportunity to improve his English, and although this was a persistent distraction from my work we developed some remarkable repartee.

To the amusement of passers-by we sang a great deal. As he splashed about outside he would carol the hygiene ditties I had taught him:

> In hot water all germs die,
> In warm they merely mul-ti-ply.

Particularly successful was an old Glasgow song which my father had taught me, sung to the tune of 'coming round the mountains':

> . . . Ye should never push yer granny,
> For she's yer mammy's mammy,
> Ye should never push yer granny aff a bus.

For the benefit of bystanders we translated this into Luganda, and the intricacies of Scots kinship behaviour provoked a good deal of earnest discussion. One day Abudu turned up with two unpleasant wounds inflicted by a panga, the East African version of the machete. He had had a fight with the brother with whom he was lodging, and to cheer him up I composed a new verse for our song:

> . . . Livingstone Wabyanga,
> He whacked me with his panga,
> But Livingstone Wabyanga is a bum.

This gave Abudu a great deal of pleasure, and thereafter he greeted all domestic mishaps with the new oath '*bum!*'

Through Abudu I learned a good deal about the life of the young dependent bachelor in Bugerere. His main preoccupation was the pursuit of money and sexual gratification. One of the many projects which Abudu devised for his financial advancement involved investing his wages in a four-gallon can of kerosene. We spent a fascinating hour discussing sales strategy, particularly how much he should charge for each Coca-Cola bottleful. I picked up some insights into petty trading in the villages, but as Abudu persistently spent his wages in advance the venture never got off the ground.

After a while I discovered that direct questioning in interviews was not necessarily the best way of learning people's attitudes and beliefs. As my own behaviour was eliciting interesting comment and discussion, I began to look for ways of stimulating the interest of people

who came to call on me. From time to time my parents sent me parcels of newspapers and magazines. The Sunday newspaper colour
supplements struck me as being sufficiently removed from reality to
provide good material for phenomenological contemplation. I cut out
many different pictures and stuck them on the walls of my room.
This was in itself no innovation, for many people had framed family
photographs, mottoes and other decorations hanging in their homes.
Once I saw a coloured sliced-bread wrapper carefully pinned to a
wall, sufficiently *bien trouvé* to have appealed to any bourgeois English eye. My pictures of interior décor, lavish culinary works and
rustic European scenes provoked much interested discussion, but the
star attraction was a series of pictures of a young lady modelling skin-
tight garments in silver lamé. Abudu would stand before them,
polishing a plate and clicking his tongue reflectively: 'wonderful
English wife'. These photographs occasioned a visit late one evening
from Mrs Amos Number One. She was a goodlooking girl and was
always in a dilemma as to whether she should sit at my feet or show
her modernity by taking the chair which I always offered her. On this
occasion she sat resolutely in the chair, and waving at my pictures
told me she wanted me to take a photograph of her. I said I should be
pleased to oblige. Amos, she continued in her primary school English,
was a modern man and it was important that he should have such
urbane pictures of his première wife as the ones of the young lady in
silver lamé. 'So,' she declared, 'I must come naked.'

I was taken aback for a number of reasons, not the least of which
was Mrs Amos's apparent assumption that the silver lamé in the
picture was the girl's epidermis. I told her that I thought neither her
husband nor my professor in Edinburgh would approve of such
intimacy. She reflected on this, and then replied with a sigh: 'Then
perhaps I shall come with a pant.'

I extended my gallery to include some of my own family snap-
shots. Scrutinising a picture of my new brother-in-law sitting smugly
on the Giant's Causeway in County Antrim, Lameka Mubiru in-
quired: 'did he build it himself?' There was greater interest in the
photographs of local people which I gradually added to my collection; one of Wasozi, the deputy mutongole, was much admired for
the fidelity with which it showed the large wart on the side of his
nose. Other experiments with visual stimuli fell rather flat. My
Edinburgh supervisor, who had been reading about cross-cultural

experiments in the perception of colour, sent me a paint manufacturer's colour chart with the suggestion that I ask people to name
the various hues. I showed this to Amos, and asked him what he
made of it. He turned it over in his hands and then told me, in as
many words, that it was a paint manufacturer's colour chart, and
would I like him to read out the names?

I was responsible for a few minor and doubtless ephemeral innova-
tions in the community. Some time after my arrival I noticed that
several of the young men were sporting beards, even sparser and less
satisfactory than mine. I invented a contraption made out of bicycle
spokes for making toast on the Primus stove, but this did not really
catch on. My aerosol insect spray attracted more interest. People
were familiar with 'Dudumaki', a proprietary agricultural insecticide
in powder form. Some of the advantages of Amos's house were offset
by the electric lights, which attracted a great deal of wild life. A great
variety of insects streamed in through the ventilators at night and
orbited the bulbs. The last person in the house to switch off would
acquire an enormous dizzying circus. The most formidable looking
intruder, in fact quite harmless, was a creature like a chipolata with
wings, which I would strafe with Shelltox when the noise became
unbearable. The aroma of insecticide brought Amos's wives trooping
in, under the impression that I was privately enjoying some potent
alcoholic beverage.

I learned to inspect my shoes carefully before putting them on, and
reacted very cautiously to any tickling sensation on my skin. I never
really recovered from plunging my arm unwarily into an empty canvas bag and suddenly finding myself covered with immense brown
cockroaches. One of the great pleasures was lying down in bed in the
evening, behind a locked door and in the secure womb of the mosquito net. I slept a little less peacefully after one night when a movement on my chest woke me; very cautiously I turned on my torch
and found myself eye to eye with the largest spider I have ever seen.
I had a similar icy sensation the first time a bat fastened itself to my
shirt; I staggered to the door and scooped it off with a whoop of
fright. It fluttered down onto a dog which was sleeping on the doorstep, and the pair of them took off into the night squeaking and yelp-
ing. The bats became part of my domestic life and many months later
in Cambridge I was neither surprised nor alarmed to waken one
morning and find one resting on the pillow beside me.

I discovered that the local people treated the insect world with a good deal of circumspection, and greater discrimination than I did. The delicate mason wasps which drifted through houses to their own little earthenware dwellings on walls and ceilings were tolerated. On one occasion when I opened my door a large centipede fell off the top of it onto my feet. It scuttled towards my bed, so I scooped it up on a sheet of paper and flipped it across the doorstep, where a group of Amos's customers were sitting. They were electrified by the sudden appearance of this strange creature. Quickly they seized their sticks and pounded it into the dust. Then they turned to me, demanding to know what mischief I was up to. Did I not know that this was *esiga*, whose sting was more deadly than the most poisonous snake?

Having already seen a number of fearsome looking snakes on my travels in Bugerere I bought a syringe of serum on one of my excursions to Kampala. It looked every bit as fierce as the snakes, and as I tried to unravel the instructions about identifying the creatures which might attack me, I resolved that if the worst came to the worst I would lie down and die quietly. The nearest I came to such a calamity was the discovery of an eight foot mamba nesting in the coffee in the storeroom next to mine. It was despatched with sticks and left for some time on the earth in front of the house. I gradually became aware, as I sat writing at my table, that things had fallen remarkably quiet. After a few minutes I heard a faint clucking sound at the side of the house. I looked out of the door and saw a strange procession turning the corner and moving past my doorstep. It consisted of twenty or thirty chickens, led by a fat and colourful but very apprehensive rooster. They stopped several yards from the snake, every beady eye fixed on it. Gradually the rooster was egged forward. He made a few preliminary sallies, tip-toeing up and fluttering back into the cluster of hens. Finally he stretched out his neck, pecked the tail of the snake and catapulted backwards with a squawk. The snake lay still. He returned and pecked it a little more confidently, then he was joined by one or two of the others, pecking and retreating nervously. Eventually every bird had pecked at the corpse; clucking with relief they gradually dispersed about their normal business.

Behind my room there were three bedrooms, dark private places each with a stout door and a strong lock. They belonged to each of Amos's wives, and were sternly defended pieces of territory. Occasionally I stole glimpses of these secret worlds full of bedding, boxes, plates, glasses and other possessions. The beds were draped around with pieces of curtain, and after some time I learned that my own un-screened bed was considered very immodest. The children of each wife slept in their mother's room, and as everyone retired at night the household broke up into its component units. Within the new architecture an old pattern was being perpetuated, for throughout East Africa a man's compound would consist of the separate huts and granaries of each of his wives. My own distinct but dependent accommodation within Amos's house sometimes made me feel a little like a fourth wife. I was drawn into his family network in some quite explicit ways. Early in my stay his mother Asinasi adopted me as her son, explaining that a young lad away from home needed someone to keep a maternal eye on him. She would call to see me after her daily visits to the Anglican church, spreading her cloth to sit on the floor of my room and enquiring whether I had written to my own mother and was saying my prayers regularly. I became very fond of the old lady and was glad to show her some filial attention by way of gifts of sugar and tea.

Asinasi also called to see her grandchildren, to whom she was very indulgent. She was particularly affectionate towards Amos's son Lukoho who, as was the Gisu custom, had been named after his grand-father, Asinasi's beloved husband. As a devout Protestant, Lukoho senior had remained monogamous, and their marital relationship had been quite different from the polygynous style favoured by Amos. Asinasi conversed with me enthusiastically about marriage; she ex-plained how the partnership which had been arranged for her had developed into a romantic attachment, the memory of which she greatly valued. She was intrigued with my opinion that in Western countries love was a prelude to marriage rather than a consequence of it. She regarded polygynous marriage as a hectic and divisive busi-ness. However, having lived in close contact with several polygynous households I feel that in many important respects the wives are more independent and more 'liberated' than their monogamous sisters. There was evidence of this in the domestic economy. In Buganda, as in many other societies, a man had to allocate a portion of his land and his home for the exclusive use of each of his wives. They could accumulate private savings, and the manager of the Standard Bank

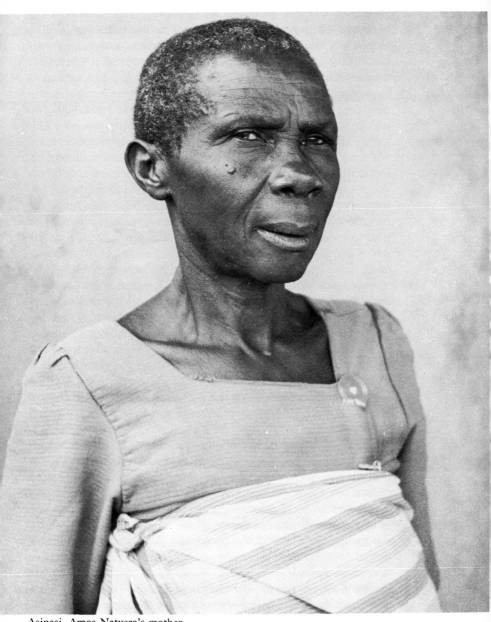

Asinasi, Amos Natyera's mother

Agency in Kayunga once told me that I would be astonished if I knew the number and size of personal savings accounts held by Bugerere women. Particularly among the Baganda, marriages were notoriously unstable, and accumulation of funds was a necessary assurance for old age. Esimafesi Salongo of Kamira told me that in twenty-six years of marriage he had had twenty-three wives, never more than five concurrently. They left 'because there was no more loving', and they 'returned to their fathers and found new husbands'. This was a record for the village, but not exceptional in the region at large.

I found the relative independence of older women very striking. Perhaps I can convey this most vividly by describing a strange encounter which took place on Easter Sunday 1966. Joseph and I had set out to meet a Muganda who had a large farm near Nazigo in Musale. We were greeted at the door of the big rambling house by an odd little man in kanzu, jacket and felt hat, who greeted us pompously and led me by the hand inside. He introduced us to the master of the house, ensconced in an armchair and drinking banana beer. There was a surreal feeling in the air, heightened by some ill-suppressed laughter from children at the doorways and windows. For a quarter of an hour I was led backwards and forwards through my introductory routine in a way which taxed my Luganda beyond its limits. Then abruptly the mood changed. The farmer, switching suddenly to good English, asked me to sit down and make myself at home. He then introduced me to his wife who, in the meantime, had changed her kanzu, jacket and felt hat for the elegant *gomasi* dress of Ganda women. She sat down in an armchair beside us, and he passed her a glass of beer.

The farmer explained that his wife had dressed up as a tax inspector to tease the Ruandan labourers. However, this Easter holiday travesty had deeper implications. He pointed to a large framed photograph above our heads in which the formal conventions of a family portrait had been significantly changed. His wife was seated in a capacious armchair in the middle of the group and her husband was standing behind her. 'Four years ago,' he explained, 'I gave her her Jubilee.' In this unusual way he had chosen to formalise a transition which many Ganda women achieve less spectacularly. After twenty-five years her independence and authority had been recognised, and she had become, in a very real sense, another man about the house.

Between 10 and 15 per cent of the household heads in any Ganda village are women. *Nnakyeyombekedde*, 'she who has built for herself', is a modern phenomenon made possible by the greater opportunities for the economic independence of women. Maria Nampa had an eight-acre farm not far from Amos's house. Her marriage had broken up twenty years previously, and in 1953 she had come to Kamira with her two little daughters. She now supplemented her income by brewing pineapple and banana beer and running a sort of bar on the verandah of her house. A Mukiga whom she described as her 'friend' lived permanently with her, as did his two children, but after I met her I wrote in my notes that she received me and dealt with me 'just as if she had been a man'.

Nevertheless, to be master of a polygynous household, *Ssemaka* in Ganda usage, remained the foremost ambition of most men. This was a concomitant of wealth and prestige within the community, and the clearest indication that an immigrant had really settled in Kamira. Most men would agree, however, that running such a household was an onerous business. Living with a group of independent-minded women, the husband would from time to time have to assume the role of peace-keeper. I was often told that sisters made the most compatible wives as they were used to living together. In a lengthy discussion of this matter, Lameka Mubiru gave me an example of the kind of domestic games a husband might be obliged to play. If one wife seemed discontented he would take her aside and whisper to her that she was his favourite, pressing twenty shillings into her hand and insisting that she should keep his special feelings for her a secret. A little later he would repeat the ruse with another wife. To me the deception seemed rather fragile and an invitation to discontent, but it was clear that calculation was typical of the polygynous ménage. A certain courteous formality prevailed in the conjugal relationships, and this probably allowed secrets to survive. This was particularly striking when one overheard a man politely address his wife in bed: 'Good morning, madam.' A feeling of reserve was also evident among co-wives, fostered by the fact that there were distinctions of senior and junior status among them. The husband would escape whenever he could into the company of other men, leaving his senior wife very much in charge; she might be described, rather ruefully, both by himself and the rest of the family, as *Nnakafuga*, 'she who rules'. Nevertheless, for most of the time relationships among wives seemed friendly and compatible, as well as being mutually supportive in matters of child-bearing and child-rearing. During my stay Amos's third wife was pregnant and very unwell, and nearly all her chores were performed for her, without complaint, by the other two.

In such a household the whole question of whose turn it was to do what was a matter of *double entendre*. One afternoon I was sitting in the courtyard in front of a villager's house, waiting for him to come up from his farm to talk to me. One of his wives was preparing matoke nearby and, simply to break the silence, I remarked: 'I see it's your turn to make supper.' She fled in confusion into the house, slamming the door behind her. Joseph, who had succeeded admirably in keeping a straight face, explained to me afterwards how cooking, eating and making love chased each other round and round in idiomatic Luganda. He took this opportunity to confide that his wife was 'wombéd', and to ask me for an advance of two hundred shillings as a down payment on a second wife. Amos told me that a man was not supposed to sleep with his wife for at least six months around childbirth, and that this was yet another reason why two or more wives were essential. He approved of the investment Joseph proposed, and explained that for a Mugisu buying a wife was a costly business. This sparked off a vigorous anthropological debate, for at Edinburgh we had always been taught that bride payments legitimised the transaction between two families and should never be regarded as a simple matter of purchase. When I tried to explain to Amos his mistake, he thumped the table and exclaimed: 'I paid two thousand shillings! I *bought* my wives!' He pointed out that the money went out of his pocket straight into the pocket of the girl's father, and that if that was not *buying* he did not know what was.

His wives certainly did not behave like mere chattels. One night Amos returned home very late after a session of drinking marwa beer and talking politics in Kangulumira. The women had locked up the house and gone to bed. Amos banged authoritatively on the back door, but no one moved. He knocked again, angrily and insistently, but the door remained bolted. His tone gradually changed to one of supplication, and then to abject pleading. Eventually Mrs Amos Number One got up grumbling. She unbolted the back door and then skipped back into her own room, locking the door behind her. Amos spent an uncomfortable and lonely night in the back parlour, and next day his mood was black. He startled me somewhat by declaring: 'Mr Sunday,

Coiffure in Kamira; a schoolgirl ties the hair of one of her father's wives

I have told my wives that they must migrate.' He knew that I was obsessed with problems of migration. However he went on to explain that life was obviously too easy for them, and that a spell down on the farm in Kamira would do them a power of good. I do not think anything came of this, but a little later he was able to reassert his authority by refusing to permit his senior wife to return home to Bugisu for a holiday, on the grounds that the coffee had to be picked. For many days the atmosphere in the house was thunderous, but Amos's will prevailed. Such episodes helped to make the basic inter-dependence of household members evident. Lameka Kigozi once told me that no friend or relative was more important to a man than his wife; only she could wash his body and care for him when he was sick.

The larger, mixed household also seemed to have some advantages from the perspective of the children. I ran an essay competition in the local private secondary school on the subject 'My Family and Our Farm'. One young Mugisu wrote a glowing account of his father's extensive and prosperous polygynous household: 'Though some of my mothers don't bring forth, I am still very proud of my family.' However, it seemed that girls tended to see things a little differently. One of his classmates, a Gisu girl of sixteen, wrote:

In my family my mother was the first to be married to my father and they received the blessed from the church. The second mother married to my father unblindly, she did not know what to do, so what she did was to take my mother's property. But I am sure there is not any man who can have more than one woman. When she came my father told her to share the house with my mummy, but the woman was cheak and refused. What my father did was to make for her a house of grass because she was still a newcomer in our home. And moreover she saw difficult things in the home.

Love and marriage were things which were very much on a young man's mind, and many of the people who talked with me assumed that I was no exception. The young rakish bachelor was something of a liability to his family. He was *mutambuze*, 'he who strolls around', and the womenfolk particularly would counsel him about finding a match and settling down. Unless he had some material security to offer he was unlikely to make much progress. One of the many Ganda proverbs declares: 'Find money and a wife will find you.' My friend Stephen, a young clerk at the Gombolola headquarters, had embarked on a serious quest for the ideal wife. He had heard of a domestic science school at Jinja, and he enveigled me into composing on his behalf the following letter to its principal:

Dear Madam,
I understand that there are in your school several girls who will shortly be completing a course in domestic science, and may be willing to consider marriage. If you happen to know of any girl who might be interested in marrying, I should be most grateful if you will let me know, so that I can arrange to meet the lady in question at your school on the fifteenth of August.
I am, Madam, &c.

We both thought this was a tasteful and discreet approach, and were disappointed to receive no reply.

As I got to know the various households in Kamira the importance of marriage in community inter-relationships became increasingly apparent to me. As I tried to turn my gut feelings about the growth of Kamira and the lives of its people into respectable academic terms, I had the disconcerting feeling that my anthropological education was slowly slipping away from me. In the progress reports which my Edinburgh supervisors demanded from me every two months, I contrived to speak the disciplinary language in which I had been schooled. Responding to my concern about family inter-relationships one of my supervisors ripped the covers off a book which he felt would shed some light, and air-mailed it to me at huge expense. It was a well-known study edited by the anthropologist Jack Goody, entitled *The Developmental Cycle in Domestic Groups*. In his introduction, the Cambridge professor Meyer Fortes explains very clearly something which is deceptively obvious: households are not static, but groups of people which are continually changing over time. They grow and decline as children move out to make households of their own. In this repetitive process, the domestic cycle, one can see how the family is related to others in the community around it in different ways at different stages in its career. The restless life of each household is an important key to understanding the life of the community as a whole.

I had already formed a great deal of respect for the Cambridge anthropologists, and on re-reading this book I felt it might provide a suitable framework for some of the things I wanted to say about Kamira. It seemed to confirm my view that, in an ambivalent way, family life everywhere is at the same time attractive and repulsive. No household can keep growing for ever, it must break up at some stage. The hearth is the centre of the universe, but the youth is torn between loyalty to and affection for his parents' hearth, and the desire to cut loose and build a hearth of his own. Domestic fission, as Meyer Fortes has called it, is a tense but inevitable period in family life. The anguish of this breach with the parental home was evident in the story of Mosa Ngobi's departure from Busoga, and in the bittersweet memories of many other Bugerere immigrants. I could sympathise, for through my nostalgia I could remember well the irksome feelings of dependence on my parents. Now, like so many others around me who had not yet made a home of their own, I was out in the social limbo of the big wide world. To the people of Bugerere I could still be regarded as a 'schoolboy', and the friendly concern for my unmarried state was most evident in the gifts of food which I received so frequently.

Having a wife seemed to make an important distinction among people in the community, separating labourers, dependent bachelors like Abudu Gidudu, and people like myself with no long-term commitment to Kamira on the one hand, from family men like Amos, whose lives had become so closely bound up with the affairs of the village. Marriage could even palliate the status of labourer, for the man who brought his wife and children to Bugerere was treated with much more respect and tolerance. He was seen as more responsible, if not necessarily more committed to the community. It was also clear that Bugerere looked very different from the perspective of the married and the unmarried man. This could be seen in the contrast between two Kamira neighbours, Kigate and Namunaga. Kigate lived in a small thatched hut on two acres of land which he had bought in 1951 from a Ruanda neighbour. His attitudes and his way of life emphasised his detachment from community life. He had been married, unsuccessfully, for a few years before he left his native Ankole to find work in Buganda. He had found life at home oppressive; his parents had died, his cattle had been attacked by rinderpest, his land was poor, he had no money, and he had fallen out of favour with his clansmen. They were, he said, persecuting him with witchcraft and so, for his own safety, he felt obliged to get out. Now he was managing to scratch a living in Kamira, and felt he might as well stay there as anywhere, for land was land whether in Bugerere or Ankole.

He said that living alone was dangerous, and that his flimsy hut had been burgled twice. Although he had lived in the village for so long he felt he could confide in none of his neighbours nor seek their assistance in time of trouble.

Namunaga, a Mugisu, arrived about the same time as Kigate and was about the same age, but his attitudes to Kamira were as effusive as Kigate's were noncommittal. Life in the village was fine, he reckoned he would spend the rest of his days there and would probably be buried in his farm. He enjoyed local beer parties, and he regarded his neighbour Nabirwa as his closest friend and counsellor. He had two wives, one of whom he had met in adjacent Kalagala village, and two children. His daughter by a previous marriage was now the wife of Mutenywa, who lived two homesteads away. Although a household of eight people were dependent on his four acre farm, he was in every respect more prosperous than Kigate.

Joseph once remarked to me that one of the advantages of being a member of a larger household was that one could escape from it relatively unobtrusively from time to time. The more a household grew, the more its members seemed to spill out into the community, seeking friends, allies and spouses. It is almost axiomatic that marriage involves going outside the family to find a mate, and that it does not simply unite the couple concerned, it brings together two family groups. These inter-relationships are important in any community, but in a village like Kamira where long-established lineage or clan groups were lacking, they were particularly significant. As I added details of each household to a large cumulative chart, I was impressed by the way in which relationships by marriage seemed to thread their way through the longer established villagers. Thirty-six of the 117 adult men in Kamira had married a relative of another villager; this meant that 43 per cent of the households were each connected to at least one other by marriage. The relative prosperity of the village which enabled a man to take more than one wife, and the high rate of separation, both increased the opportunities for inter-marriage. Typically, a man would arrange to introduce a neighbour to his sister or cousin, and would act as intermediary in negotiations with the girl's parents. In this way, Wamembi married Wirege's half-sister in 1953; he told me: 'For two months I prepared my home, buying a bed and household things which were needed. Then I built a shelter on my yard, and on the appointed day there were drums, dancing and plenty of marwa beer.' Such a wedding party was an opportunity for local participation and enjoyment, unlike the marriages which were arranged outside the village. Wamembi recalled that for a day and a night his homestead was a noisy and convivial focus for the people of Kamira and a good many others besides. Perhaps the atmosphere was similar to the weddings which I have attended between two members of my graduate college in Cambridge; the ceremonies do not simply unite the couples and their families, they leave the community itself with a closer sense of solidarity.

The 'in-law' relationships formed strings on my chart of the villagers: Dongo, a Mugwere, had married a cousin of Amos Natyera; Kigozi Lameka had married the sister of one of Amos's wives. The longest string, counting all kinds of relationship by kinship and marriage, extended through eighteen Kamira households. I have no doubt that I was the only person to have seen the string in its entirety; nevertheless it was important, for on occasions like funerals and weddings parts of it would be 'activated' and talked about by the people themselves. The complete chart of village inter-relationships brought to light some interesting facts. The tendency was for men to marry the women relatives of longer-established villagers. Luka Manyala, the first of Kamira's present settlers, had married ten wives, but it was striking that all of them had come from home in Bugisu; he explained that his brother kept him posted about likely girls there. However, his daughter had been married to Wagama, another Gisu villager, and his sister to the Sudanese, Israeli Bune. The fact that these two marriages had since broken up seemed to have no adverse affect on the relationships between the men. Manyala spoke to me very warmly about Bune, and Wagama cited his erstwhile father-in-law as his most trusted village friend. The fact that more recent settlers tended to marry into established families, and not the other way about, indicated the strategic interest of village inter-marriage. Various alliances were the subject of much gossip, particularly where the material rewards to one party or the other were obvious. Village opinion could be very censorious if it was felt that a man was courting a widow or a divorcée with a view to getting his hands on her property.

This kind of feeling obliged a man like Masanga to play his cards very carefully. Nandundu was the widow of a Mugisu who settled in Kamira about the same time as Luka Manyala. When her husband was still alive her younger sister came to live with her, and she was followed by her prospective husband, Masanga. Masanga's problem was that he had no property of his own, either at home in Bugisu or in Bugerere. He rented a separate plot of land on a year-to-year basis, growing annual crops like maize and cotton. In 1965 Nandundu's husband died, and Masanga made himself indispensable as the man about the house. Nandundu gave her sister two acres of her farm and insisted that she should now marry Masanga. When I spoke to him, he was still diffident about the arrangement, speaking of the two acres as 'my wife's land'.

Fourteen of the existing marriages in Kamira were cross-tribal. It did not surprise me that earlier mixed marriages, such as that between Bune and Manyala's sister, should have broken down, for there must have been many problems of domestic adjustment. Language was undoubtedly an obstacle, and the tendency was for Luganda, the lingua franca of the community, to become the lingua franca of the mixed household. Matters of diet, domestic routine and styles of living can not have been easy to reconcile, and it was clear that in such a household the problems and processes of integration were at their most intricate. I felt that those who succeeded were truly the new people of Bugerere, and regretted that I did not have the opportunity to live at close quarters with a mixed family.

In some respects I found it perplexing to think of Kamira as a village of in-laws. My anthropological reading had told me that in most parts of East Africa in-law relationships were conducted in formal and not exactly friendly ways. A young man was obliged to treat his wife's father with great deference, and to shun his mother-in-law altogether. In Kamira this did not pose a very serious problem, as most parents-in-law lived outside the village. However, when they came visiting special accommodation had to be provided for them; some people had built little huts among their coffee trees, at a discreet distance from their own houses. I discussed this once at a beer party, and there was general agreement that strict formality was on the wane. One man pointed at a neighbour and remarked: 'he is my wife's cousin; if our grandparents could see us drinking together like this, they would have been shocked.' In the conventions of many East African peoples, brothers-in-law were expected to treat each other with a stylised boisterousness which anthropologists have termed 'joking behaviour'. This involved taunts and sexual badinage which I found a little alarming on the few occasions I observed it. It certainly seemed an uncomfortable style for day-to-day relationships among neighbours, but in Kamira it had been diluted to a kind of bonhomie which would have been considered unexceptional among brothers-in-law anywhere. When I drew attention to the proliferation of in-law relationships in Kamira, they were invariably acknowledged with approval. Wamembi remarked: 'This helps us to work together', and indeed, in-law ties seemed to provide a pretext for friendly co-operation in such things as house-building or coffee-harvesting. Such friendly reciprocity, I was often assured, was seldom possible between full brothers. Of course, the bonds between households were sustained as much by the wives as by the husbands. Although Amos and Kigozi were good friends, the close relationship between their two households was sustained mainly by the two sisters to whom each was married.

On her regular visits to see me my 'mother' Asinasi would express concern that at twenty-three years of age I was still unmarried. Several efforts were made to find me a wife, or wives in the case of a delectable pair of six-year-old twins who came hand-in-hand to call on me now and then. As a long-term investment I found this offer particularly difficult to resist, but I remained unwed and, bearing in mind my Professor's advice, quite chaste. On the subject of marriage there was a difference of opinion between Asinasi and my real mother, who had counselled against returning to Edinburgh with a black wife.

6 Bernardo Gizaza

During my absence in Bugerere there were a number of changes in my own family. My sister married and moved out of our parents' home to a small town in the Scottish Borders. She sent me a piece of wedding cake, but the dainty silver paper box arrived empty. Our grandmother, a lively and affectionate woman who had an important hand in our upbringing, died. The household was further reduced by the demise of our elderly family dog. My mother felt these changes keenly and dwelt on them in the letters she wrote to me. The house suddenly seemed very large and empty. I found it hard to imagine how different things would be when I eventually returned home. I felt sure that I had made my own break with the family nest and would return to Edinburgh as an independent son. Nevertheless, my letters home were ambivalent about this, seeming to look for a sense of continuity and an assurance that in spite of all my new experiences, the things I valued would remain fundamentally the same.

There were many other people in Bugerere who watched the mails as avidly as I did. The poste restante facilities at Kangulumira consisted of a large cardboard box full of letters and packages, many of which had become grubby and tattered by being picked-over by dozens of anxious hands. A letter addressed to a village could be delayed for months, as it was the responsibility of the parish and village chiefs to ensure that it reached the right person. In spite of the expense, many people used the registered post as the only reasonably secure method of communication.

The few letters which I was shown seemed brief and formal, epistolary conventions masking personal sentiment. No doubt many of my own letters home were inhibited in the same way; they were certainly more lengthy and verbose. The migrant's letter would often include a string of messages to and from other people, and it seemed that those who could not read or write were very dependent on this indirect form of communication. Sometimes marriages, funerals and other get-togethers would provide an opportunity to compose a joint letter home. At a Kuku drinking party I attended a young man was acting as scribe, scratching out with a ball-point refill the messages dictated to him by the people present: 'Tell Zeno, father of Modi, that the child Namu has died.' My donation of a new pen and several sheets of clean paper was much appreciated. It occurred to me that if I had the linguistic ability I could have learned a great deal about the migrants and their problems by setting myself up as a letter-writer. Radio Uganda provided an important service by broadcasting 'Personal Announcements' on its vernacular services. In this era of the transistor radio the quickest and surest means of informing dispersed clansmen of a funeral was to send a postcard to the radio headquarters.

The most popular times for visiting home were January and February after the cotton harvest, and August and September when most of the maize and coffee had been sold. The frequency of visits seemed to depend on the distances involved, and their duration on whether or not the migrant still had close kin at home. Baganda would make regular two- or three-day trips home, but a Kuku would be lucky to get home once in three years and would stay for two or three months. All visitors would act as couriers, bringing messages and gifts to and from other villagers. Only a quarter of the people in Kamira never went visiting outside Bugerere; these were mainly older people whose parents and brothers and sisters had either died or dispersed.

Amos Natyera had rhapsodised to me on many occasions about his Gisu homeland and I was glad to accept an invitation to accompany him on his next trip to Mount Elgon (see Map 3). He proposed to travel in the ruined Land Rover which he had bought that year, and I was instructed to keep our excursion a secret otherwise every Mugisu in the vicinity would be pestering Amos for a ride. We left under cover of darkness one Saturday morning, carrying a Kamira villager, Wadwaya, and six bags of maize meal which Amos hoped to sell advantageously in Bugisu. We had to pause in a garage in Jinja to solve a carburettor problem, and as the sun rose higher in the sky Amos hopped around the car impatiently. It was unlicensed, uninsured and mechanically unsound, and he knew that by 11.00 a.m. the police patrols would be out on the main roads. Not far from the town of Tororo we were flagged down and a zealous young constable made a catalogue of our misdemeanours. He took from my fingers a twenty shilling note which I just happened to be holding, and told me that in future I should find a more respectable driver. As he proceeded to draw up a series of charges Amos restrained me with his hand; pleading in kitchen-boy English with the supercilious young policeman he seemed an iota of the man I knew. As we proceeded on our way, he was philosophical: 'Now you have seen how we suffer.' I was very vexed, and we commiserated with each other over a pot of fresh Gisu coffee in a café at Mbale.

We spent the next two hours driving around the town trying unsuccessfully to dispose of the maize, and then took to a series of narrow hill tracks to the area where Amos was born. We paused once to deliver a parcel of food to a relative of Bernardo Gizaza, again to arrange to pick up the son of another Kamira villager on our return journey, and a third time to join a noisy marwa beer party at the home of one of Amos's clansmen. On each occasion there was a rapid exchange of news, and discussion of the most profitable way we might dispose of the maize. We then climbed to Nkokonjeru, one of the shoulders of Mount Elgon. Amos pointed with excitement as we caught occasional glimpses of the peak, a faint outline high above the lush green valleys. We stopped at the village of Busano in the midafternoon to visit the parents of Mrs Amos Number One—always called 'Nabusano' after her native village. We were greeted with more marwa beer, and given a package of food to take back home to their daughter. Amos gave the father a generous cash gift, and coyly refused to confirm my suspicion that he had designs on Nabusano's extremely attractive sister. Later we drove down the Manjiya valley to Bulucheke, and as we neared Amos's birthplace we stopped more frequently to greet friends and relatives. Amos reckoned that we could spend the night at the home of one of his mother's brothers, but when we arrived his wives told us that he had gone to visit a sick relative. They gave us a gloomy account of the poverty of life in Bugisu, eyeing the maize meal in the back of the Land Rover. Amos emptied out half a sack for them, and then with a final flourish of generosity pulled all the notes and loose change out of his pocket and thrust them into their hands. As we drove off the women looked greatly heartened, and I congratulated him on his munificent gesture. He confided to me that on such excursions he always distributed his cash about his person, as emptying a pocket always looked more generous than peeling a few shillings from a wad of banknotes.

We pressed on, with Amos pointing to homesteads here and there, naming relatives of himself and other Kamira people I knew. By this time my concentration was slipping, for we had drunk large quantities of marwa beer and eaten nothing. I should explain that marwa is taken by a group of people sitting on small stools around a single pot, which is replenished now and then with fresh beer and hot water. Each drinker has a long flexible tube with a small filter on one end to keep out the grains of millet. The conviviality of this arrangement demands an element of mutual trust, and Bagisu have become very adept at judging how fast someone is drinking by the movement of his cheeks and throat. In my case our hosts were not concerned that I was getting more than my share, but that I should drink heartily. Each time we stopped my intake was carefully monitored, and I was rebuked if there were any signs of pretence as I sucked on my tube. The result was that as the Land Rover lurched through the twilight my stomach and brain were awash. Amos, however, was exhilarated, and driving with great verve. As we were heading down a narrow, winding track we were caught in a short sharp rainstorm. Amos braked sharply as we approached a precipitous corner, and on its bald tyres the Land Rover became a sledge. We plunged off the road and into space. Some divine hand had placed a small grove of bushy trees in our trajectory, and the vehicle came to rest in them almost vertically. We clambered back to the road, shaken but with only a few bruises, and found a group of ten or fifteen men returning home drunk after a marwa beer party. They were greatly amused by our plight, and to Amos's vexation they had a long and raucous debate about whether or not they should help us, and how much their assistance would cost us. Eventually they hauled the Land Rover back to the road for a shilling a head. It looked a little more battered than before, but the engine started and the wheels went round. We continued on our way very cautiously, with Amos still mortified by the behaviour of our rescuers: 'Now you will think badly of Gisu people.'

By the light of the moon and our one remaining headlamp we arrived at a large homestead, and I was greatly relieved when Amos assured me that here we would spend the night. It was the home of the Hon. David Kimaswa, a Gisu member of the National Assem-

A Gisu family at Kamira drinking *marwa* beer. A labourer is topping-up
the pot with boiling water

bly and yet another relative of Amos's. Although we were late and unexpected guests we were warmly received and given cups of sweet tea. The best bedroom was vacated for us and I slept gratefully.

I rose shortly after dawn to discover that Amos was already out visiting his father's grave. The morning was cool and bright and the valley around the house was very beautiful. The hillsides were intensely cultivated and later Amos picked out for me his father's former share of the clan lands: a fragment here, another there, a small terraced plot half a mile away. The self-contained farms of Bugerere suddenly seemed rich and spacious. David Kimaswa announced that he wanted to spend the day showing me his constituency; I think Amos regretted that he would not be my guide, but he was now freer to attend to his own affairs. We drove to a mountainside village where Kimaswa wanted to speak to some of his Democratic Party supporters, and I was taken on an energetic climb by a group of youths. The path snaked up through coffee trees, turning steeply over the tin roofs of homesteads below us. As we climbed through strands of morning mist I found the altitude tiring, but an elderly man who accompanied us bounded ahead impatiently. Our goal was a plump imported Jersey cow, grazing contentedly high up on a narrow grassy ledge. Above us, cultivation gave way to fragrant conifers which reminded me of home. On the way back, some of the boys gave me a dramatic demonstration of the speed with which people could run down the mountainside. After midday we returned to Kimaswa's house and my first meal since leaving Bugerere: matoke, rice, maize cake, chicken and curried goat.

In the afternoon Kimaswa drove me to the Kenya border twenty miles away, pointing out the overcrowding and overcultivation which so seriously threatened the prosperity of his constituency. As we sat in the car waiting for another sharp rainstorm to pass over, he told me that the temperamental climate had fostered an aggressive and restless spirit among the Bagisu. Pointing to a dark, narrow valley he said there was a sombre and menacing side to the Gisu character. There were numerous witch-finding cults and strange prophetic churches, symptoms of a malaise which afflicted the area. Where the mountain slopes made communications difficult, brigands flourished. I began to sympathise with the many Bagisu who had found refuge in the relatively placid hills around Kangulumira. Nevertheless, there were many ways in which Bugisu looked more prosperous than

Bugerere; Kimaswa showed me new schools and clinics, flourishing co-operative societies and other evidence of public progress which made Bugerere look like a wasteland.

On our return to Bulucheke we found Amos in sentimental mood. After a day of family visiting and a good deal of marwa beer, he was gesturing expansively at 'our school' and 'our hill'. Before our departure he took me up to his father's grave and pointed to the pieces of land he proposed to reclaim by some means for his retirement. As he stood on the hillside evoking dead ancestors and distant cousins, he seemed to draw the web of kinship tightly around him. Bugerere and the collection of new friends, neighbours and in-laws which comprised Kamira, seemed very distant. As we drove back through the night we argued endlessly about the merits and demerits of home and abroad until, not much before dawn, we passed again through the Mabira forest south of Kangulumira, and the tall trees reawakened his earlier vision of the promised land.

Bugisu offered me another perspective on the migrant's ambivalent feelings about home. The kind of success which Amos enjoyed in Bugerere did not escape the attention of relatives at home, and settlers used to grumble about the predations of visiting kin. One way of keeping them at bay was to send small presents regularly. I was told: 'If I don't send things to my family, they will all come here saying "Ah, how your coffee is thriving! You must be very rich! Alas, your brothers at home have nothing to eat . . ." so I send them some money.' Usually amounts ranging from five to thirty shillings were sent to one or two specific relatives, although much larger sums might be sent as a subscription to a funeral or hospital fees. A great deal of food was sent, usually such portable items as beans, groundnuts, a particularly good cutting of coffee or some Pepsi-Cola. Rather than sending presents, some people looked after a young relative and paid for his education at a school in Buganda. Contact with home was sustained mainly through parents, and when they died visits and gifts would dwindle.

There were a few cases in which a migrant's family, and thereby his loyalties, were more sharply divided. Wamubireggwe had two homes, one in Kamira and one in his native Bukede. He was a prosperous farmer, with fifteen acres in Kamira and a herd of cattle at home in Bukede. He had invested in a taxi which plied between

Kangulumira and Mbale, and as he and parts of his family commuted monthly between the two farms he was undoubtedly his own best customer. He acknowledged that this arrangement did not make much sense, and he was the only long-established resident of Kamira who stated unequivocally that he proposed to quit soon to concentrate on his cattle. His regular absences made him something of a stranger within the community. Such a split could only occur if the migrant had sufficient land of his own at home, which was rare. Occasionally a migrant would inherit land, confronting him with the dilemma of whether or not to return. Mulengule unexpectedly inherited fifteen small plots at home in Bugisu; he had already moved his wives and children back there, and it seemed unlikely that he would retain his four acre farm in Kamira much longer. Some people considered Mulengule a lucky man, for once a migrant had settled in Bugerere the family heads at home were much more likely to favour a needy relative there when property was being distributed. I asked all the people I interviewed if they thought it at all likely that they might sometime inherit land at home; about 40 per cent of the newcomers thought they had some chance, but only 9 per cent of those who had been in Bugerere more than sixteen years were optimistic. A slightly higher proportion felt that they could get a piece of family land at home if they really needed it, but most of them reminded me that one of their main reasons for leaving was to relieve pressure on resources. By passing up their small share of family property they had enabled a younger brother to marry and establish his own farm. In crowded areas like Bugisu no land could be left idle, and a plot left in the care of a brother was more difficult to reclaim the longer it was entrusted to him.

The settlers in Kamira seemed to recognise that as they became more involved in the new community it was increasingly difficult to devote time and attention to affairs at home. Bernardo Gizaza was a remarkable exception, and his decision to return to Bugisu after sixteen years in Kamira came as a surprise to everyone. He had come to play a vital part in the emerging social order of the village, and his departure shortly before I left Bugerere seemed to call into question my understanding of what commitment to the community meant. By the demise of his elders, Gizaza had risen *in absentia* to a position of eminence in his clan at home, and after some heart-searching he had decided that he could no longer resist the call to return to Mount

Bernardo Gizaza at home in Kamira

Elgon and fulfil his ancestral duties. Shortly before I left Bugerere he came to ask me to take some photographs of his family and farm in Kamira. He seemed genuinely regretful about leaving, but said he had many friends in Kamira whom he would come to visit from time to time. He told me that he would never have considered leaving had his new clan office not assured him sufficient land and mature coffee trees.

Gizaza's departure renewed my feelings of perplexity about the migrant's permanence, and how much it mattered in the growth of the community. Was my concern for the relationship between personal commitment and the growth of the new society misplaced? Did the comings and goings of individuals have any real effect on continuity and order? In an ordinary, established village elsewhere it might make no difference, but the future of Kamira seemed much more directly dependent on the attitudes and actions of its first generation of settlers. How was the village diminished by Gizaza's departure? It was in conversations with him, more than with anyone else, that I began to feel the presence of a moral order; he seemed to see in Kamira something greater and more durable than the sum of its individual inhabitants. For him the village was not, nor should it be, simply a crude *pax* which allowed immigrants to exploit the material opportunities of Bugerere. It was a home in the making, competing with and gradually displacing sentimental attachment to that other home which the migrant had left. But Gizaza's decision to quit and become a custodian of the moral order in his Mount Elgon home was not an act which diminished the society which he had helped to create in Kamira.

One reason why I found my conversations with Gizaza so instructive and satisfying was because his view of Kamira was more complete than anyone else's. He knew all its settlers by name and, if I had wished to compromise him, I could have pressed him to tell me many intimate things about them. By contrast, the local knowledge of a newcomer like Kafifi or myself was trivial and inexact; we would make mistakes about such basic details as the name of the deputy chief or the boundaries of the village. Moreover, the newcomer's view of the community, and to a great extent its view of him, tended to be amoral, reserved; Kafifi treated his neighbours with polite caution and saw no reason why they should be much concerned for his welfare. Yo, who had had his plot for only ten months, told me: 'I am no-one here, if tomorrow is not good, tomorrow I shall go.' By contrast, Gizaza was knowledgeable, influential and respected; his outlook was moral in that he had some clear convictions about what *ought* to happen in Kamira. His advice about how the boundaries of a farm should be marked was unquestioned, and he was quite prepared to answer my hypothetical questions about the rights and wrongs of neighbourly relations.

Gizaza was no white-haired sage, but he was undoubtedly *ssemaka*, a man of family and property; he had five wives and eleven children, and nine acres of prime village land. He seemed to epitomise the connection I was trying to establish between the 'mechanics' of community involvement—a secure economic foothold and an established family—and an emotional attachment to the village. My blunt question: 'Please tell me how you find the condition of life in Bugerere' was usually answered in terms of the prosperity of the individual's farm and family. Mozi, a Southern Sudanese immigrant of thirteen years' standing, was enthusiastic: 'Here my children keep alive because there is food; I use my hoe well, and we have money for clothes.' Domestic setbacks could make people pessimistic; in an uncharacteristically gloomy moment, Mosa Ngobi once told me: 'We should all get out of this place (Bugerere) and leave it to the porters.' In interview, all but seven householders gave me a positive opinion of life in Kamira. They were more cautious when I asked them if they intended to stay in the village for the rest of their lives: thirteen were undecided, and six said they would probably quit. Three of the latter were young men living on plots allocated to them by their fathers; as a new generation anxious to make independent lives of their own, their restlessness suggested that the cycle of emigration might be about to recommence. Newcomers were careful about committing themselves to the village: only five of the seventeen who had been in Kamira less than six years assured me that they would stay. Of the twenty-one householders who had been in the village more than fifteen years, only Gizaza was considering leaving.

I had some misgivings about the relevance and tactfulness of my ultimate question: 'If you were to die suddenly, would you be buried here in Kamira?' This produced a good deal of gloomy but interesting speculation. One or two newcomers said they would get a bus home as soon as they began to feel poorly. Others, notably the Baganda, said they would go straight into an unmarked grave in their banana plantation. Some felt it was proper to be buried in ancestral land at home, but reckoned it was more a matter for their family and clan elders at home to decide. One Mugisu told me he had set aside some money, and given careful instructions that when his time came he should be parcelled up and driven home in the boot of a taxi. Before his decision to leave, Gizaza had assured me that he would be buried in Kamira beside his teenage son and a couple of his infant children; the former lay in a handsome cement grave near Gizaza's house. People from such distant places as Southern Sudan tended to shrug the question off, saying that the soil of Bugerere was as kind to a corpse as the soil of home. The only real fear was that one's body might not get buried at all. Although villagers seemed to feel confident that they would be disposed of with dignity, labourers I spoke to had a horror of being abandoned to the dogs and vultures. For myself, I knew that I would go back to the sanctuary of Kampala if I felt really ill; an attack of dysentery was as much as I could cope with in Kamira. It is intriguing how morbid people become when they travel away from home. Insurance companies thrive on summer holiday tourists haunted by fears of airliner catastrophe and fatal exotic diseases. Throughout the world, one of the first acts of social organisation among immigrant or resettled people is the formation of a funeral club to ship home corpses and indemnify dependents.

The word most frequently used in Kamira's favour was 'safety'. Behind the repeated assurances that the village was indeed a secure place to live there was a kind of ideological assertion: safety was something devoutly to be wished. The comments of newcomers had a curiously negative tone: 'Since I came to Kamira there has been no trouble for me, no one has beaten me, no one has burned my house . . .' Women like Maria Nampa particularly relished the respect shown to persons and property in Kamira. When she lived with her own and her husband's kin she had been given no peace to to make a living by herself. Namboso, another woman settler, told me: 'Here no-one can interfere with me or my farm.' One of the explicit aspects of this ideology was that safety could be assured because of, not just in spite of, tribal differences. Patience and toler- ance were essential, and the Bagisu never tired of telling me that if they were the sole inhabitants of Kamira, community life would be hectic. Again, it seemed arguable that such a positive face was put on tribal differences because they were potentially so disruptive. Cer-

tainly, the piecemeal way I collected information on attitudes brought
to light some latent distinctions among the groups in Kamira. Ostensibly the most committed were the northerners, mainly Sudanese:
all of them were happy in Kamira and all reckoned they would be
buried there. Although most of the Baganda were content, half of
them reckoned they would be buried at home; nevertheless they
showed the greatest tendency to marry locally and spent the least
amount of time away on visits from the village. For some reason the
Soga, Kede and Gwere people showed the least commitment in all
respects, but the numbers involved were too small to allow me to
draw any firm conclusions.

From the beginning I felt it was important to try to find out how
much the people in Kamira depended on each other. The best evidence of this would have been a complete catalogue of every villager's
movements each day; this was clearly impossible, although I did
make a daily record of a selection of people for short periods. As
usual I had to fall back on a series of hypothetical questions, some of
which proved informative in unexpected ways. I asked each householder: 'Say you were in some sort of private trouble or difficulty, or
needed some special sort of help quickly, to whom would you go?'
As each person named another on whom they felt they could depend,
I drew a line between their homes on my village map. Virtually all the
lines were confined within Kamira itself, providing me with the most
explicit evidence I had so far obtained that the village was a distinct
social unit. Of course, my question implied immediate assistance, so a
pattern of interdependence among relatively close neighbours was to
be expected. Occasionally the sense of dependence was qualified: 'I
would go to my neighbour X and ask him to lend me money to go
home and talk to my brother.' There was a tendency for people to
depend on a fellow-tribesman, which was also hardly surprising.
What was most interesting, however, was the way in which a few
individuals were singled-out as particular foci of dependence within
the community. One of the king-pins was Simewo Mazaki, cited by
eight householders, all of them settled for more than ten years. Five
people said they would rely on Bernardo Gizaza, and Manyala,
Salongo and Bune were other established settlers who commanded
similar trust.

By the time I fitted this information together I was not surprised to
discover that this particular group were apparently village patrons.

I had already become dependent on them myself, for Amos had picked them out early in my stay as people who could tell me most about Kamira and how to secure the co-operation of its inhabitants. Although I had the support of Musoke, the village chief, it was clear that this in itself did not make people feel obliged to talk to me. I could see from the start that the success of my work would depend on the backing of others who were personally much more involved in the community than Musoke. As I doubted my own ability to spot the leaders, I decided to ask the villagers themselves whom they reckoned to be the 'senior man'—'*omuntu omukulu*'—in Kamira. This seemed the best formulation, for I was anxious to avoid putting my own ideas into their heads. The newcomers tended to cite Musoke or his deputy, Wasozi, as I myself might have done. Other settlers mentioned Manyala or Salongo, but the longest established villagers were almost unanimous that the 'senior man' was Bernardo Gizaza. For them, it seemed that 'senior man' was a clumsy circumlocution; they would ask: 'Do you mean, who is *Mutaka*?' They would agree that Manyala and the others were all *Bataka*, but they also accepted Gizaza's own assertion that he was *the* Mutaka.

The first time I heard this I was greatly surprised, for I understood Mutaka to be the Ganda term for a clan head. It seemed a very odd way of describing a leader in a village where clan identities counted for virtually nothing. I consulted my Luganda dictionaries and asked other scholars in Kampala for their opinion. It became apparent that in modern usage 'Mutaka' had a range of meanings, some of which were quite apposite in the context of Kamira. The root of the word was *ettaka*, meaning soil, or land in the legal sense. It seemed true to say that the Bataka of Kamira were custodians of village land, for it was they who approved and witnessed farm boundaries. Later I discovered that in his doctoral thesis Martin Southwold had also examined the meaning of the word; sometimes, he noted, it was used to describe people who had lived in a village for a long time and had buried relatives there. This description certainly fitted Gizaza. I concluded that in Kamira, indeed in Bugerere at large, the word had three kinds of significance: it connoted priority of settlement, some kind of controlling influence over economic resources, and a moral responsibility for local people. In other words, the Bataka were closely concerned with security within the village, and as their doyen Gizaza undoubtedly held the position of a political leader.

Wasozi, the deputy mutongole chief of Kamira

Amos, that great political connoisseur, seemed to recognise this. Although he clearly respected Gizaza, he was reluctant to accord him particular eminence. Amos was not recognised as one of the Bataka, but as a local businessman he was aware of their economic influence. Perhaps it was this which prompted him to say on one occasion: 'I would not tell Gizaza and the others what I think deeply.' From the perspective of the newcomer the Bataka exerted an obscure but pervasive influence, evident from the very beginning when they escorted him round the boundaries of his farm. By contrast, the authority of Musoke, the village chief, was formal and circumscribed, but in several respects more frail. The political purchase of the official hierarchy over the villagers was significantly attenuated by the influence of the Bataka. Wasozi, the deputy chief, had been elected by the people of Kamira and performed most of Musoke's official tasks for him, but he was undoubtedly a puppet of Gizaza and the others. He was certainly respected by the community, if only for the conscientious way in which he performed his unrewarding task, but no-one said they *depended* on him, and only the relative newcomers regarded him as the 'senior man'. Answering my question, he himself said he depended on Gizaza; with no apparent sense of contradiction he designated him as the 'senior man' of Kamira.

By the time I left Kamira, Gizaza knew as much about me as I did about him. He was an intelligent man, and was concerned to understand my relationship with the government authorities, and the purposes to which I proposed to put the information I was collecting. This prudent interest was palliated by his great charm and concern for my welfare. I was in no doubt that Gizaza's personality was a vital part of his acknowledged eminence. The amicable Mazaki, doyen of the beer-drinking set, might be a favourite confidant, but Gizaza was undoubtedly the leader, charming but firm, heedful but discreet. I regret that I never asked him what *he* thought was the basis of his authority. I suppose that I assumed it was my anthropological business, not his, to draw such conclusions. When I asked him instead what tasks he performed as Mutaka he emphasised the moral and communal aspects of his role. For example, it was his duty to see that anyone who died in the village had a decent burial, particularly those who had no kinsfolk nearby to undertake the arrangements. Gizaza would institute a fifty-cent house-to-house collection to buy a cloth for the corpse, and if the deceased had no land of his own he would be buried in Gizaza's farm. On the occasion I was sick he and Manyala came to visit me, and when I told them I thought I was going to die, both assured me that I would be given the nicest possible funeral.

When I heard that Gizaza proposed to leave Kamira I was intrigued to know who would succeed him. Gizaza himself was in no doubt: the new Mutaka would be Israeli Bune. This was so unexpected that I raised the matter again when I was having a meal one day with Manyala and Mazaki, and they confirmed the choice of Bune. In his background and physical appearance he could hardly have been more different from the southern Ugandans who predominated in Kamira. He was jet black with alien-looking facial scarifications; he spoke Luganda fluently but with the distinctive lisp of the northern peoples, many of whom file their front teeth into points. Bune was not at all reticent about his tribal identity, although many Kuku were obliged to work as labourers in Buganda, nor was there any suggestion that he was trying to pass himself off as a Muganda. He never wore the Ganda *kanzu*, but always dressed smartly in a checked shirt and dark trousers. He was one of the first villagers I interviewed; he answered my questions slowly and carefully, and I returned to talk to him on several occasions. I found him charming and self-effacing, and he was one of the people who understood very quickly my interest in the new, mixed society of Kamira. He had left home in the Southern Sudan in 1942 'to look for money'. First he worked as a labourer in Bunyoro for five shillings a month, then moved to Buganda when he heard that farmers there were paying twice that amount. Attracted by even brighter prospects he moved to Bugerere at the end of 1942, and for the next seven years worked for Ganda farmers near Kayunga. In 1949 he moved south to become one of the pioneering settlers of Kamira. Although political troubles in the Southern Sudan made travelling difficult, he tried to visit his father once a year, taking with him presents of money and clothes. He dismissed at once my suggestion that he might return to live in the Sudan: 'I came here as a young man and everything I have is here, I have nothing to return to.' He was a well-known figure among emigré Kuku and had played an important part in finding land for them in the Kangulumira area.

When I met him his family life was in some disarray. His first wife had been Manyala's sister, but she had left him many years before.

His second wife, a northern girl who had borne him three children, had also left, and while he was on a trip to the Sudan his third wife, another Mugisu, had disappeared taking her children with her. He thought she had gone to Nairobi and had applied to the police to trace her. He now lived with his teenage son, to whom he was very closely attached, and one of his youngest children. He had a farm of about four acres and in 1963 earned nearly £200 from his coffee. He also ran what might be described as a labour pool: nine Barundi lived in a relatively comfortable building on his compound, and he sub-contracted their services to farmers in the Kangulumira area. Mazaki was his close friend, but he designated Gizaza the 'Big Man' of Kamira: 'He settled many of us on our farms, he speaks well and gives us good advice.'

Manyala and the others were agreed that in spite of his lisp, Bune also 'spoke well'. This was an essential quality for the Mutaka, for it implied the capacity to give a carefully considered opinion and to mediate authoritatively in discussions and arguments. Gizaza told me that it was the duty of the Mutaka to intervene in a dispute among the established villagers and persuade them to resolve the matter informally. Newcomers were more inclined to take their grievances straight to the mutongole chief, who in turn preferred to present the matter directly to his superiors rather than attempting to arbitrate personally. Established settlers disliked getting involved with the police or officialdom, particularly in matters affecting their own security. Boundary lines would get overgrown and from time to time arguments would break out about who had the right to dig where. In such cases there were strong pressures on the established villagers to settle things among themselves. It was known that the law dealt capriciously with tenants on *govumenti* land and that litigation might have unfortunate consequences for everyone.

The parish chief knew the Bataka and counted on their assistance in village government. Officialdom was often in evidence in Kamira, usually in the person of Wasozi, cycling soberly around the village issuing tax receipts or delivering messages. Although Musoke's deputy, he often dealt directly with the parish chief and when he appeared in court at Kangulumira he was usually addressed as the mutongole. Musoke seemed determined to continue 'serving the Kabaka' as long as he could, but there was little doubt that Wasozi would soon succeed him. Wasozi's main problem was that increas-

A Ganda farmer playing *mweso*

ingly the affairs of state were transacted in writing; he had left school early 'because of the urge to fornicate', but four years' service with the King's African Rifles had given him some practice with the three Rs. He got on well with Musoke, sharing with him a passion for *mweso*, the Ganda version of the ubiquitous Arabic board game Mankala. As an established villager and Manyala's cousin, he made a good bridge between the old chief and the community. Both of them made it evident that when they acted zealously it was under pressure from superior authority. Periodically the parish chief would drive through the village in his car, and as an inevitable consequence Wasozi would be obliged to organise *bulungi bwa nsi*, 'labour for the public good'. This mainly involved remaking and draining the roadway, and clearing unhealthy patches of undergrowth. If there was some official message to pass on to the people Musoke was supposed to summon a village meeting, but he and Wasozi usually found it simpler, although more arduous, to make individual house-to-house calls. Many of Wasozi's tasks were distasteful but he particularly disliked having to turn out in the middle of the night to deal with some breach of the peace.

The official alarm signal was '*nduulu*', a kind of Red Indian war whoop; anyone who heard it was expected to rush from his bed, prepared to arrest a thief or douse a blaze. On two occasions I stumbled through the night in my underwear to assist a neighbour in distress. Both were false alarms; as we stood around with our torches and sticks at the ready, our neighbour would count his chickens and then tell us apologetically that he was sure he had heard a thief. With our night's repose shattered, it seemed quite appropriate that there should be strict penalties for the improper use of *nduulu*. At night the front door of each house in Kamira was closed as firmly as in any English suburb. Honest citizens up late were expected to carry a light and call out '*mirembe*', 'peace', to anyone they encountered. Everyone was more tolerant than I of the drunks stumbling home from Kangulumira. Once, one of them banged on my door in the middle of the night and I rose in a rage and socked him on the jaw; I knew this would be regarded as intemperate and intolerant, and went back to bed fearful of repercussions. Thankfully there were none. Later I asked some of the villagers how they would have dealt with such a situation, and all of them said that unless their doors were actually beaten down they would keep mum, or call out: 'Please go away.' I reflected that they had made more progress than I had in cultivating a stiff upper lip.

The established settler dreaded falling foul of the law. One morning I tried to take a photograph of a procession of government prisoners making their way up the hill towards Kangulumira. The askari in charge quite rightly remonstrated with me, asking if I would like to have my picture taken in such demeaning circumstances. I apologised, but next day was taken aback to receive a visit from one of the prisoners. He explained that he was a respectable farmer from Kangulumira and had been gaoled for six months because he could not pay his tax. I anxiously repeated my apologies but he waved them aside: on the contrary, a photograph would have served as an object lesson to others. He posed for me in his khaki prison shirt and shorts, and when he was released from gaol I gave him a copy of the picture to hang up at home as a warning to his children. Kalisti Mukasa was the only established villager formally charged with an offence during my stay in Kamira. He was a Muganda and lived quietly with his wife and small niece on a couple of acres in the centre of the village. His case was eventually dismissed by the gombolola chief, but during the whole episode he was very upset and did no farmwork. He had given hospitality to his wife's sister and her son after they had been involved in a domestic quarrel. The angry husband suddenly arrived in Kamira and accused the son of stealing a transistor radio. He sought out the parish chief, and Musoke was despatched with an askari to arrest the boy. Mukasa refused to allow him to be taken away because he was too young, and it was for this obstruction that he was later charged. His neighbour Namwandu stood bail for him; Mukasa explained: 'I was afraid that they might lead me through the village tied up with a rope.' Musoke himself dealt with this delicate affair, and according to Mukasa, did so with tact and consideration. The neighbours were very sympathetic, and I was one of a number of people who called daily to hear the latest news.

Amos's fiery temperament kept getting him into trouble. One hot afternoon a friend parked his car in the shade by Amos's store. A stranger came and lolled against it, and ignored Amos's curt order to move. The ensuing scuffle turned into a fist fight, and with surprising alacrity the Kangulumira mutongole appeared on the scene. He listened to several accounts of what had happened then with a shrug

Amos, with his shirt ripped, explains his fight to the mutongole chief of Kangulumira

said he would take the matter to the parish chief. When Amos cooled down he sought out his opponent and persuaded him to accept sixty shillings; the pair of them then sent a message to the chief saying the matter had been resolved. Amos told me: 'I did not want to get a reputation as a trouble-maker.' Shortly after this episode a villager from Kangulumira stole a ball of twine from Amos, who earned praise for not pressing charges. Where labourers and other riff-raff were not involved, magnanimity was much appreciated.

With Joseph's assistance I studied the legal records at the Gombolola headquarters. The gombolola chief dealt mainly with tax defaulters and infringements of health regulations such as not digging a proper latrine. Nearly half of the cases brought before the circuit magistrate involved assault and robbery, and a further 25 per cent were cases of petty theft. The magistrate agreed that the great majority of offenders brought before him were young labourers from Ruanda and Burundi. Local settlers were mainly involved in liquor offences, particularly the illicit distillation and sale of *waragi*, or 'Nubian gin'. Only four of the 347 cases dealt with by the chief and the magistrate between April 1964 and March 1965 concerned land. Elsewhere in Uganda this would have been a major theme of litigation, and the fact that so few boundary disputes reached the courts was further evidence of the active role of the Bataka. When I discussed this with Gizaza he pointed out that inheritance had not yet become a major problem in a village like Kamira. One reason why he was being pressed to return home was because there were twelve succession disputes awaiting his mediation in Bugisu.

I was surprised that such a small proportion of the cases originated at beer parties. The authorities seemed much more concerned about the production of *waragi* than the noisy and occasionally riotous consumption of millet, banana and maize beer. While I was in Uganda, waragi was in fact adopted as the National Drink, the plain white spirit being given a suitably patriotic flavour—banana. Its illicit village equivalent was an opaque liquid which scalded the belly and punched a hole in the head if taken too quickly. I was surprised to be told one day that an old man in a neighbouring village had 'died of hunger'—such a thing seemed very unlikely in this relatively prosperous area. On further enquiry I was told that he was a waragi addict and that after his final binge his jaw had clamped tight. His family could find no way of getting food into him and he had wasted away.

Although I felt it was my anthropological duty to attend the beer parties in Kamira I never really enjoyed them, particularly when they took place at Amos's house. His wives would spend several days brewing marwa in a huge oil drum, and on a Saturday or Sunday large numbers of people would gather round the house with their pots, stools and tubes. Mrs Amos Number One dispensed the beer at fifty cents a calabash, while Amos himself walked from group to group topping up each pot with hot water from the electric kettle I had given him. A lot of noise was generated and, as the day wore on and the beer became more diluted, tempers started to fray. It took several days for the stench around the house to clear.

It was comforting to discover that other people like Kigozi and Mubiru disliked these occasions as much as I did, preferring more abstemious entertainment at home. The Bagisu and the Northerners were the most avid drinkers, the Baganda and Basoga being less enthusiastic. Each party had a tribal emphasis dictated mainly by the brew and the identity of the host. The conviviality had an abrasive quality which made me feel uneasy. Occasionally I was teased or insulted, and to start with I thought that my presence was resented; however I discovered after some time that this was the idiom of the occasion. Now and then the whole company would pillory an individual for some social misdemeanour like suspected adultery or stinginess. Watching the established villagers censure each other's behaviour in this way, it occurred to me that the beer party might be more an instrument of social control than a source of social disruption. If criticism became too stringent there was always that morning-after exculpation: 'I'm sorry, I was drunk at the time.'

It was this aspect of the beer parties which discouraged people like Mubiru from attending. They preferred to stay at home and drink sweet tea, or walk to Kangulumira for a cold Pepsi Cola. As a newcomer, I shared their preference for more private recreation; I particularly enjoyed going to someone's home for a leisurely meal, where the most wicked pleasure was smoking hemp. I reciprocated by inviting one or two friends to drink cold lager with me in the evenings. Although women attended the beer parties, their main recreation was taking tea at each other's homes. If I had been able to join them on these occasions I would undoubtedly have learned a great deal more about the life of the village. I knew that as a bachelor my view was partial and that, like any other immigrant, a wife and children would have broadened my perspective on Kamira greatly.

In the afternoons and evenings, transistor radios blared throughout Bugerere. The weekend request programmes brought numerous reprises of Jim Reeves' 'I Love You Because', Millie's 'My Boy Lollipop' and the Beatles' 'Words of Love'. These are tunes which still evoke the red earth, green leaves and black faces of Uganda for me, although during my stay I heard a great deal of music which was more authentically African. I occasionally listened myself to crackly shortwave broadcasts of orchestral music, as unintelligible to my neighbours as their music often was to me. Amos was surprised that Beethoven's Pastoral Sympony could make me feel serence and slightly melancholy: 'Are they praying?' he asked. He looked doubtful when I told him the peasants were cavorting on the village green after a storm, and was astonished when I started to hum along with the orchestra.

Amusing conversation has always been one of my favourite forms of recreation, but I found this very difficult in Bugerere, not only because my Luganda was weak. Cracking a joke or telling a funny story is the most drastic test of linguistic and cultural competence. The anthropologist Laura Bohannan has described superbly her efforts to tell a group of Tiv elders in Nigeria the story of Hamlet; after many interruptions the old men reformulated and reinterpreted the story to their own critical satisfaction, leaving her more informed about the Tiv and more perplexed about Hamlet.* I longed to be able to tell my friends in Bugerere a funny story, so I studied their humour carefully. I concluded that the cuckolded husband was a favourite theme so one evening, over a bottle of cold beer, I embarked on a joke about a Scots farmer who annoys his wife by persistently returning from market drunk. Eventually she decides to lock him out of the house, but after an hour of silence her curiosity takes her out with a lamp into the farmyard to look for her spouse. She finds him bedded down with a large sow in the pigsty, crooning his wife's name amorously. This provoked a little polite laughter from Amos and the others, and a lot of serious discussion about pigs, wives and Scots farmers. Much later it occurred to me that my story was too impersonal, that my Scots farmer was too much of a stranger to the Kamira community. A Cambridge friend once admonished me after a party: 'people here don't tell funny stories, they tell *anecdotes*'. I am sure

* Laura Bohannan, 'Miching Mallecho, that means witchcraft', in J. Morris (ed.), *From the Third Programme*, Nonesuch Press, London 1956.

that the same principle applied to Kamira; I should perhaps have 'personalised' my story in this manner: 'my brother-in-law Jim, who is a farmer in Scotland near where I live . . .'

The humorous side of village gossip was much appreciated, and even if the joke was at the expense of a particular villager it provided a focus of interest and amusement for everyone else. Although much of the gossip I picked up was too circumstantial for a newcomer like myself to understand, it seemed to have positive as well as negative functions. When either the welfare or the good conduct of a villager were at issue, Kamira could become a kind of corporate busybody. Even malicious gossip could express a general concern for proper behaviour, which suggested that people were not content to keep themselves to themselves on a live-and-let-live basis. Gossip could be creative, for as action and reaction were evaluated, new ideas about how settlers ought to live in the village were elaborated and disseminated.

I can think of no better way of explaining these things than to tell the story of Kafuko and Mebulo. I came across fragments of this story as I talked separately to the people involved, but it was only shortly before I left Kamira that I heard a relatively complete account from Bernardo Gizaza.

One of the earliest settlers in the village was a Murundi who had worked for many years as a labourer in Buganda and had saved enough money to start a farm of his own. He rented two and a half acres of Nsibiirwa's *mailo* land and in 1949 brought his wife to live with him in Bugerere. His plot, between Manyala's and Salongo's, was fertile and in the first two or three years while his coffee trees were maturing he had good crops of cotton and matoke. They had a daughter, Kafuko, but while she was still very young her mother died. Her father felt that he was too old to remarry, and when he died in 1964 Kafuko was not yet sixteen.

There were no relatives to hand and it was Gizaza and Manyala who stepped in and made the burial arrangements. Accompanied by Wasozi they went through the village collecting contributions, and many of the people of Kamira attended the simple ceremony. For several weeks one of Gizaza's wives slept in Kafuko's house to keep the girl company. Shortly after the funeral, a Murundi called Kalimanzira arrived in the village, declared he was the dead man's brother and heir, and moved into the house too. He told Gizaza and the others that he used to have a farm of his own near Kangulumira but that after a lengthy visit home he had returned to find he had been dispossessed. There was no one who could vouch for this, or for his claim that he was Kafuko's uncle, and as Kafuko neither knew nor liked him, Gizaza, Salongo and the others met to consider what should be done. They made two decisions: Kalimanzira's claims to the property should be firmly resisted, and Salongo should act *in loco parentis* to Kafuko until further notice. As Kafuko had known Salongo and his family all her life the arrangement seemed a good one.

Kalimanzira was told to leave Kafuko's house, so he joined the Barundi in Bune's labour pool. It was while I was leaving Bune's house one day that he presented himself to me. He declared that he, too, was a villager and that I should interview him at his house. He stopped a passer-by who was returning home with a large pineapple and demanded it as a gift for me, making vague noises about paying a handsome price for it later. Feeling himself compromised the villager reluctantly handed it over; when I discovered the full extent of Kalimanzira's eccentricity a few days later, I despatched Joseph to seek out the poor man and reimburse him for his pineapple. After some fuss about the most convenient day and time, Kalimanzira arrived unexpectedly at Amos's house one afternoon and walked me down through the village to 'his farm'. He apologised for his tatty clothes, saying that he had been busy working in his farm; he greeted everyone we passed with elaborate courtesy, and they solemnly returned his salute. When we arrived at the house Kalimanzira called Kafuko 'my daugher' and had her fetch wooden chairs for us. She sat down nearby with her baby, peeling matoke and listening dead-pan to Kalimanzira's ravings. The interview left me in no doubt that he was crazy but it was several weeks before I discovered that he was not in fact Kafuko's father. When in due course I returned to talk to Kafuko as mistress of the house she explained that as he was some kind of friend of her father she felt obliged to show him tolerance. When I told Gizaza later about my encounter with Kalimanzira he laughed and said that no doubt he had hoped that I might intervene on his behalf.

Kafuko told me that she had had her baby by a young man called Mebulo who lived in the village. He was not her husband but her 'friend'; there seemed nothing remarkable about that, but I made a note to look out for him as I proceeded with my survey of the village. He had a small thatched hut on a tiny strip of land to one side of Manyala's farm, almost opposite Kafuko's house. I had a great deal of difficulty contacting him as he never seemed to be at home, but eventually Manyala passed on the message that I wanted to see him. I met him one Sunday afternoon, and as we talked I became more puzzled about his circumstances. He was about thirty, and had been working as a labourer for Manyala for eight years. He said he had not been home to Burundi for several years, and regarded Bugerere as his home. At the time I met him he was working in a coffee processing plant several miles away, although he also worked occasionally for Manyala. What I could not understand was why Manyala should have given a mere labourer a piece of land to build a hut; 'He likes me' Mebulo told me, unhelpfully. When I asked him if he was married, he told me he slept 'over there', pointing to Kafuko's house. He had a lot to say about Kalimanzira, explaining that he was not Kafuko's father but a rascal who was trying to get his hands on her land.

This made me reflect on Mebulo's own interest in Kafuko. If he moved in with her as her husband he would acquire a small but flourishing farm, a fine newly built house and a family to go with it. He would no longer be a mere labourer, but an established member of the community. I decided to ask Manyala what was going on. He told me that the affair between Kafuko and Mebulo had become apparent when, shortly after her father's death, she had had her baby. Manyala felt in some way responsible as Mebulo was his man; although he had no land of his own either in Burundi or in Bugerere he seemed an honest enough fellow, so after talking the matter over with Gizaza and Salongo he lent Mebulo a small plot to build a hut and grow some food of his own. It was agreed that if Mebulo had any pretension to settling in the village it would be best if he did not continue to work as a labourer there. It was through Gizaza's good offices that he was given the job in the coffee factory at Seeta.

So, at the time I arrived in Kamira, Kafuko was the ward of Salongo and Mebulo was effectively the ward of Manyala. Shortly before I left the village I sought Mebulo out and asked him more directly about the affair. Yes, he said, Manyala had forbidden him to live with Kafuko, although he spent the nights with her. He wanted very much to marry her, but he saw no advantage in antagonising his patron. With a certain gleam in his eye he told me that Kafuko was pregnant again and that the birth of his second child must surely mark his acceptance as *paterfamilias*.

To Gizaza and the other Bataka, their intervention was essentially out of consideration for Kafuko's minority. She was considered too young to be able to handle her own problems, and as the orphan of an established and respected villager it was the responsibility of the Bataka to protect her from adventures like Kalimanzira. No one said anything explicitly against Mebulo, but, as Gizaza remarked, 'We must get to know him better.'

This story gave me much satisfaction, not just because of the detective-work which had gone into unravelling it. The actions of the Bataka reflected in a gratifying way aspects of a village ideology which I had already identified: their judgements were affected by categoric ideas about the difference between labourers and settlers, but the tribal identities of the *dramatis personae*—Barundi, Basoga and Bagisu—had at no time been brought to bear on the issue. The events provided tangible evidence of a new moral order in Kamira, and I found myself agreeing with Gizaza that the Bataka had acted judiciously and responsibly when confronted with an anomalous situation. In the sequence of crisis, discussion and corporate action it was pleasing to see the capacity of the villagers to concern them-selves with each other's welfare. However, it was also apparent that the Bataka were not acting without self-interest. Kafuko's welfare was intimately connected to the security of other community members: access to village land, and the privileges and responsibilities of community membership were at stake, and these things were as much a matter of concern to them as the fate of Kafuko herself.

Looking back, I can see that my discovery of social order in Kamira had important effects on my personal adjustment to life in the village. I felt more confident and more secure. On the one hand I felt that I had met the professional challenge of survival in an African village, and that furthermore I had made one or two anthropologically interesting discoveries. But more important, I no longer regarded Kamira strictly as an academic exercise, a source of raw data which I had to knock into some plausible shape. My early visits to each household were to elicit information from strangers, but my later visits were to converse with friends. The more I got to know about the village, the more I felt at ease. Using my licence to pry, I had tamed my surroundings more quickly than many other newcomers. In moments of introspection I asked myself sternly if there was not, perhaps, too close a connection between my happiness and my understanding of social order in Kamira; was there a darker side to the village which subconsciously I did not wish to see?

My tidy research plan had taken account of the possibility that I might become too absorbed in the affairs of a single community. The more I learned about Kamira, the more I discovered how much there was to learn, and the feeling that I would have to leave so many stones unturned vexed me. Nevertheless, by October 1965 I knew I ought to be moving to another part of Bugerere and a new village. I hoped that there I would be able to re-evaluate what I knew about Kamira; for example, were there Bataka elsewhere, and did they perform the same functions? Comparison would give me a better idea of how typical and how distinctive the village was. At the same time I had to try to avoid using Kamira as a yardstick, and to discipline myself to approach what might well be a very different kind of community with an open mind. As I contemplated leaving the sanctuary of Amos's house I knew this would be difficult, and that I would have to depend more than ever on my interview schedules and other 'scientific' paraphernalia to help me keep my eyes open.

7 Kitimbwa

The unsettling, but by now familiar process of finding somewhere to live and work began again. Joseph and I made several preliminary sorties northwards, armed with some precise ideas about what we were looking for. I had set my sights on Kayonza, headquarters of the Sabagabo gombolola (see Map 3), because from the maps and censuses it appeared to be the focus of the most recent immigration to Bugerere. If only I could find somewhere to live thereabouts, I could then look for a very new community which would compare well with Kamira.

As usual, our first call was on the gombolola chief. He received us with the courtesy and good will I had come to expect of Ganda civil servants, and spoke enthusiastically about the large tracts of untenanted land still available around Kayonza. The new settlers were taking up land for as little as twenty or thirty shillings an acre and were, he said, a very mixed bunch. He feared that after the urbanity of Kangulumira I might find the denizens of Sabagabo uncouth. I asked him about the Banyala, whom I understood to be the indigenous people of the area, and the chief told me that he was himself a Munyala. His father had been a follower of Kakungulu and now, a generation or two later, many of these 'Bakungulu' were returning to their homeland from other parts of Uganda. The fervour with which he spoke about the history of Bugerere and the repatriation of his people made it seem that Sabagabo was becoming a kind of Zion for the Banyala. I wondered how this affected their relationship with the other new and uncouth immigrants in the area.

I was surprised to discover that Kayonza consisted of the gombolola headquarters and not much else besides. There were only two stalls selling sardines, soap and kerosene, and settlement in the vicinity was much more sparse than I had expected. After two hours of enquiry we found the only rentable accommodation, a small shack beside the main road. The owner, a bleary-eyed old man in a grubby kanzu, opened the flimsy door and let us peer inside. I stepped in and my head hit the tin roof. There were no windows or ventilators, and the small dark cavity was filled with a pungent fug. The old man pointed out that the walls had been freshly plastered with cow dung, and that as a European such amenity would cost me dear. We thanked him politely, and said we would need some time to consider his offer.

We left Kayonza with flagging enthusiasm, and our quest for cold beer took us several miles down the main road. There we came upon a new roadside settlement which had not yet got onto the map. A large Pepsi-Cola sign led us to a trading store, a shady verandah with three plastic chairs, an immense kerosene refrigerator, and two bottles of beer. It turned out that Joseph knew the storekeeper, who had moved north from Kayunga to make his fortune. This, he informed us, waving proudly at the two rows of ramshackle buildings facing each other across the hump of the main road, was Kitimbwa town.

As he talked, it became apparent that Kitimbwa, not Kayonza was the centre of new settlement in Sabagabo (see Map 5). There are new 'towns' like Kitimbwa on main roads everywhere; on aerial photographs they look like flies clustering on a vine. In the early afternoon the place looked uninviting, even morbid. The unavoidable focal point was the corpse of a cur in the middle of the road, and the scavenged remains of taxis and lorries lay here and there. People slept in patches of shade, oblivious of the gramophone screaming hoarsely in the store behind us. Chunks of flesh turned slowly in the sun above the butcher's stall on the other side of the road.

I sent Joseph back next day to Kitimbwa to find us somewhere to stay. I had come to depend on Joseph's help, and we had agreed that he would accompany me when I left Kamira, and work with me on a full-time basis. I anticipated that there would be greater language problems among the new immigrants in Sabagabo, and in any case I valued his assistance as aide, clerk and navigator. I also found that his presence kept interviews moving smoothly; he made the introductions and contrived to be as much the assistant of our victim as mine. After each session he completed his own page of comments, which I appended to my notes. He gave a description of the individual, the house and the farm, and evaluated the interview as a whole. We both developed a keen sense of when things went well or badly, and his own reactions helped me to judge the reliability of the information

William Lubega

we were collecting. In addition, he kept a diary of local events which provided an informative and amusing accompaniment to my own record.

When Joseph returned from Kitimbwa he handed me a tiny key. He had scoured the town and with some difficulty had persuaded a shopkeeper to rent me part of his premises. The man looked rather shifty so Joseph had decided to clinch the deal straight away; he bought a shilling padlock and put it on the door as a tiny token of my occupancy. Joseph himself had arranged to stay with his friend in Kitimbwa. He spoke guardedly about my accommodation: it was fairly spacious, not too expensive and could be quite comfortable when it was cleaned up. We set out again next day so that I could see for myself. We found a couple of old men sitting on the doorstep with empty beer pots and drinking tubes, looking forlorn. Joseph had thought it unwise to tell me in advance that my new home was a shebeen.

The building was made of timber, mud and reeds, plastered inside and out with cement. Behind it was a large square in which the weekly market was held, and in front of it was a patch of well-trodden earth, a ditch and the road. The owner was a tall, unsmiling Munyala called William Lubega. He had a farm nearby and had put up this building quite recently; one half of it was a shop with a small room behind it and the other half was the shebeen. Lubega told us that he had got tired of drunken brawls and had no objection to my moving in. We opened the door to an exhalation of stale odours; the room was about eight feet by twelve, and although at the moment it was foul it could certainly be made habitable. Immediately next door was the butcher's stall which had a distinctive sour smell of its own. I could see no latrine, no water supply and none of the other amenities to which I had become accustomed at Amos's. I gave Lubega a month's rent in advance and arranged to move in two days later.

My neighbours in Kamira commiserated with me when I told them I proposed to live in Sabagabo for a few months. Nampata, a woman who lived opposite, made up a parcel of food for me, saying: 'I hear they are hungry up there.' As I was packing up my possessions and loading them into Amos's truck, Gizaza called and told me that he wanted to accompany me to Kitimbwa to make sure that I had settled in comfortably. When we set out northwards, Joseph and I leading the way on the motor cycle, two or three other villagers were sitting on my baggage in the back of the truck. We paused in Kayunga to buy an oil-drum and some zinc guttering with which I proposed to solve the water problem. When we arrived at Kitimbwa I directed a thorough purge of the shebeen. When my baggage had been moved in, Gizaza turned to the crowd which had gathered outside and addressed them. He was, he said, Mutaka in Kamira and had known me as his own son in that village. I had become a good friend of the people there, and he exhorted the people of Kitimbwa to welcome me and help me with my work. When he finished there was some polite applause. I was most impressed by this generous testimonial, and as my friends drove off home to Kamira I was overwhelmed by nostalgia. As an antidote, I at once set about putting my new home in order.

Having considered the priorities, I asked Lubega first about the latrine. He took me to the back of the house and pointed to a small tumbledown shack with a straw roof on the edge of the market place. The pit was shallow and the wooden frame over it looked treacherous. There were large chinks in the walls and huge cockroaches everywhere. Joseph found me a carpenter who cleaned it and patched it up. For a few days it was the most popular amenity in town, and returned quickly to its former squalid state. I had it put in order again, then I claimed it as my own with Joseph's shilling padlock. I rigged up the barrel outside my door and during a short rainstorm the following afternoon I watched with satisfaction as the water poured into it off the roof. I had to leave it for a few hours to let the red dust in it settle, and when Joseph and I returned in the evening from an interview I was eagerly anticipating a wash and a leisurely cup of tea. In the bottom of the barrel I found a quarter of an inch of red sediment: my neighbours had already emptied it. Grimly I summoned the carpenter, and next day my water supply had been secured by another shilling padlock.

The same carpenter made me a table and some chairs, and sealed the gap in the roof between my room and Lubega's shop. The place was infested with rats, attracted by the food and sacks of grain, and by the butcher's stall next door. They came over the wall, along a beam and down my mosquito net to forage in my room. It was distressing to feel them running over my legs at night.

My growing bunch of keys seemed to tell me that I felt much less secure here than I did at Amos's. Lubega felt in no way responsible for me and although one of his wives and a child lived in the room behind the shop, I was in no sense a part of his household. It took me a long time to accustom myself to life in Kitimbwa. People from the surrounding countryside would congregate there, and on market days the noise and disorder became almost unbearable. It was often difficult to sleep at night, which did little to improve my temper. At dawn each morning a bus queue would form on my doorstep and sometimes, to their astonishment, I would rise, open the door and beg them to be quiet. Once again I had to accustom myself to being the local freak show, and spent a good deal of time explaining to inquisitive callers who I was and what I was doing in Kitimbwa.

One of my first visitors was Bonny Moses Sekasi, a man of about my own age who worked part-time as treasurer of the local Co-operative society. He had a charming and relaxed manner, and we became good friends. He enjoyed Kitimbwa, and did much to make my stay there pleasant and instructive. He told me that he, like Kitimbwa, was 'looking for progress', and said that he sought me out because 'talking to people and reading books brings on a general knowledge'. His ambition was to be 'one of the élite', and his recipe for success was 'working hard, sociability and education'. He insisted that we should talk in English, and each day we conversed about the affairs of the world very much as I had done with Amos in Kamira. Sekasi was a Muganda who had come to Bugerere with his father, an ex-serviceman, when he was eleven years old. He left school when he was nineteen, but his Junior Leaving Certificate was not sufficient to secure him the place in agricultural college which he had hoped for. He proposed to take a job as tea-packer for Brooke Bond in Kampala and tried to persuade his father to help with night-school fees. His father refused on the grounds that the money was needed to educate his other brothers, so instead Sekasi accompanied him to Kitimbwa and helped him to establish a new farm. However, arguments developed about Sekasi's share of the profits, so shortly after he married in 1964, he found a seven acre *mailo* tenancy of his own, six miles away.

Sekasi had some experience of clearing and breaking-in new land, and when I visited it his farm already had an appearance of order and efficiency. He was growing and selling annual crops of cotton, groundnuts, maize and beans, but it would be three or four years before his carefully-tended coffee trees would come to fruition. Each day he cycled through the maze of small paths to Kitimbwa, often with his wife perched on the carrier. He was optimistic about his farm and his prospects in Bugerere: 'Life is not hard, the land is profitable and it is our investment.' However, life was not without mishap, and he was greatly affected by the death, shortly after my departure from Bugerere, of his newborn daughter.

Like the other main road towns throughout Bugerere, Kitimbwa had already become a focus of party political activities. As part of his plans for personal progress, Sekasi had become secretary of the Kabaka Yekka branch, and was able to tell me that I had been the subject of a special meeting shortly after my arrival. He had assured them that contrary to their suspicions I was not a communist agent; he brought me a small delegation of party officials, who departed in due course with promises of friendship and co-operation. I found it more difficult to dispose of a persistent rumour that I was an agent of the Bakungulu, planning to dispossess the other immigrants in the area. Sekasi tended to laugh this off, saying that in Sabagabo everyone was suspicious of everyone else.

Sekasi procured for me the services of Abudul Tief, a recent immigrant from Busoga whose prime qualification was three years of domestic service with an Asian trader. This disposed him to expect beatings as part of his daily routine, but he had also learned to make excellent curries. He worked like a demon and had none of Abudu Gididu's lighthearted informality. He was not interested in learning English, and confined himself to getting his tongue round *sauce chasseur*, a few dehydrated packets of which I had bought in Kampala to liven-up my daily matoke. He took a very professional view of his chores and regarded it as a recrimination if I did anything myself. One morning he held out his hand and said to me sternly '*Maxwell!*' Bewildered, I asked for an explanation; he pointed at my pocket and repeated 'Maxwell!' I pulled out my handkerchief and he snatched it, added it to his pile of laundry and marched out. My habit of washing my own handkerchiefs had apparently upset him, but I was never able to discover why he called them 'Maxwells'.

A few days after my arrival in Kitimbwa, Sekasi brought the mutongole chief, Edward Nsubuga, to share one of Tief's curries with me. Nsubuga was thirty-four years old, tall, serious-minded but not without a sense of humour. He was a Muganda from the distant Ssese islands in Lake Victoria, and in 1952 he had been an early

Nsubuga, the mutongole chief at Kitimbwa, listening to a dispute

immigrant to this part of Bugerere. Having been to school in Kampala he considered himself no bumpkin; he was a keen advocate of 'Kitimbwa town', envisaging that it would soon rival Kayunga as a political and commercial centre. His local popularity rested at least in part on his regular sponsorship of beer parties and traditional music sessions, but he was also well known for his sense of judgement and fair play. In his diary, Joseph recorded a typical incident in which Nsubuga lost his temper and struck one of his wives; he then called together some neighbours, 'tried' himself, and imposed on himself the fine of a new dress for the injured party.

Nsubuga's realm was large, covering six square miles and including nearly two hundred homesteads. In the previous three years the population of the area had grown so rapidly that the boundaries of his *Kitongole* were in some disarray. There were now four distinct village subunits: Kyato, Wabiyinja, Budada and Kitimbwa. The first two had deputy chiefs and Nsubuga himself had direct charge of the other two. He was a staunch advocate of the unity of the four villages, but it was becoming evident that prior authority would soon insist on subdivision. To the cartographers and the Ganda hierarchy, Nsubuga's realm was known as Kyetume, but local people always referred to it by its new focal point, Kitimbwa. Nsubuga and his deputies took me on a guided tour of the four villages, pausing now and then to argue among themselves about where boundaries lay. Settlement was much more dispersed and homesteads more sequestered than in Kamira. Whereas 80 per cent of the Kamira homesteads were arranged along the main roadway through the village, here paths seemed to straggle in all directions. Houses looked newer and poorer and were hidden in patches of scrub and long grass. The soil was not nearly so rich; the matoke plants were fewer and smaller, and millet and sweet potatoes were much more in evidence. When I compared the homesteads in the Kangulumira and Kitimbwa areas, I discovered that the former grew four times as much coffee and the latter twice as much cotton. The Kitimbwa farms were larger but were used much less intensively. There was more open grazing land and many of the farmers we met kept a few indigenous 'Nganda' cattle.

My pursuit of gridline intersections in the countryside around Kitimbwa took Joseph and me further and further from the well-beaten tracks towards the frontiers of new settlement. Twice the motor cycle carried us deep into the undergrowth and then died, obliging me to push it for miles, cursing loudly while Joseph followed at a discreet distance. Eventually the net which I was painstakingly spreading over Bugerere caught for me a very special fish: an immigrant in the act of cutting a homestead for himself out of the undergrowth. He was firing piles of dried brushwood, his body gleaming with sweat and streaked with cinders. The sense of action and urgency made my questions seem otiose: why was he here?—to make money, why else. He was a young man from Ruanda, a labourer who had worked for a farmer near Kangulumira. Soon he would make a farm of his own out of these five acres of wilderness. He had paid 150 shillings for his tenancy on a *mailo* estate, and at the moment he neither knew nor cared who his new neighbours might be. As he had little money his most pressing task was to plant food.

This encounter was a timely reminder of the problems of survival which confronted the new immigrant. The prime concern was to secure a livelihood, and by comparison my interest in the niceties of community development seemed dilettante. My preparatory reading had left me in no doubt that migration was fundamentally a matter of economics, 'the pursuit of a higher level of real income, or, more precisely, of a new equilibrium between economic activity and the enjoyment of leisure', as one economist sagely put it.* The individual migrants themselves repeatedly told me that it was the quest for money and food which had brought them to Bugerere. In the face of such insistence it seemed unwise to ascribe to the newcomers any Utopian ideals; even the irredentist claims of the Bakungulu or Amos's dream of the tall trees could be reduced quite easily to straightforward material ambitions. It did not seem too cynical to suppose that even Bernardo Gizaza's concern for community well-being was a function of his privileged material circumstances.

It is more than likely that this particular turn of thought was prompted by the fact that, by the end of 1965, I was broke. Efforts to find extra funds had so far come to nothing so I wrote to my sponsors, the Scottish Education Department, asking for help. The SED suggested that I might qualify for a cost-of-living supplement and invited me to complete a form and send them grocery, laundry and other bills. As I read the letter, Tief was sitting outside on the

* P. G. Powesland, *Economic policy and labour: A study in Uganda's economic history*, E.A.I.S.R., Kampala 1957, p. 1.

doorstep, pounding my shirt in a plastic basin; I wondered how I might set about extracting from him a bill for his services. It seemed that my sponsors in the grey winter of Edinburgh found it difficult to apprehend my circumstances, so I wrote them a long, colourful and slightly desperate letter. I pointed out that the £50 allowance they had made me for photographic expenses was generous, but in the circumstances useless, as I could only claim it retrospectively. Appealing to their Presbyterian consciences I told them that I had not only spent all my savings, I was now in *debt*. I received by return of post a cheque for £200.

My style of life had been neither prodigal nor frugal. My main extravagance was beer, and in Kangulumira I could buy bread, and fresh Kenyan milk and butter. The best cuts of lean meat cost 1.50 shillings a pound, and I benefited from the African customers' preference for the fat and chewy parts. Every afternoon a hooting taxi brought fresh *talipa* (perch) from Lake Victoria to Kangulumira and Kayunga, and a wide range of vegetables was readily available in the market place. People passing Amos's house would often offer to sell me eggs; I learned to decline politely the ones which arrived by bicycle as they were usually scrambled. Life in Kitimbwa was much more austere, and as there was not much surplus food available locally I had to shop in Kayunga. I kept a procession of chickens for the pot, scrawny birds with bald necks, all of whom I called Vera after a character by the cartoonist Giles. I wondered what some future employer of Tief would make of being offered 'curried Vera' for supper.

I arrived in Sabagabo during a period of particular local privation. There had been a prolonged dry season and most of the shallow water holes had dried out. Many people were obliged to walk up to fifteen miles to the river or the bore-hole at Kayonza, and two or three shillings was being paid for a four gallon can. Sekasi told me that water was carefully conserved for drinking, and food which was normally boiled or steamed was now being roasted. Matoke was in short supply and most people were reduced to eating maize, or the famine crop cassava. For many days my barrel was empty, and having to fetch a can of water from Kayunga taught me a new respect for this most valuable of commodities. Where there is no pipe-borne supply, drawing and fetching water involves considerable effort; in the Ganda household, upsetting the water pot is a minor catastrophe, and if someone does it on purpose it is a drastic gesture of vexation. However, no-one would dream of locking up water and I am sure my neighbours were offended by the lid on my barrel; for my part, I could not understand why they did not make more effort to conserve rainwater. When it rained they would gather it in pans and basins, or let it run down the stems of banana trees into pots and gourds. Rain in the wet season would make people sleepy and lethargic, but a sudden thunderstorm in the dry season would bring relief and exhilaration. I remember standing outside with a feeling of elation as the cold water soaked my clothes, while around me the naked children screamed and danced through the falling curtains of rain. Within minutes my barrel brimmed over, and I filled every receptacle I could lay my hands on with fresh, clear water.

For the many newcomers to the Kitimbwa area the drought brought great hardship. The Baganda used to say of the immigrants from distant places: 'They don't know how to eat.' Although this referred mainly to their inappropriate diet it also had metaphoric significance, suggesting more general problems of adjustment. New settlers from the Southern Sudan seemed to have the greatest difficulty. I came to know one of them, Lario Sula, quite well. He told me that his first concern was to find money to cover such official demands as tax, and that providing for food and shelter necessarily took second place. His problems had recently been exacerbated by the arrival of a refugee family who were living with him on his small four-acre farm. He continued to grow and eat cassava, the staple food of the Kuku people, and it seemed that he and his family had not yet accustomed themselves to the more nutritious matoke. One writer has described this traditional staple food of the Baganda as follows:

[About a year after planting] the first bunches of fruit came to maturity. The stem was then cut down and the fruit steamed and eaten as a starchy mash or, if it belonged to the sweet variety, was converted into beer. Meanwhile the stem had put forth fresh suckers, so that, when fully developed, the grove contained clusters of up to twenty stems in varying stages of maturity and, taken as a whole, could normally provide food at any season of the year. . . . This kind of tropical gardening is in many ways the most satisfactory form of subsistence economy that man has ever evolved.*

Sula grew some matoke but sold nearly all of it. It was clear that he

* C. C. Wrigley, *Crops and wealth in Uganda*, E.A.I.S.R., Kampala 1959, p. 7.

had not yet learned how to use his land to the best advantage. For example, he did not know that beans could be interplanted with cotton, or that matoke was an ideal cover-crop for young coffee.

Sula worked in his farm for about seven hours each day, mainly keeping down the weeds which seemed to grow much more vigorously than anything he planted. Given the limited energy on which he could draw, this was certainly a hard day's work. He rose at dawn, drank some water and after four hours of work he returned home, washed and had his first meal of the day. Typically this would consist of cassava-flour cake with a little vegetable stew. After a brief siesta he would work until about 5.00 p.m., when he would return to a similar meal. Afterwards he would sit outside his house, watching people passing by on their way to and from Kitimbwa. As he had no money for a lamp, the family would go to bed at nightfall. As a Christian, Sunday would bring him more relaxation and a richer diet —perhaps a meal of matoke and fish or, if there were visitors, some meat.

All newcomers were obliged to take work very seriously. 'I never have time to enjoy myself,' Mugawula complained, 'this business of looking for money is too exhausting.' He rose at first light and worked until mid-day, and his visits to Kitimbwa were brief and purposeful: 'I was there just ten minutes, buying soap.' By contrast Lukhoza, a Munyala who had been established in Kitimbwa for sixteen years, never seemed to work for more than two hours at a stretch. He was a former client of Lubega's shebeen, and as part-time collector of market dues he had a regular excuse for going to town. The farm was run by his two wives who always seemed to be on hand when he needed them, with his meals cooked and his bathwater ready.

The enormous increase in cash cropping in Uganda during this century had involved men in farming very much more than they had been in the past. The essays which the Bugerere schoolchildren wrote for me made it clear that the whole household was now involved in farming activities:

Our farm is approximately five acres. About two acres are the coffee estate, one and a half acres for bananas and the rest part is for other crops, e.g. [ground-]nuts, cotton and beans. The mother takes great care of the bananas garden so that it may produce satisfactory food for the family. The father also does the same and keeps his coffee estate clean throughout the year.

When we wake up early in the morning we go into our farm, we children, and start digging or picking coffee. In our farm we do not grow coffee only but we also grow cotton, bananas, potatoes, maize and other kinds of food and vegetables. In our farm we also have some cows, goats and hens and those animals are looked after by our mother. The work of the father is to check and see whether everything is clear.

If the *paterfamilias* traditionally had an easier life, he also had a richer diet. Nutrition experts have always been vexed by the prohibition throughout East Africa on women eating eggs. One of these experts, Dr F. J. Bennett, visited me at Kitimbwa and took me on a most informative excursion through a number of nearby farms. He gave me botanical names and descriptions for many plants which I had come to know only in vernacular terms. He was very much concerned with the modern farmer's preoccupation with money, pointing out that people paid much less attention than they did in the past to food crops, and many varieties of vegetables, herbs and shrubs were disappearing from Ganda gardens. Simple medicaments and remedies could no longer be found in and around the homestead, and instead people went to town to buy Aspro and other proprietary medicines. An enormous variety of plants thrived naturally in Bugerere, and it was striking that many immigrants had remarked on this to me; nevertheless, the diaries which I collected indicated that the diet of ordinary people was extremely dull and monotonous.

It struck me as odd that people seemed little concerned to vary or enrich their diet, because it was a commonly held view that 'man is what he eats'. The wealth and talents of white men and élite Africans were often ascribed to the richness of their diet. As in many peasant societies, 'food' was synonymous with the dietary staple and for the Baganda a meal without matoke was a meal without food. Insects provided a valuable but fortuitous source of protein. One night at Amos's I was woken by a strange commotion outside my door; I opened it and found the night air filled with thousands of small, beating wings. After a rainstorm swarms of white ants had taken flight from the ground and had been attracted to a light left burning outside Amos's store. My neighbours were cramming them into pans and baskets, and into their mouths. When I tried to do the same the squirming sensation nearly made me vomit, but next morning for breakfast I enjoyed a plateful of them lightly fried in butter.

The lack of protein was most sadly evident in the malnutrition of children around Kitimbwa. Occasionally when Joseph and I visited homesteads we would see children with the unmistakable signs of kwashiorkor: with reddish hair and bloated bellies they would sit in unsmiling torpor, watching us with dull eyes. Of the thirty-eight children who lived in Budada village when I arrived at Kitimbwa, three had been buried by the time I left. I found these funerals very affecting; one evening I went to offer my condolences to a family of recent immigrants from Teso district, and found that quite a large group of people had already assembled for the first night of mourning. Their solemn eyes reflected the light from a single oil lamp, hanging from a stick which had been pushed into the mound of fresh earth. Nine of Lario Sula's thirteen children had died, and he gave this as his main reason for moving to Bugerere. Nevertheless, during my stay he buried his ten-year-old son, and each time I went to visit him the grave beside the threshold of his hut was a poignant reminder that for some families Bugerere was not yet a land flowing with milk and honey. When I got to know Sula better I asked him about his bereavement. He seemed to regret most his inability to share his grief with his new neighbours; very few of them had come to the burial, and it was on this occasion more than any other that he had found himself thinking sadly about his distant home in the Sudan.

Confronted by these tribulations I felt very helpless. The little boxes of vitamin pills which I handed out seemed a puny response to the hardship around me. It only prompted people to believe that I was a doctor and was able to help them in moments of real crisis. On a number of occasions I was obliged to give first aid. In a country where nearly everything is transported by bicycle, it was inevitable that pillion passengers would get their feet caught in the spokes from time to time. Children were the main victims, and as my remedies tended to be simple and drastic I was always impressed by their stoicism. While he was hoeing one day, the deputy chief of Wabiyinja lopped the end off his big toe and hobbled round to me to have it dressed. I gave him graphic warnings about the dangers of gangrene and told him that if he did not go to the Ntenjeru clinic he should at least come back every day so that I could change the dressings. On the third and fourth days he did not appear, so I called to see him at his house. He explained apologetically that he had been unable to visit me the previous day because he had been playing centre-forward in a village football match.

Lario Sula spreads millet to dry at his home in Budada. Behind him is the
grave of his son, and in the background the huts of the Kuku refugee
family with whom he shares his homestead

By this time I was resigned to the fact that anyone who was sick, mad, lost, bored or simply curious, gravitated to my door. One day a boy of indeterminate age appeared and settled down on my doorstep. While I was working I flipped a cigarette end out into the dust near him, and he reached over, picked it up and smoked it. It was then I noticed that he had no hands. His appearance was very distressing: he had thin gingerish hair, a yellow, malnourished face, filthy ragged shorts pulled up under his distorted belly, spindly grey legs, and grotesque feet infested with jiggers. For two days he sat watching me. He seemed unable or unwilling to speak, but on the second day Joseph managed to find out something about him. Apparently he had lived with his mother who, to punish him for stealing, had tied cloth and grass around his hands and set fire to them. When she saw that she had maimed him she fled, abandoning him. Now he was a young itinerant beggar in a poor rural area. For two days I bought off his silent indictment with food and money. It seemed altogether beyond me to take responsibility for him, and in my remorse I blamed the people of Kitimbwa for showing him even less compassion than I did. At last, he rose from my doorstep and shuffled off out of town, leaving me with an unpleasant mixture of guilt and relief, and very little self-esteem.

I was often challenged by the people we met to explain how my work in Bugerere would benefit them. I had always hoped that what I discovered would in some way contribute to the improvement of their lives, but Kitimbwa gave me many doubts. I had seen myself as a kind of intellectual mediator for the people of Bugerere, but now I felt I was simply acquiring a further education at their expense. Their own understanding of what I was about seemed to show an uncomfortable realism: as a result of all they had told me I would get fame and promotion in my own country, not to mention the profits from the sale of my book. I had been careful to avoid any pretence that I could help people individually and had instead argued that it was within my power to communicate to the world at large the problems and aspirations of all the people of Bugerere. I had not yet thought very seriously how I might do this, nor had I dwelt on the possible abuses to which those in authority might put the information I was collecting. The people themselves seemed to find the idea of a book about Bugerere quite satisfactory, mainly because it would serve to explain them to their own descendants. My efforts to 'understand the ways of the people' and record local history had a more parochial interest for them than for me, and few of them seemed enthused by the possibility that my writing might have wider political influence. Again, this was a realistic appraisal of my endeavours, but at the time it did little to encourage my hope that my social anthropology might have some positive instrumental value.

I therefore seized enthusiastically on an invitation from pediatricians at Mulago hospital in Kampala to assist them in a study of child nutrition. Dr Bennett introduced me to Dr Rainer Arnhold, a Californian pediatrician who periodically left the coughs and colds of his well-fed patients at home to give his services to hospitals in poorer countries. He had been seeking out anthropologists like myself in the hope that they could contribute information about particular localities and individual households which might enhance the Mulago medical studies of child nutrition. After we had made careful arrangements with the chiefs and local officials, Arnhold arrived in Bugerere with a group of students to weigh, measure and test as many children from the Kangulumira and Kitimbwa areas as we could round up. Our main concern was to examine all the children under the age of five from Kamira and Budada villages, and then to consider their nutritional status in the light of their family background, details of which I was able to provide. The study threw an interesting light on the problems of settlement, but raised more questions than it answered. It suggested that once the immigrants had overcome the immediate privations of establishing themselves, they regarded the physical welfare of their youngest children as a high priority. As I suspected, the most recently arrived northern families in the Kitimbwa area were experiencing the greatest hardship, but it was striking that after three or four years' settlement their children were among the best cared-for. It was more surprising to discover that a high proportion of the apparently malnourished children came from households with the largest cash incomes, families from Buganda, Busoga and Bugisu. There was no evidence of wilful neglect, but it was clear that in each case the family had overcommitted its land to coffee, cotton and other cash crops, and was producing insufficient food for its own growing needs.

Bugerere could give its settlers the food, clothes and shelter they needed and make some of them rich besides, but there were still many uncertainties in the search for security and the pursuit of material ambitions. The weather, crop prices, the best techniques and many other things were never fully predictable, not even by the most experienced and prescient farmers. For the newest immigrants very few things were certain, and even the established settlers acknowledged readily that family health and welfare depended on forces beyond their immediate control. Success and prosperity were continually threatened by what, as students, we used to call Sod's Law: there is always someone or something Out There working to undo everything we try to do. While I sought to render some of these forces intelligible by rational sociological explanation, the people themselves took more direct prophylactic and remedial action.

The market places of Bugerere were full of medicines. The range was enormous, but a very large proportion were concerned with household protection. There were mass produced 'swears' costing a few shillings, little bags of medicine which could be hung around a child's neck or over the door of a house. More potent prophylaxis could cost as much as £50, more than many households could hope to earn in a year. These were special prescriptions containing rare and powerful ingredients: a shaving of rhinoceros horn, twigs from the nest of a particular bird, a hair-ball from a lion's stomach, a fragment of a small dried tuber, and so on. The specialists in the market place talked to the customers and made up a specific, appropriate to their needs and financial means. I consulted one of these specialists at Kitimbwa, giving him twenty shillings and saying I wanted some general protection for myself, my wife and children. Although he did not know me, he pointed out that as I was a bachelor my request was both silly and impracticable. I settled for some personal insurance, so he took a splinter of bark, a small bean and a sliver of my thumbnail, tied them up in a scrap of barkcloth and handed it to me. I asked him what I should do with it, and he waved his hand vaguely. I complained that having paid twenty shillings I felt a little disappointed, so he threw in for good measure a handful of herbal tobacco. If I smoked it in the evenings it would attract prospective wives to my door.

I bought several other things in the market place: aphrodisiac roots and cures for sterility and stomach upsets, a porcupine quill to guard cotton seedlings and some cowrie currency to pay a Ganda diviner. I made several attempts to consult one of these diviners, but they were very difficult to locate and at the last minute my plans were

A seller of magic and medicines at the market place in Kitimbwa

always frustrated. It was evident that they mistrusted my motives, not without reason. They were mainly concerned with the diagnosis of *mayembe*, the Ganda black magic which most of the people I met either respected or feared. I found it very difficult to make sociological sense of people's attitudes to these things; they would say that there was a lot of malicious magic about, it was necessary to be on one's guard against it. It seemed to me that if magical prophylaxis was to be really effective in a mixed community like Kamira it would have to be generally recognisable. The northern labourers would tell me rather smugly: 'the medicines of the Baganda mean nothing to us', an attitude which can have given the anxious Muganda little peace of mind. In very rational terms, the effectiveness of swears seemed to depend on a community of knowledge, for the most expensive medicine would be unlikely to deter an ill-wisher if it was invisible or if it had no meaning to a foreign intruder. On the other hand, if people simply *believed* in the universal efficacy of an expensive swear, this rational view of medicine was probably irrelevant. If people felt confident that intruders would be annihilated regardless of tribe or creed, that was probably sufficient, but I was sure there were enough newcomers like myself blundering about with apparent impunity to call such a sanguine view of prophylaxis seriously to question. I saw the beginnings of a theoretical proposition: complex magical beliefs and practices belonged within the established community, where mutual knowledge, as well as schisms and suspicions, were highly developed. On the other hand, the magic of the new, heterogeneous community would tend to be simple and overt. While expensive, mystical and invisible concoctions were certainly used in Bugerere, the prevalence of mass-produced swears was very striking. They were to be seen everywhere, on children, above doorways, on trees and even on bicycles, and they were apparently used by people of all tribes. It was as if a simple common language of magic was appearing to cope with the insecurities which all immigrants shared.

There was a Ganda hit-record about *mayembe* which warned the ambitious young man that if he got rich his neighbours would put a spell on him. The closing verse declared that 'we, the new generation' should put aside such superstition. This was typical of the ambivalent and slightly embarrassed feelings of 'modern, progressive' people on the subject of witchcraft and sorcery. I was annoyed and perturbed one day when Joseph told me that the diary he had been keeping for me had been stolen. I had warned him to guard it carefully, as people would not take kindly to the knowledge that their actions were being observed and recorded in this way. Moreover, I had the strongest suspicion that Joseph had been neglecting his diary, and that the 'theft' was a ruse. I warned him darkly that his salary and future prospects hinged on the speedy return of the diary. Joseph informed me soberly that he would visit a diviner he knew in Kyaggwe county and would discover from him what had happened to the diary. Two days later he told me that the mission had been very satisfactorily accomplished: he had returned from the divination and, lo, there on his table lay the diary. I found this episode very perplexing, mainly because it indicated that we understood each other less perfectly than I had supposed. I then reflected that he probably found many of my ways bizarre and inexplicable. My life was dominated by ritualistic schedules and procedures which I am sure he found irrational, although he accepted them without demur. I knew that he was disconcerted by the process which reduced each interview to the formal anonymity of a punched card. Although I tried to explain the cards to him, he showed a strange reluctance to touch them, as if they represented a potent quintessence of our activities in Bugerere, and of the lives of the people we had met.

The Europeans in Uganda had a reputation for religious enthusiasm. Scientific education had followed very much in the wake of this, and it was probably even more difficult for a Ugandan to distinguish between the rituals of magic, science and religion than it is for us. One afternoon while Joseph and I were visiting a homestead near Kitimbwa we were taken aback to find a huge white cross in the middle of the courtyard. It was made of thick banana stems laid out on the ground and covered with white paint; around it was a circle about ten feet in diameter in the same material. With some excitement I wondered if I had stumbled on a strange religious sect. Our interview with the homestead head was uneventful and when I asked him, with trepidation, about his religious beliefs he replied mildly that he was 'Protestanti'. At last, when I felt I had secured his confidence, I asked him directly about the strange symbol lying in the courtyard beside us. He shrugged and said that he had thought I might be able to tell him. Several weeks previously some white men had arrived in a Land Rover and built the cross in front of his house. They had warned him that he must not disturb it and had given him a pot of paint, telling him to recoat the cross once a week. They said that some time later they would return in an aeroplane and would expect to see that he had looked after the cross well. Now he was apprehensive because he had almost run out of paint and increasingly he was finding the clumsy object a nuisance to himself and his family.

Later I asked Sekasi what he made of this, and he told me that he had indeed seen a small aeroplane flying slowly over Kitimbwa. At last the truth dawned on me. I returned at once to the perplexed farmer and told him he could dismantle his cross and throw away the white paint. It was a ground-marker for an aerial photography survey of the main road through Bugerere. Although he seemed to find this explanation no more convincing than any other he had been offered, he was plainly glad to be relieved of his weekly painting ritual.

Although the people I met in Bugerere were prepared to label themselves (in roughly equal proportions) as Catholics, Protestants and Moslems or even, as a rather quaint residual category, 'pagans', active congregations were not very much in evidence; nor was an ostensible commitment to Christianity or Islam an obstacle to engaging quite comfortably in practices which the orthodox would undoubtedly have regarded as 'pagan'. The injunctions of the Christian churches against polygamy were politely ignored, and in a society where the actuarial risks in everyday life were high, people bought whatever insurance, magical or otherwise, they could afford. The world religions were little in evidence around Kitimbwa. With no churches in the vicinity, Christmas was a strikingly secular occasion. On Christmas eve I threw a stylish dinner party for Bonny Moses Sekasi, Nsubuga and several of the other men-about-Kitimbwa. I provided enough drink for everybody, and each of them did likewise, with the result that everybody made a beast of himself.

I woke up at dawn on Christmas Day feeling evil, staggered through the debris of our party and opened the door. Something horrific blundered into the room and sat heavily on my feet. I found my spectacles and brought it into focus: it was the freshly-severed head of a cow. Outside in the street the butcher was cutting the rest of it into pieces, while the people of Kitimbwa queued to buy their Christmas lunch. Someone with an unpleasant sense of humour had propped the head up against my door. I staggered outside and, bent double, made my own contribution to the revolting spectacle. I then

The butcher at work in his stall at Kitimbwa

retreated, locked the door, drank the hair of the very large dog which had bitten me, and retired to bed for two days.

January was a tense and difficult month in Kitimbwa. It was the time of the cotton harvest and everyone was obsessed with money. The Co-operative store looked strangely seasonal to me, with snowy white cotton strewn over the ground and drifts of it lying against the walls of the building. The officials, one of whom was Bonny Moses Sekasi, were turning out each bundle as it arrived and prodding it suspiciously, for it was well known that people added stones and other rubbish to increase the weight. The Co-op did not have enough money to make cash payments, so Sekasi was engaged in the unpleasant task of issuing credit slips. A sense of grievance hung over the town, for a scrap of paper was a cruel return for an arduous year's work. Some people had cut their losses and sold their cotton well below the official price to Asian traders, who always paid cash. To make matters worse, coffee and other commodity prices were very low. Feelings of bitterness and frustration were much in evidence, and there is no doubt that many migrants were wondering why they ever made the effort to move to Bugerere. There was no money to pay the labourers and they in turn became aggrieved and frustrated. Suspicions were rife and disturbances at night became more frequent. Market days were particularly hectic, and one afternoon a suspected thief was caught by an angry mob and beaten until he coughed blood. Joseph's diary bristled with such happenings: a woman waylaid by thieves on her way home from market, a spectacular fight between a taxi driver and the butcher, a murderous assault by one of our neighbours on his wife, and a tooth-and-nail scrap between two local women outside Lubega's shop. The Standard Bank agency at Kayunga was in a state of siege. The manager arrived in a fortified Land Rover twice a week and unloaded a large steel trunk into the otherwise empty building. He put a cushion on the trunk and sat on it while his guards allowed the customers to filter in one by one. Now and then he rose to make deposits or withdrawals, lifting the lid of the trunk with one hand and holding the holster at his hip with the other. In spite of these precautions the agency was held up again and the unfortunate manager knocked unconscious.

One night Kitimbwa was aroused in a particularly impressive way. I was wakened by my camp bed rocking to and fro and the empty beer bottles jangling. I clambered out of bed in alarm and once more the earth rocked beneath me, knocking me off balance. My first thought was that I was ill, but the screams and shouts of my neighbours told me that they had shared the experience. In fact we were feeling the shock waves of an earthquake which had its epicentre in the Ruwenzori mountains to the west of Uganda. We heard later that the town of Fort Portal had been badly damaged, and felt grateful that we had been spared the worst. This was one of many disturbed nights and somehow it seemed quite in the order of things that Kitimbwa should be shaken in this way. As I tried to get back to sleep I found myself thinking naively that Kamira would surely have stood firm.

8 Budada

Of the four villages which comprised Nsubuga's realm I chose to study Budada in detail (see Map 5). Its boundary lay a convenient three hundred yards from where I lived and Nsubuga had assured me that the majority of its inhabitants had arrived very recently. For my purposes it seemed very suitable, and my only concern was that Lubega, to whose menage I was loosely attached, had his farm there. I had already learned that he was disliked by some people in the village but I hoped it would be evident to them that he was neither my patron nor a close friend. The situation echoed my living and working arrangements in Kamira in some respects: in both places I lived outside the boundaries with a merchant who had a farm in the village. However the similarity ended there, for my relationship with Amos and his family was quite close, and he did not have as much influence in the village as Lubega.

I had great difficulty mapping the boundaries of Budada, which were physically much less distinct than those of Kamira. It was a little smaller, consisting of about six hundred acres of *govumenti* land. All of this was apparently tenanted although, unlike Kamira, the village did not give the impression of being 'full up'. I estimated that about a fifth of the land, mainly in the low-lying area to the north, was uncultivated. In my census I counted 43 homesteads and 191 residents. There were only 10 labourers, most of them working for farmers like Lubega; this meant that the ratio of labourers to households was only a third of what it was in Kamira. The population was settled at much less than half the density of Kamira and on average the Budada household had an acre-and-a-half more land. It was immediately evident that although it was much less crowded Budada was also much less prosperous.

After one of my early explorations I wrote in my notebook that this seemed a much more *private* village than Kamira, where the houses stood candidly along the main roadway and paths. Some of the homesteads in Budada were so well hidden that it took me several weeks to discover them. I found one by following an old man down an obscured path which hitherto I had not noticed. The house itself was one of the most weird I have ever seen. It stood in a small shady hollow and was in every respect the familiar tin-roofed box, except that it was completely covered in huge spiderwebs. I was able to grasp the six foot mainstay of one of these webs and shake it vigorously without breaking it; the spider, whose globular body was about an inch in diameter, scuttled up into the eaves. The evil creatures were everywhere, black and brown, poisonous red and even blue. The appearance of order and industry was most striking. There were no dusty skeins of web blowing about, and there was a chilling sense that this macabre colony was not simply tolerated by the householder, it was well tended. The elderly Nyala couple who lived there were affable enough but I was quite unable to discover from them the reasons for all this. I had to be content with the unsatisfying explanation that it was a private 'religious duty' which they had undertaken.

Other people in Bugerere expressed many opinions on the Banyala, some guarded and some outspoken, but the only point of agreement seemed to be that they were strange people. After meeting several of them in their homes I felt bound to agree. They seemed to elude stereotype; many of them struck me as dour and cagey, they could easily be roused to anger and their sense of humour was undoubtedly on the dark side, but their most distinctive characteristic was unpredictability. This confounded my earlier assumption that as the indigenous people of Bugerere their culture and temperament would be much more uniform than the other immigrant groups. Instead, I found them individualistic, eccentric and divided amongst themselves. By contrast, the conformity and unanimity among the very mixed group of established settlers in Kamira was striking.

Settlement in Budada had grown up around a group of Banyala who had moved south during the 1940s and 1950s. They provided an unstable core for community growth which was evident in the life of the village as I came to know it. The settlement history, which I have charted on figure 3, was very different from that of Kamira. Budada took its name from a man called Kadada, who was apparently the original settler in the area. He died in about 1945 and the remnants of his family moved away. Eriasafu Lukoza was the only present householder actually born in the village. His father had joined Kakungulu's retinue and had eventually settled in Lango district on the other side of Lake Kyoga. Lukoza had lived in Budada with his mother until his father's death in 1929, when they moved to Lango to look after the family property there. When Lukoza's mother died in 1949 he returned to the farm in Budada which in the meantime had been in the care of his father's brother. It was this uncle who greeted me on my first visit to the homestead. Joseph and I walked into a spacious compound shaded by tall trees and called out at the open doorway of the house. There was no response, and we were about to leave when a wild old man in a loin cloth came bounding out into the sunlight. To our consternation he danced around us, whooping and thumping his chest vigorously.

We withdrew hastily, but returned a few days later in the hope that the entire family was not insane. We met Lukoza, who proved pleasant and helpful once he understood our business. As we talked the old man reappeared, but on this occasion he sat down beside us and quietly smoked his pipe. Choosing what I hoped was a propitious moment I asked him pointedly if he felt well. He cackled with glee, and Lukoza explained that his uncle had mistaken us for tax inspectors and that, as madmen were exempt, he had thought it prudent to act accordingly. As we walked back to Kitimbwa Joseph shook his head and repeated: 'Mr Sunday, I wonder at these Banyala. . . .'

Settlement history of Budada

Settlement of the present (1965) population of Budada. In brackets: average size of landholding acquired during each period.

Tribes or countries of origin:

ⓖⒶ Ganda	Ⓝ Nyala
Ⓚⓘ Kiga	Ⓝⓨ Nyoro
ⓀⓊ Kuku	ⓇⒶ Ruanda
Ⓛ Lango	Ⓢ Soga
ⓊⓊ Lugbara	ⓉⒶ Tanganyika

ⓖⒶ Newly arrived immigrant

o Established immigrant

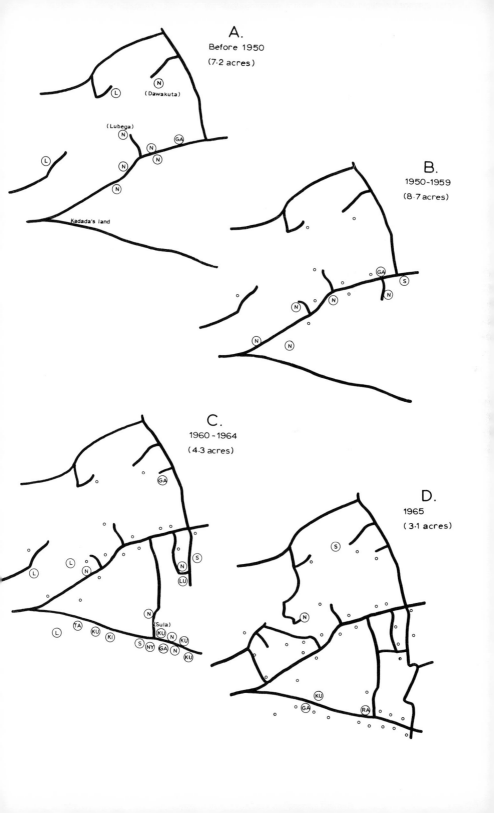

A.

Before 1950

(7·2 acres)

B.

1950-1959

(8·7 acres)

C.

1960 -1964

(4·3 acres)

D.

1965

(3·1 acres)

Kazoba, the longest-established of the present householders, came to Budada in 1935 from his home village, some twenty-five miles to the north. The land at home was poor and leopards and other wild animals made farming difficult and dangerous. He knew Kadada and, taking his advice, cleared and settled on an adjacent piece of land. He was followed in 1943 by his half-brother Mutagasa, who was attracted to the area by the prospects for cotton growing. A cluster of Banyala began to appear around what is now the central roadway through Budada. Nsamba, the first Muganda to arrive, settled to one side of this group and two Lango tribesmen claimed substantial areas of low-lying land to the north, accessible by a separate path from the main road at Kitimbwa.

Lubega's father was one of the early Nyala settlers, and he was followed a year later in 1949 by his half-brother Dawakuta. When his father died in 1954 Lubega inherited ten acres to add to the five he already held himself. The houses of Lubega and Dawakuta were buried deep inside their respective farms, and although their land was adjacent, walking from one house to the other involved a complicated, circuitous detour. In due course I discovered that this was one manifestation of the deep enmity between the two men.

The next groups of Nyala settlers who arrived during the 1950s also strung themselves out along the central roadway. Nearly all of them came from the Sabaddu gombolola of Bugerere, and each newcomer had some kind of kin relationship with a previous settler. After 1960 a wave of newcomers from a variety of different tribes swept into the village, settling mainly on the southern slopes (see Figure 3).

By the time I arrived late in 1965 the pattern of settlement in Budada was quite clearly divided. Dominating the centre of the village was the Nyala core with Lango and Ganda appendages to the west and east. To the south was the new strip of settlement which in its density and tribal admixture closely resembled a segment of Kamira. This part was virtually 'full up', and it was clear that further settlement would increasingly involve the intrusion of newcomers into the Nyala sphere of influence. Numerically the balance was in favour of the newcomers, as 63 per cent of the population of the village had arrived after 1960. Nevertheless it was clear that in other respects the Banyala held the upper hand. They constituted 43 per cent of the village, and it so happened that the proportion of Bagisu in Kamira was identical. The latter could also be regarded as a 'core

The homestead of an established Nyala settler in Budada village. The woman is gathering up maize cobs which have been spread out in the sur to dry

group', but their role in the settlement history of Kamira was very different. They were distributed much more evenly throughout the village, and the earlier and more recent settlers were intermingled. Perhaps more important, the Bagisu did not think of themselves as having any prior claims in land. Intermarriage, among themselves and with other families in the village, was a prominent feature of Gisu relationships in Kamira. The Banyala were quite different; for example, Dawakuta had married ten times but none of his wives came from the Budada area. Instead, ties of kinship prevailed and, viewing the schisms and squabbles within the Nyala core group, I found some truth in the frequent Gisu assertion that a village of brothers is unlikely to be a happy one.

Conversations with the householders of Budada made it clear that the village lacked the atmosphere of freedom and security which the people of Kamira valued so highly. When they talked about their fears and suspicions I came to realise that the Budada settlers had made much less progress towards securing their rights in land. Every household, Nyala and Kuku alike, was overshadowed by an implicit but occasionally outspoken question: who owns the land? In Kamira and Budada everyone knew the final answer: it belonged to the *govumenti*; but everyone, including the government land agents themselves, knew that amongst all the other competing interests this had little significance.

The most severe threat to the security of the village arrived in Budada in 1964, in the person of George Willison Luwano. To everyone else in the village he was simply 'the Mukungulu', a man who had aquired land by deceit and represented a threat of further invasion. As descendants of Kakungulu's retinue, several of the other Banyala could also be described as Bakungulu, but unlike Luwano they had found their own land in Bugerere. Luwano's grandfather was a Munyala who had travelled with Kakungulu's retinue to Busoga district and settled there. Local hostility eventually obliged the family to move to Lango district where a growing number of displaced Bakungulu were gathering. Irrendentist fervour reached a peak in the early 1960s, and it was this group which petitioned the Kabaka for resettlement in Buganda. The Ganda authorities gave their consent in principle and Sebunnya, the lands officer whose wedding I had attended at Kayunga, was given the unenviable task of finding vacant *govumenti* land for some of them in the Kitimbwa area. He was confronted by a familiar problem: the rate of settlement had long since outpaced his capacity to keep records. Nevertheless, Sebunnya identified fifteen acres of apparently untenanted land on the nothern side of Budada and told Luwano it was his. To the established villagers the ultimate insult was that this land was designated *mailo*, or freehold.

When Luwano arrived to take possession the village showed its sense of outrage. Segujja and Lubega denied him access and Luwano was obliged to make a difficult and circuitous path through the swamp from Kyato village. He managed to claim three acres of marginal, low-lying land which Lukambaga, a Muganda who had lived in Budada for eleven years, strenuously protested was his. Supported by the Banyala core group and, apparently, by the mutongole chief Nsubuga, he took the matter to court, demanding Luwano's eviction. The complicated issue had not been resolved by the time I left Budada, and Luwano was hanging on grimly to his miserable scrap of land. He was fiercely ostracised and the only person who would speak to him was Ayonge, a Lango whom he had known for many years. He complained to me bitterly of this treatment but felt sure that his claims would soon be upheld officially. It seemed unlikely that this would make him more acceptable to the people of Budada; although legally his rights were more permanent and more secure than anyone else's, in reality he was the most underprivileged member of the community. 'I cannot build a permanent house here,' he told me, 'the people would burn it down'. Every time he tried to make a pathway through the swamp it was obliterated. In the meantime, most of his family continued to live in Lango. Lukambaga spoke bitterly of 'this Mukungulu with five wives'; it was as if the intrusion of a well-established household into the community by such devious means added insult to injury. Some of the feelings aroused reminded me of the predicament of Kafuko in Kamira. The hostility to Luwano was a rare instance of unanimity among the people of Budada; they seemed adamant that not even the government had the power to intrude a new family into the community by an artifice of which they did not collectively approve.

If the case of Luwano evoked strong feelings about who did *not* own the land in Budada, it did little to dispel the uncertainty about who *did*. I was puzzled by the reluctance of several of the Banyala to tell me precisely the boundaries of their land. This made it impossible for me to chart landholding in the village, as I had done in Kamira. However, the newcomers on the south side were as specific about their boundaries as the Banyala were vague. The latter seemed to take a conveniently pragmatic view, as Sebunnya had discovered when he tried to mark out land for Luwano. Newcomers like Lario Sula had been obliged to buy land which had mysteriously, and in his case improbably, become the property of an earlier Nyala settler. For Sula, the only virtue of this was to pacify and formalise his relationship with his Nyala neighbours. As things turned out, even this was a misjudgement. When the Kuku refugee family moved in with Sula in 1964, he was obliged to cultivate right up to what he understood to be the boundaries of his land. His Nyala neighbour Mutagasa, who had sold him the land, was filled with resentment and arbitrarily reclaimed a portion of it. Sula sought the assistance of Lamene, a fellow-Kuku who spoke Luganda well, and together they confronted Mutagasa. In the heated discussion which followed, Mutagasa apparently delivered his riposte in ethnic terms: 'Back there in the Sudan, nobody owns land—you just roam around here and there—so why should you own land here?' Sula took his case to Nsubuga, who had witnessed the boundaries and collected a fifty-shilling fee, but the chief was plainly apprehensive about confronting an established Nyala settler. He had postponed consideration of the matter for so long that Sula had abandoned hope of redress.

The Banyala seemed very ready to capitalise on their reputation as the indigenous people of Bugerere and the original settlers of Budada, but their pragmatism in matters of land tenure was undoubtedly a two-edged weapon. By far the most bitter and protracted disputes were among the Banyala themselves. The wide uncultivated strip between the farms of Lubega and Dawakuta was fiercely contested by both. As land in the village became more scarce, so Nyala resentment of the newcomers increased. Fearing the kind of predation which Sula had suffered, the recent settlers anxiously planted boundary trees and cleared broad pathways around the perimeter of their farms. Many of them dared not leave the village in case someone sold their land in their absence. Filipo Mugawula, an elderly migrant from Kigezi district, was particularly beset by feelings of insecurity. He had worked for eleven years as a labourer near Kangulumira eventually saving up enough money to pay for four acres of land in Budada. He suffered from acute stomach pains and a visit to Mulago hospital confirmed that he had an ulcer. He was afraid to go for treatment in case someone took his land from him while he was away. He told me mournfully that he would soon be dead, but that he had come a long way to get a farm of his own.

In spite of these insecurities, land in Budada was undoubtedly cheap. The highest price was apparently paid by Motidienga, another Kuku tribesman: his four acres cost him 432 shillings and in addition he had to pay a 'chicken' of fifty shillings to Nsubuga. One of the many imperfections in the market for land was the higher price charged frequently, but not consistently, to the Sudanese immigrants. In 1963 the average price seemed to have settled at about sixty shillings an acre; meanwhile newcomers to Kamira were paying more than twenty times that amount, plus a 'chicken' of as much as five hundred shillings. It would have been interesting to know, but almost impossible to discover, how much the price of land in Budada had been held down by that other prevailing 'cost', the insecurity of tenure.

Feelings of insecurity tended to focus on suspicion of the Banyala, and evidence to support this was not lacking. Fanatya, a Musoga, had the misfortune to spend several months in Luzira prison for a traffic offence, and when he returned to Budada he discovered that all his coffee trees had been cut down (a favourite act of vengeance) and his car burned. He was convinced that his neighbour, Lubega, was responsible, but was unable to muster any proof. The Lango people expressed a closer affinity to the Banyala than anyone else, but even they were critical. Ayonge remarked bluntly: 'The owners of this country do not speak to us as brothers, and when they are angry they tell us that we [Lango] are as wicked as our tribesman Obote [the Ugandan President].' The Banyala were often accused of jealousy and spite; Fanatya complained: 'They can not bear to see another man succeed.' A Muganda, Serunjoji, spoke at length of the capriciousness of the Banyala, then switched suddenly into English: 'They have no *inside love*, and they are too interested in magic.' My own view was that they were intemperate. I was once an innocent party to a marital scene in the village. While I was talking to a group of people one morning the younger wife of Sentongo came running over to join the discussion, interrupting a journey to fetch water. A moment later, Sentongo himself came pedalling up the pathway and heard his wife utter a peal of girlish laughter. He hurled his bicycle to the ground, picked up her empty water can and proceeded to bang her about the head with it. The rest of us watched with embarrassment. As Sentongo drove his wife off home with shouts of abuse, one of the bystanders remarked: 'That was not nice; a sensible man would not have beaten his wife out here in the village, he would have taken her home.' Joseph shook his head and said again: 'I wonder at these Banyala. . . .'

Tribal identities played a much larger part in community relationships in Budada than they did in Kamira. When football teams lined up at Kitimbwa they did so on a tribal basis, very often simply 'Nyala versus The Rest'. By contrast there was an established village football league at Kangulumira, and there the onlookers could be heard shouting 'Kamira!' or 'Kigayaza!' Football at Kitimbwa was certainly not a new idiom for tribal warfare, indeed the games I saw seemed quite friendly and relaxed. Furthermore, individuals of different tribes could be on very cordial terms with one another, just as some people in Kamira seemed very friendly towards their labourers. However, tribal characteristics were the subject of frequent discussion in Budada, and prejudices and preferences were openly declared. Newcomers were sometimes guarded in their judgements, but only because they knew the matter was contentious; one of them said in answer to my question: 'I cannot tell you which tribe I like best, I do not want to get myself into trouble.' Among all these critical opinions I was somewhat surprised to discover that the Ganda were on the whole the most popular. This may have owed something to the personality of Nsubuga, who was generally regarded as a fair and sensible chief. He himself commented in detail on several tribes. He was critical only of the Lango, an attitude which no doubt reflected the national political enmity which existed between them and the Baganda at that time. He found the Sudanese the most polite and co-operative of all the immigrants; they performed public labour and paid their taxes without demur, which was more than he could say for the Banyala.

Tribal characteristics formed a basis for discussing the differences between 'Us' and 'Them' in much the same way that settlers distinguished themselves from labourers in Kamira. In fact, I only began to think seriously about the class difference in Kamira when I discovered that this counted for very little in Budada. Comparing the two villages it was very tempting to jump to the conclusion that

Kikumeko, a young Nyala settler in Budada, asking the spirit of his dead grandfather if he would like some food. After some domestic mishaps, a diviner told Kikumeko that the spirit had come to stay for a while and needed hospitality. Kikumeko made him a little hut (spirits, of course, do not need full-sized huts) and served him a diminutive lunch and supper each day

'class' had displaced 'tribe' in Kamira, and that the two kinds of category were mutually exclusive. However, on closer consideration it was clear that the difference was only a matter of emphasis: in Kamira people were well aware of tribal differences and these continued to play an important part in interrelationships; in Budada there were intimations of a class division in the attitudes of the Nyala core group towards the newcomers and land in the village. What was important was that the settlers of Kamira chose to express their unanimity against a distinct class of labourers, while the schisms among the people of Budada were acted out primarily in tribal terms.

The labourers in Budada were not at all obvious, not only because there were fewer of them but because it was difficult to distinguish them from settled villagers. In marked contrast to Kamira I never heard them spoken of as a threat to community life. While settlers in Kamira took great care to avoid being identified as labourers, people in Budada, particularly the newcomers, were glad to earn some cash when the need and the opportunity arose. Bernardo Pata, an immigrant from Busoga, divided his time quite evenly between casual labouring jobs, his own five-acre farm, and a nearby shebeen. Mulindwa, a Ruandan, had a small house and a half-acre plot in the village, but worked full-time for a farmer near Kitimbwa. Most families in Budada depended on their own labour but the Munyala Gawedde employed two men—a fifth of the available labour force. They were both from north-western Tanzania and seemed to live at close quarters to Gawedde and his family. One of them had a wife and three children and was looking for a farm of his own in the vicinity. There was no suggestion that any of these people were outcasts from the community.

If the Banyala in Budada had been more united among themselves it is probable that tribal relationships would have been much more tense than they were. The most spectacular crises tended to be Nyala family affairs and it seemed that the other villagers looked on with a mixture of curiosity and apprehension as their fractious neighbours let off steam among themselves. One of these crises erupted shortly after Christmas, and I was struck by the way that the Banyala, immersed in their imbroglio, showed a carelessness about the feelings of other members of the community which I knew the people of Kamira would have found very shocking. The first I heard of it was a commotion one moonless night in the room behind Lubega's shop.

Some people were trying to calm an hysterical woman. Eventually they put her to bed where she lay groaning deliriously for the rest of the night. In the morning my discreet enquiries revealed nothing more than the obvious fact that the woman was ill.

I next encountered the matter two days later when Joseph and I met Sentongo striding through the village in a state of great agitation. Shaking with rage he told us that he was on his way to make an official complaint to the mutongole chief. Someone had made magic on the pathway near his house. He was outraged because he was innocent of any malice and he and his family felt gravely threatened. He continued on his way to Kitimbwa, complaining vigorously to the other people he met. Soon everybody knew about the magic and was avoiding the area around Sentongo's house like the plague. Intrigued, I told Joseph that I wanted to investigate. He counselled strenuously against this, but accompanied me to a point about a hundred yards from the scene. Feeling a little apprehensive I marched towards Sentongo's house and came on a shallow hole about two feet in diameter in the middle of the path. There were chicken feathers scattered all around it and nearby lay a sharpened stake covered in dried blood. Inside the hole were pieces of burned flesh, herbs, twigs and charred remains of other unidentifiable objects. Although I could not understand what it meant the scene was pervaded by feelings of violence and malice. I took some photographs and beat a hasty retreat.

During the next two days I tried to reconstruct what had happened. Everyone was talking about this latest piece of Nyala mischief and fanciful accounts of it were going the rounds. I tried to base my own version on what I had seen and by asking the protagonists themselves a few blunt questions. It appeared that Lubega's sister had left her husband, who lived five miles away, and sought refuge with her brother in Budada. She claimed that her husband was a thief but he was persistent in his attempts to get her back. When more practical means failed he resorted to sorcery; she went mad, and to dodge the malicious forces she was hidden in the room next to mine. Lubega then consulted his friend Bakisula, a young Musoga from Wabiyinja village, who was well known for his talents as a *muganga*, witch-doctor.

I got to know Bakisula quite well, and found him the antithesis of the archetypal witch-doctor. He always looked very dapper, in crisp white shirts and neatly pressed trousers. As a Kitimbwa dude, he was fond of pop music and cold lager, and his house was solidly built and well furnished. There was no doubt that his life-style was supported by a substantial income from his magical skills. He was respected and feared by some, but several people, including Lubega, cited him as their most trusted friend. His manner was relaxed and helpful and I learned a great deal from him, but when I tried to question him about his profession he was smilingly non-committal.

Bakisula told Lubega to buy a goat, hens and barkcloth in preparation for a nocturnal exorcism. They chose a quiet spot near Sentongo's house, and there were many lurid accounts of how this piece of business was actually performed. Was Sentongo implicated, and did Lubega intend him any harm? This I could not discover. Certainly, no effort had been made to clear the residue of the exorcism and it must have been very plain to the participants that Sentongo and his family would have to pass that way. Sentongo vigorously protested his innocence of any involvement in the affair, and it was notable that he made no attempt to seek a magical remedy but took his complaint straight to the civil authority of the chief, letting the whole village know in transit how offended he felt. Nsubuga was bound to agree with him that to leave public traces of what purported to be a family affair was a breach of the peace and a threat to persons and property. Bakisula explained that he was obliged to use a public pathway as this was the artery of communication through which the medicine travelled to its appointed goal. He had been as discreet in his choice as circumstances would permit. Nsubuga insisted that he should clear away all evidence of his magic, but it was a long time before the feeling of menace left the area. Needless to say, Lubega's sister made a speedy recovery.

The major schism among the Banyala in Budada was between Lubega and his uncle, Paulo Dawakuta. Having heard that many people were afraid of Lubega and having found him taciturn in my early dealings with him, I was apprehensive about interviewing him. I cornered him in his farm one Sunday afternoon and found him surprisingly forthcoming. He told me that he had been born in Busoga of Nyala parents, and came with his father to Budada in 1949. Until his father's death five years later Lubega worked as a building labourer at the rail-head town of Namasagali on the opposite bank of the Nile. At one stage he probably owned about thirty acres, including the land he inherited from his father, but by 1965 he had sold

John Bakisula, the 'witch-doctor' at Budada

nearly half of this. He said that he enjoyed life in Budada; there was enough food, he could choose his own friends and he could ignore the people he disliked. Money was the most important thing in his life, and if he had more of it he would expand his shop in Kitimbwa. He had married fifteen times and when I met him he had five wives; he also had ten children, and another seven had died in infancy or childhood. Lubega described how he was related to two or three of the other Banyala in the village, but at no point did he mention his uncle, Paulo Dawakuta.

Nsubuga laughed when I said I proposed to interview Dawakuta, for he had a reputation as a lonely and embittered man. Thinking that I should allow myself ample time for persuasion, I took the bull by the horns and walked round to visit him one evening quite early in my stay. The house was large and decrepit, secluded among a grove of trees. Water draining down the hillside around it had cut deep gullies in the bare red earth. Joseph called out at the doorway and Dawakuta presented himself. He was a tall man, dressed in an embroidered cap, a long white kanzu and wellington boots. His features were heavy and the corners of his mouth and eyes were inclined downwards, giving him a very dejected appearance. Nevertheless, his manner was brisk and to the point: he would listen to what we had to say, but only for five minutes. He led us indoors, and Joseph and I sat down side by side on a motheaten sofa, facing him. Pinned on the walls around us was an impressive collection of illuminated mottoes. Most of these were cryptic epigrams, but I jotted some down and worked out translations later with Joseph's assistance. The prevailing theme was mistrust and suspicion, and the whole gallery amounted to a compendious injunction to the visitor to behave himself. 'If you come to my house, keep your eyes off my wife', 'Don't sit there and watch my house burn down', and so on. I explained in as much detail as time allowed, and with as much charm as I could muster, why I had called. He said he would think about what we had told him and let us know later whether we could return and ask him questions. Next day he called on Joseph (avoiding Lubega's shop) and told him he would answer our questions for five minutes that afternoon.

The interview lasted nearly four hours. In one of the most informative sessions I had ever had in Bugerere we discussed everything from the price of coffee to our favourite colours, but Dawakuta kept

Paulo Dawakuta of Budada

returning to a central theme: his fear and hatred for Lubega. Lubega, he said, had poisoned his cows and tried to burn down his house; he and his henchmen prowled around the village at night with guns, and he, Dawakuta, went in perpetual fear for his life. With Bakisula's assistance, Lubega had become reckless in his use of magic. Greed was his motive, and he seemed determined to hasten the day when he would fall heir to Dawakuta's property. Dawakuta was fifty-nine years old and although he had been married ten times he had fathered only one child, a daughter who was now married and had a family of her own. If Lubega craved money more than anything else, Dawakuta craved a son and heir of his own. Dawakuta had been a senior and respected man in Budada, but his nephew had turned the people against him. Now his attitude was one of undisguised bitterness and cynicism, he no longer cared what his neighbours thought of him. Did he have a friend to whom he might turn in a moment of crisis? 'I have no friend; if I make you my friend, we may be friends for a year and then we fight and you become my enemy—there is nobody one can trust.' Which of the many tribes in Bugerere did he find easiest to get along with? 'None, even the Banyala, for they can be the worst of all.' Under this carapace, Dawakuta was undoubtedly a sad and sensitive man. He was strangely tender towards his last remaining wife, and spoke with touching warmth about a brother who was confined to a leper colony. After a surly start, he revealed himself to us with a candour which I feared he might soon regret. To assure him of my discretion and good intentions I visited him as often as I could, but after that first long session he slowly withdrew, without recrimination, into his shell.

Part of the animosity between Lubega and his uncle had been caused by a struggle for leadership within the core of established villagers. Dawakuta told me: 'I used to be Mutaka in this place, but now the people no longer respect me.' For his part, Lubega roundly declared: 'I am the Mutaka of Budada.' Answering my question about 'the most important man in the village', ten householders, seven of them Banyala, said it was Lubega. Only two remained loyal to Dawakuta, although I was told that he had commanded a great deal of respect until his nephew's rise to power in about 1957. Lubega was even appointed mutongole chief for a brief period, but his leadership proved too divisive; after many complaints the office was taken from him, and Budada was placed in Nsubuga's charge. For virtually all the newcomers, more than half the village, Nsubuga was 'the most important man'. If the predominantly Nyala core group was ready to regard Lubega as Mutaka, it was clear that the office meant little or nothing to the more recent settlers. When I pressed him on this point, the Sudanese Dema declared: 'If you want to know who is the leader here you must ask the Banyala.' His attitude was similar to some of the newcomers to Kamira: until one became an established member of the community the man who mattered most was the official chief.

Inevitably, I found myself comparing the position of Mutaka in Kamira and Budada, and the very different personalities of Gizaza and Lubega. Although not everyone may have called him 'Mutaka', Gizaza's status as doyen of the Kamira settlers did not seem to be a matter of political intrigue as it had been in Budada. Lubega's entrepreneurial talents extended to politics and his approach to leadership was aggressively partisan; Gizaza, on the other hand, had successfully become the moderator of conflicting interests within Kamira. It seemed that the consolidation of a new office like the Mutaka depended on consensus within the community that leadership was a matter of necessity and virtue. In this way a vital distinction could be made between the office and its incumbent: it would not matter so much if an individual Mutaka was corrupt or fallible so long as people believed that Mutaka-ship itself was a good thing and worth preserving. In this regard, it seemed that the people of Kamira had made much more progress than the people of Budada.

Both communities had taken the term 'Mutaka'—which seemed to have currency in Bugerere—but in each it had acquired a different meaning. This was evident in the behaviour of the two men: while Gizaza sought authority by settling disputes and trying to discriminate between right and wrong, Lubega sought power by intimidation and friendship, magic and money. In their respective quests both men had met with considerable success, but the implications of their behaviour for the life of each community were quite different. Gizaza's authority could be transferred more or less intact to Bune, but Lubega had had to wrest his position of leadership from Dawakuta.

Perhaps the different status of the two men could be summarised by saying that while Gizaza's eminence was moral, Lubega's was amoral. I found some evidence for this in the information about 'the most important man' and the 'friend in need' which I collected in both villages. In Kamira, the two choices tended to coincide: an individual would regard Gizaza or Mazaki as both leader *and* friend. In Budada, leaders were not friends. Not one of the ten people who regarded Lubega as the most important man in the village also regarded him as their most trusted friend. In fact, only one villager, the young Nyala bachelor Gandu, regarded Lubega as a 'friend in need', but when I asked him who he thought was the most important man he gave me the typical response of the newcomer: 'I have not been here long enough to make up my mind.'

There was much greater coherence of sentiment and interrelationship in Kamira. By comparison, the network of friendships and neighbourly collaboration in Budada was thin; for eight householders the 'friend in need' lived in another village, again suggesting that as a community, Budada was much less self-contained. All that I have said may have given the impression that Kamira was a more benign place to live. In my opinion this was true, but when I counted up the opinions of the people themselves I discovered one of the many paradoxes in their behaviour and attitudes: although in Budada fewer people were enthusiastic about life in the village, more of them were ostensibly committed to settlement there. Ninety per cent of the householders in Kamira gave me a positive opinion of their village, compared with just 56 per cent in Budada; however, while 95 per cent in Budada declared that they would live out their lives there, only 77 per cent were similarly committed to Kamira. Did some people in Kamira not know how lucky they were? Or were the Budada immigrants asserting their permanence to counteract their own feelings of insecurity?

By February 1966 I was immersed in a sea of facts and figures, impressions of personalities and events, and fragmentary theories about what was going on in Bugerere. I was so absorbed in my own experiences that I found it very difficult to make objective sense of what I was discovering. An invitation to read a paper at the annual conference of the EAISR at Kampala brought an important turning point. I struggled for many weeks to think of something coherent to say to this august gathering. Eventually I picked what I thought was a safe and self-contained topic, and wrote a short account of the historical background to immigration to Bugerere.

After three months, absence, returning to Makerere University for the conference was like a stepping out of the wilderness into a brave new intellectual world. This was the first academic conference I had ever attended and I was greatly impressed. There were dozens of social scientists from all over East Africa, sociologists and anthropologists, economists and political scientists; there were scholars from Africa and many other countries, professors and new graduate students. As I read my way through the mountain of duplicated papers I began to realise, with a sinking feeling, how trivial my own contribution was. However, I met many people with interests similar to my own, seasoned fieldworkers who asked flattering questions about my work and greenhorns who boosted my morale by seeking advice. Before long I was immersed in discussion and was astonished to hear myself expatiate on the problems of migration and settlement. The new feeling of identity with the cosmopolitan community of scholars was completely intoxicating. With this new access of confidence, when my time came I virtually ignored my paper and talked instead about the people of Kangulumira and Kitimbwa. Semakula Kiwanuka, the urbane Ganda historian detailed to comment on my efforts, declared politely that what I had said was more informative than what I had written. At the end of the session an American visitor pumped my hand and thanked me for 'a stirring presentation'. Needless to say, I felt greatly encouraged.

9 Kigozi and Kabu

February 1966 was a momentous month: the Russian space module *Luna 9* made a soft landing on the moon, Buster Keaton died, Britain bought fifty FIII swing-wing supersonic low-level bombers from the USA, President Nkrumah of Ghana was ousted in a police-military *coup d'état*, and I was rescued from my chronic financial plight.

Several months previously I had heard that the African Studies Centre at Cambridge proposed to make a social and economic study of large-scale farmers in southern Uganda. One of the directors of this projects was Audrey Richards, whose study of migrants in Buganda had been my prime source of information about the situation in Bugerere. I wrote to her, saying boldly that even if they had already appointed their research officers I should be pleased to assist the project in any way she thought fit. One Sunday afternoon several weeks later Simon Musoke from the EAISR arrived at Amos's house with a car full of his family and an invitation to meet Audrey Richards in Kampala that evening. As I felt I needed time to brace myself for a meeting with the great lady, I begged to be allowed to follow him to the Institute early next morning. Dishevelled and covered with oil from my delinquent motor cycle, I presented myself to her; as her visit to Uganda was short, our meeting was brief and I felt that I had given a very poor impression of what I had done and could do. However, a few weeks later I heard from her again: she proposed that I should work for six months with the Big Farmer project and said she would apply for extra funds for my salary and expenses. I should spend three additional months working in Bugerere and three more in Cambridge during the summer of 1966. Neither I nor my patient bank manager in Edinburgh could believe my good fortune.

I planned to spend the extra three months from March to June in Kamira, tidying up my work in the village and looking for big farmers in the Kangulumira area. During my last few weeks at Kitimbwa I explored some of the problems of identifying the big farmers and discovering what kind of people they were. My new collaborators had not yet arrived in Uganda, so I had no idea how they proposed to set about the project. The people I had met so far seemed to think that anything over about twenty acres constituted a 'big farm', so I decided to use this as an arbitrary starting point. The survey I had made of the Kitimbwa area proved very useful and before very long I had assembled a collection of twenty people who, in one way or another, farmed more than twenty acres.

The first thing I discovered was that a family could 'farm' twenty acres and still be as poor as a family which farmed only two. Being a successful or wealthy farmer was obviously as much a matter of quality as quantity. The only common factor among the twenty people I interviewed was that, with one exception, they were all either Baganda or Banyala. This was not difficult to explain: only they had access to *mailo* freehold land, and the larger estates were amost invariably *mailo*. But in all other respects my collection of 'Big Farmers' were a very mixed bunch. Farm sizes ranged from twenty acres to nearly two thousand and annual cash income from about £30 to £3,000. There were a few elderly Banyala with large crumbling houses and ill-tended groves of coffee trees, and there were a few former civil servants who had retired to the country and used their capital and influence to build up flourishing agricultural enterprises. To the local people these were the '*bagagga*', the rich men whose large estates and cosmopolitan interests set them apart from village life. They depended heavily on hired labour, and when I visited their farms the extremes of the social class hierarchy became sharply evident. This renewed my resolve to make a particular study of the labour relationship both with the Big Farmers and the local community when I returned to Kangulumira. I was sure that in the fertile south of Bugerere I would find the most prosperous farmers, the highest proportion of labourers and the most pronounced social distinctions.

I had purposely not visited Kamira for about four months, because I felt it might distract me from the difficult task of getting to know Budada. I had not expected that much notice would be taken of my absence, and the enthusiasm with which I was welcomed back took me by surprise. When I called on Amos at the end of February he killed the fatted cock and we drank large quantities of cold beer. The front room, with my picture gallery still more or less intact, was cleared for me and two days later I was bidding farewell to Kitimbwa. The small group which saw me off made it evident that although I may not have become an established member of the community, I had at least made some very good friends.

The great news when I returned to Kamira was Gizaza's decision to quit the village and return to Bugisu. Almost as momentous was the news that Lameka Mubiru had agreed to buy Gizaza's nine acre farm for 'an immense sum'. Village gossip offered many different estimates, but eventually I managed to wheedle the exact price out of both men: Mubiru had agreed to pay the undeniably immense sum of twelve thousand shillings. Like householders in an English suburban street, the other settlers showed a lively interest in the deal as an index of the soaring value of their own property. I was intrigued for two main reasons: firstly, Mubiru's purchase indicated a possible turning point in the pattern of settlement in Kamira, for Gizaza's land was not being fragmented to make way for four or five new immigrant families, it was being taken over *en bloc* to double the land resources of an established settler. Secondly, the land was not, strictly speaking, Gizaza's to sell, for like most of the other people in the village he was a government land tenant. He was entitled to some compensation for standing crops, but the value of his coffee trees came nowhere near twelve thousand shillings. In any case Mubiru was clear that he was buying land, not compensating Gizaza for his coffee trees; indeed, he told me that he proposed to cut them all down and establish a fenced pasture for imported cattle. At 1,333 shillings per acre he had agreed to pay more than five times the price of the most expensive *freehold* land in Bugerere. This was dramatic confirmation of the way in which the price of *govumenti* tenancies had outstripped the value of *mailo* land ownership, to which only the Baganda had direct access. The deal was particularly interesting because Mubiru was himself a Muganda, and could surely have bought himself a large *mailo* estate elsewhere with the same money.

I now had an immediate interest in Mubiru, because soon he would almost qualify as a Big Farmer, according to my twenty-acre criterion. Amos remarked, with a certain gleam in his eye, that Mubiru would soon be a *mugagga*, a rich man; he might even be a big man in the community—after all, the tall tree which was Kamira's most prominent landmark would now be his. Mubiru was abashed to find him-

Lameka Mubiru and his wife

self the focus of so much speculation and gossip; all he wanted was to get down to the arduous business of making the farm pay. He said that in the meantime he would continue to live on the eight-acre tenancy which he held on the strip of *mailo* land along the south-west side of Kamira. Every year he was obliged to pay his landlord four hundred shillings in rent; this rankled because, as he pointed out, tenants on *govumenti* land had virtually no rent to pay. *Mailo* rent was proportional to farm yield and therefore the subject of much argument, but Mubiru could hardly conceal the fact that he was a prosperous farmer. In 1965 he sold eighty bags of coffee, some cotton, maize and matoke, and fifty bags of 'English' potatoes under contract to a government hospital. His cash income of around ten thousand shillings provided the basis for his investment in Gizaza's land.

Although apparently well off, Mubiru was certainly overstretched financially. This was a characteristic of many of the successful farmers I met in Bugerere, indeed I suppose it is no more than one would expect of ambitious entrepreneurs anywhere. Mubiru had the kind of household which befitted the established and prosperous settler: it included three wives, nine children and an assortment of nephews and nieces. In many respects he was the archetypal businessman: ambitious, God-fearing, industrious and thrifty. His enterprise, particularly the potato contract, weighed heavily on his family and his present resources. In his examination of the young children of Kamira, Rainer Arnhold picked out seven who appeared to be under-nourished; two of these were Mubiru's. It was startling to discover that the fathers of the other apparently underfed children included Amos, Bune, Manyala and even Bernardo Gizaza—men who, in cash terms, were among the wealthiest in the village. It seemed that these men were squeezing money out of their farms at the expense of the physical welfare of their own families, and it was sobering to reflect that from a child's point of view it was probably as advantageous to belong to a newly-arrived and impoverished family from the Southern Sudan as to have a wealthy and businesslike father.

Before I cast my net more widely in the Kangulumira area I decided to look more closely at the biggest farmers in Kamira. It was evident that they stood somewhat apart from the rest of the village and were more absorbed in their own affairs than in the life of the community. Although quite respectable, men like Wamubireggwe,

Mulengule, Mubiru and Lameka Kigozi were certainly not regarded as Bataka. It was as if social and economic eminence were not quite compatible, although it was true that Gizaza managed to combine the qualities of community leadership with a good deal of business acumen. I had already discovered that Big Farmers were not necessarily successful farmers in economic terms; it now appeared that they also might not be important men in a social sense.

I paid a call on Lameka Kigozi, who farmed his eighteen and a half acres of land intensively, immaculately and profitably. I once asked Kigozi if he owned a suit, for the best dressed I had ever seen him was in a rather elderly sports jacket and carefully pressed flannels, returning from a shopping trip to Kampala. He retorted that, for a farmer, smart clothes were an unnecessary extravagance. He could be seen on his farm most days wearing a tattered felt hat drawn low over shrewd, slightly hooded eyes, and with the tails of his shirt hanging down over a pair of old corduroy trousers which he always kept rolled up to the knees.

He was born thirty-six years previously in Bulemezi county, where his father was still a peasant farmer. Kigozi was older than his brother and sister, the other children of his father's only wife. Kigozi received a good education, attaining Junior 3 grade, and then he went to Kampala to take a technical course. He failed his exams and in 1953 returned home somewhat embittered. He got on well enough with his father but the small piece of land available for him was too small and too impoverished for a young man of his ambition. He had already fathered his first child and wanted very much to set up his own home independently. His cousin Mukasa had gone to Kamira a year previously and had spoken to Kigozi expansively about the good prospects there. When a three-and-a-half acre plot fell vacant there in 1955, Kigozi scratched together the 650 shilling asking-price and moved in with his wife and child.

Kigozi told me that his sense of failure diminished when he reconciled himself to the fact that it was 'God's wish' that he should be a farmer. He was clearly very industrious, and when a fellow villager decided to quit Kamira in 1958, he made a successful bid for the eleven-acre farm. He set to work at once on the reorganisation of his property, building a house on his new land and installing his labourers on the first plot, about a quarter of a mile away. His next land deal was only a year later: he bought nearly five acres from a near-neighbour, and by arranging a clever series of exchanges was able to extend the boundaries of his main farm.

I was introduced to Kigozi early in my stay in Kamira by Musoke, the mutongole chief. He was, I was assured, the best farmer in the district. I met him frequently thereafter and we conversed in a mixture of English and Luganda. His ambition and asceticism marked him off from most of his fellow villagers; I never met him at the drinking parties, which he scorned: 'We came here to make money, not to throw it away.' Although frugal, there is no doubt that he regarded the welfare of his family as the first priority. He had eleven robust and cheerful children, ranging in age from about twelve to a few months. He spoke about them frequently, and his plans and present labours were centred on them. He was an independent-minded man, and spoke critically of both the government and some of his fellow villagers, but his life was very much enclosed within his homestead. When I met him he was building a new bungalow-style house out of cement blocks, with a storehouse and garage built-in. He neither smoked nor drank, and his ideal recreation was to relax with a cup of tea and the radio after supper. He looked forward to Sundays and the prospect of almost continuous light music and request programmes from Radio Uganda.

Kigozi married his second wife in 1959 and a third, on his cousin Mukasa's recommendation, in 1965. He told me that, as a farmer, he needed at least two wives, but he confessed that he was worrying about how he could manage to put all his children through school. He thought that six was about the optimal number of children for a man of his means. Kigozi made regular visits—as many as eight a year—home to Bulemezi, taking with him generous gifts of food and money. There were always three of his children living, turn about, with his parents because 'they now have no children of their own'. Family relationships were important to him and I once asked him who, apart from his wives and children, mattered most to him, and he replied: 'Your father will soon die, and so you cannot depend on him too much. Your brother will always be your helper in time of need—so long as he is a good man. If my brother were a thief, of course, I should have nothing to do with him.' It was striking that Kigozi did not cite another villager as his 'friend-in-need', not even his cousin Mukasa.

Lameka Kigozi, with two of his sons

His very limited involvement in the affairs of Kamira were reflected in his attitudes to leadership. If anyone caused trouble on his property he would send for the mutongole chief straight away, rather than summoning the assistance of his neighbours. However, he reckoned that he would remain in the village and would probably be buried in his farm there. He remarked: 'It is not easy to move from one place to another; where would I put this one'—he put his hand on the head of the nearest child—'if I were to leave Kamira? There is no land for me now in Bulemezi.'

Kigozi told me his recipe for success: 'You must work hard and look after your affairs carefully; profit—that's what matters most.' Occasionally I met him leading an Indian-file of labourers between one of his two parcels of land, hoes over their shoulders. He made sure the five of them worked hard for their monthly wages of seventy shillings, but there is no doubt that, with the food and accommodation he provided, they were better off than most. Kigozi estimated that in 1965 he sold 120 bags of coffee, 10 of cotton, 10 of groundnuts and 20 of maize, as well as small quantities of tomatoes, aubergines and potatoes. A few years before, he had attended a week's course at the Ntawo farm school and had returned full of bright ideas about clearing and respacing his coffee, and treating sections of his land with chemical fertiliser. His greatest pride was his 'herd' of three cows, two native and one an imported Jersey, to which he devoted two valuable acres of land. With the veterinary officer's advice he had fenced this scrupulously, sown suitable pasture and built a concrete water tank. Early in 1965 his Jersey cow was artificially inseminated and he was duly rewarded with a fine calf. Although the milk yield was only enough to meet his family's needs he had ambitious plans to increase his dairy stock. Kigozi took an experimental and individualistic approach to his farming; he was critical of officialdom, with the exception of the veterinary officer, he mistrusted the government-inspired Farmers Clubs and the marketing Co-operatives, and he sold all his crops through carefully selected private dealers. He proposed to invest in a 'Landmaster' rotary cultivator, and relished the prospect of being able to thin down his labour force. Needless to say, he was continually on the lookout for more land. He told me once that he would have no difficulty putting a couple of square miles to good use—probably by starting a cattle ranch.

When I asked one of Kigozi's Sudanese neighbours who he thought

Kigozi making cement blocks for his new house

was the most important man in Kamira, he pointed silently across the roadway to where Kigozi's new house was beginning to rise from a neatly-trimmed lawn of paspalum grass. On one side of the lawn stood a green Opel car, battered but still pretty impressive. Kigozi's homestead was distinguished by its spacious openness—coffee trees clustered closely around most of the other houses in the village. Kigozi told me that he tried to be a good neighbour, minding his own business but sending gifts of milk or food to people he knew to be in difficulty. He was aware that some were jealous of his success and might not scruple to use 'those troublesome African medicines'. He said he could not afford to worry too much about this, but the more he felt threatened the more he looked to his professed Roman Catholic faith for support. Although at times he was irritated by my persistent questioning he seemed to regard my visits as a gratifying opportunity to reflect on his achievements and plans.

I suppose that Kigozi and Mubiru were both men who had risen above their peasant neighbours and preferred to think of themselves as commercial farmers. However, by the time I had met twenty or thirty 'Big Farmers' in the Musale area I had reason to wonder just how permanent this transition into modern agricultural enterprise might be. Both men were engaged, on behalf of their large and grow-ing families, in a battle with the productivity of their land; Kigozi was holding his own, but Mubiru was in difficulties. When Kigozi's children were all safely educated, some of them with jobs in the city and others with farms of their own, would he continue to accumulate land and build up his herd of cattle? The experience of other Big Farmers suggested that he would not. The wealthiest of them told me that they knew that many wives and many children did not make sound economic sense in the long run. If a man had just one wife and a couple of children he could hire labourers and build up a really successful farm which he could pass on more or less intact to his son. As it was, all these wealthy men had big families, which meant that in due course the big farm would be fragmented into many small units. All the evidence suggested that big farms waxed and waned, and were seldom passed over as going concerns to a new generation. This suggested the significant conclusion that big farms did not have very much to do with the consolidation of social class distinctions.

Some of the Big Farmers I met were expanding their enterprises fast, using their land intensively and profitably; others seemed to be running-down their farms and would apologise for abandoned coffee plantations or overgrown pasture. All of them had large numbers of children, on average three times as many (i.e. roughly ten) as the ordinary farmers in my Kangulumira area sample. The main difference was that the 'declining' Big Farmers had more adult children and were themselves in their mid-sixties, while the 'expanding' farmers were usually in their forties or fifties and still had children of school age. I was a little surprised to discover that the connection between the family and the farm was as intimate for the Big Farmers as it was for the ordinary people of Kamira or Budada. One of my main aims was to try to define 'success' in the Bugerere context, and in conversation with the Big Farmers it was plain that this was measured both in terms of material prosperity *and* a large household. To be wealthy and have no family, an unlikely circumstance, was as great a cause for commiseration as to have many children and no means of looking after them.

The road to success of course involved many things besides the stimulus of a large family; knowledge, experience and access to other vital resources played an important part in the careers of the most prosperous farmers. Nineteen of the thirty-eight Big Farmers I interviewed had been educated as far as Primary grade 5, compared with only a fifth of the people in my Kangulumira area sample. They also had more experience of the wider world, serving in the army or working in the towns before taking up farming. The wealthiest of them had cars or trucks and travelled regularly to Kampala and Jinja; they read newspapers and listened to the radio, and lent their support to the political parties. Like Kigozi, they were keen to experiment and diversify their activities—some of them had invested in shops or taxis—but were suspicious of the government institutions which were supposed to be abetting agricultural development. This did not prevent them from taking substantial government loans for farm improvements and from soliciting the advice of agricultural extension officers when they needed it. Seventeen of them kept basic farm accounts and records, and twenty-two had a current bank account.

The most distinctive feature of the Big Farmers was that, with only two exceptions, they were Baganda. In other words, they were a completely unrepresentative sample of the Musale population at large, in which the Baganda were a 30 per cent minority. In 1964 the social anthropologist L. A. Fallers remarked: 'We may hazard a guess that when and if "class consciousness" in a Marxian sense does develop it will not be the Baganda who produce it but rather the immigrants . . . a native middle class set above an immigrant proletariat.'* It seemed to me that the Big Farmers neither regarded themselves, nor were regarded by others, as a class apart. It took me a long time to make a list of them, visiting chiefs, combing through tax registers and examining air photographs, and still I have no doubt that there were more than thirty-eight people who farmed more than twenty acres in Musale. Ordinary people I asked could name one or two Big Farmers, because they lived nearby or were conspicuously wealthy, but the impression they gave me was that wealthy men came one-by-one, not in groups or classes. However it was clear that virtually everyone in Bugerere knew that if you had a farm of more than twenty acres, the odds were that you were a Muganda.

On the big farms I visited, the contrast between Ganda and immigrant, between employer and labourer, was clearly evident. What surprised me was that the labourers seemed to have a much more harmonious relationship with the most prosperous farmers than with the ordinary villagers. This was primarily because wages were better and were paid more promptly, and working and living conditions were more agreeable. The biggest of the Musale farmers, a former civil servant with a 1,300 acre estate, had a labour force of 120 men. They were housed in specially built lines and even had their own football pitch. There was a quite sophisticated organisation of foremen and gang leaders, which brought with it attractive opportunities for promotion and higher rates of pay. Wages for the ordinary labourer ranged from thirty-five to over one hundred shillings a month for the more specialised tasks like tending imported cattle. Every day prospective employees queued up to see the foreman, and nearly all were turned away. The farmer himself received me in a large, comfortably-appointed house. An energetic and enthusiastic man in his early fifties, he told me that he had spent the morning working with a fencing gang and that with his sleeves rolled up and a mattock in his hands he had inspired new zeal in his men. The scale of this enterprise put it in a class of its own, but many of the advantages enjoyed by the labour force were shared by the other Big Farms. This was reflected in the fact that a very high proportion of their

* L. A. Fallers, *The King's Men*, Oxford University Press, 1964, p. 149.

A big farmer superintends the loading of *matoke* into his lorry, near Kayunga

labourers (82 per cent) were employed on a permanent basis, whereas ordinary farmers preferred to hire men casually or by the month.

Buganda has provided a market for immigrant labour for many decades. Foreign-owned estates accounted for only a small proportion of this, for economic development was mainly an indigenous affair, a response by local farmers to new opportunities for growing cotton and later coffee. The colonial government and its successors saw no reason to discourage this situation in which labour from the poorer peripheral areas contributed to the economic prosperity of Buganda. The lack of local opportunities in the north or west did not deter successive governments from demanding tax; indeed, these demands were used to promote the flow of labour into the productive areas around Lake Victoria. Ruanda and Burundi provided a striking example of a colonial government (Belgian) which demanded tax while doing little or nothing to stimulate opportunities for earning it locally. It was this which caused—and still causes—the massive annual exodus from these countries. Ruanda now lags far behind its neighbours in the development of commercial agriculture, which means that ordinary people are still obliged to sell their labour very cheaply in Buganda rather than exploit their own land at home. One of the many anomalies I encountered in Bugerere was a Ruandan who earned thirty shillings a month labouring on a farm which was less than half the size of his own at home.

The labourers I spoke to seemed agreed that tax was the bane of their lives. Double-liability was the worst hazard: a labourer who worked in Buganda for more than four months was obliged to pay tax there, and although payment in his own country was supposedly taken into account there seemed to be few personal safeguards. Evasion was the most common tactic, which of course redoubled the harassment to which the labourers were subjected. Minor officials pursued defaulters zealously, and when they set up roadside checkpoints people—by no means only the labourers—could be seen picking their way through the fields on either side.

According to the 1965 Agricultural Census of Uganda, 37 per cent of all farmers in Buganda hired labour. My own surveys indicated that 60 per cent of the Bugerere farmers hired labour, 38 per cent of them on a seasonal or permanent basis. Two main reasons suggested themselves for this exceptionally high rate of employment: as an area of new agricultural development Bugerere was undoubtedly more prosperous than neighbouring parts of Buganda, and there was a keen demand for labour to reap the benefits of the fertile land; at the same time, opportunities for settlement provided an added inducement for landless young men to look for work in Bugerere. About a quarter of all the settled householders I interviewed had been 'porters' before finding land of their own. It was clear that the abundant supply of cheap labour was a key to the rise of the Big Farmers in Bugerere; when I compared notes with my new Cambridge colleagues who were working in other parts of Buganda I discovered that there were more wealthy farmers and more labourers in the Kangulumira area than anywhere else.

Hiring 'porters' was a firmly-established aspect of farming in Buganda, even for people who owned no more than a couple of acres. One effect of this was to diminish collaboration between households in Ganda communities and to put a price on ordinary work done on the farm. There was a good deal of variation in the way labourers were actually used; while tasks were quite specialised on the Big Farms, the smallholder would expect his 'porter' to turn his hand to all sorts of tasks, from harvesting coffee to baby-sitting. Each labourer was supposed to have an employment 'ticket', a monthly record on which the master was required to inscribe daily payments. This card was intended to safeguard the interests of both parties but in fact it was the cause of much confusion: no-one seemed to know for sure who was supposed to keep the card, and as employer and employee were often illiterate not many cards were properly completed. The prudent labourer would keep his card tucked into his pants where, during the course of the month, it would slowly disintegrate along with other vital documents like tax receipts.

Work was usually organised on the basis of a *kitalla*, a strip of land about twelve feet wide and of variable length. The nature of the task, hoeing, weeding or picking coffee, determined the length of the *kitalla*. This had the effect of reducing negotiations about terms of employment to daily arguments about yards and feet, rather than hours and minutes, or shillings and cents. It seemed that the more effectively he argued, the more the labourer was talking himself out of a job. The rate of pay remained static at a shilling a *kitalla*, and while its length was slowly whittled down, so too was the working day. In Bugerere in 1965, a *kitalla* amounted to about two and a half hours' work— hardly worth migrating for. This suited the small farmers very well, but made the working conditions of the labourers increasingly depressed. Those who could not work more than one *kitalla* a day for a single master tried to find more than one master, which meant holding more than one ticket. This had led to the tendency for small labour pools to develop, groups of 'porters' living together in some wretched hut, hiring themselves out by the day or by the month to a large number of villagers. In this way they were more estranged from the community than the labourer who chose to live with his master, earn only a shilling a day, and provide a wide range of extra services in exchange for board and lodgings. Bigger farmers like Kigozi told me that it was absurd to pay four men to do the work of one; his men worked three and sometimes four *kitalla* jobs a day, and it was evident that they took great care not to abuse what were undoubtedly privileged working conditions.

However, 1964 and 1965 were bad years for coffee farmers. Prices had fallen steeply, labour hiring had been cut back and Bugerere was full of 'porters' sitting around waiting for their wages. For the established farmer, a 'good' labourer was one who did not complain, but the growing number of hungry and dissatisfied men who congregated around the villages and in the townships did nothing to relieve the mounting tension. Petty crime increased and the reaction of the local people was becoming increasingly venomous. For example, in February 1966 the *Uganda Argus* reported: 'Yowana Kakwaya (porter) of Mpumudde village, Gombolola Musale, Bugerere, was beaten to death by villagers after he had been caught with a stolen cock.' On one occasion I saw a battered labourer being carried up the hill into Kangulumira with the remains of a purloined chicken still clutched to his breast. He was prudently feigning death until he reached the sanctuary of the Gombolola chief's office.

I soon realised that I could hardly depend on the 25 per cent of Bugerere householders who had once been labourers for an understanding of the porter's way of life. They had crossed the pale, and their attitudes to the depressed working class were particularly acerbic. Although they were quite prepared to admit that they had once been labourers, they were not inclined to dwell on their experiences. One of them told me that he thought the opportunities for settlement in Bugerere fostered an unhealthy attitude among the labourers: 'they come here to look for land, not to work hard'. The availability of labour was taken very much for granted, and when some porters

A young Rundi labourer working in the Kangulumira area

refused to continue working until they had been paid, their employers were very offended. The smaller farmer and his wife in particular were rediscovering the drudgery of farmwork.

Now and then, as my surveys proceeded, a gridline intersection would throw up a grubby shack inhabited by labourers. One afternoon Joseph and I called on five Rundi porters who were living together in a tumbledown hut not far from Kangulumira. My sudden appearance made them very nervous, and although I beamed at them encouragingly they remained taciturn. After further cajolery one of them, who said his name was Petero Ngulabanga, was pushed forward by the others as their spokesman. I decided to treat him as the head of the household, and while his fellows crowded round interjecting gruff comments now and then, he told me that he was about thirty years old and had a wife and three children on his small farm at home in Burundi. He had worked in Buganda for six years and returned home each October for about two months. He came to Bugerere 'because usually they pay well here', but now he and the others were fed up because they had not been paid for nearly five months. Ngulabanga said that the farmer he worked for had wrung his hands and said he was broke, but this did not seem to have prevented him from acquiring a new transistor radio. Ngulabanga felt there was no point in complaining and had resigned himself to waiting until the cotton crop was sold. In the meantime his boss bought his patience with enough food to keep him from starvation.

When the five of them were assured that I had not come to quiz them about tax, they were more forthcoming about their experiences. Finding somewhere to live was even more of a problem for them than it had been for me. Most farmers were unconcerned about how or where their labourers lived, and they reckoned they were fortunate to be allowed to live in this crumbling, grass-roofed hut, and to grow a little cassava and maize in the area immediately around it. Their idea of high living was to buy a piece of meat and cook a tasty supper here at 'home'.

In Kamira I got to know David Balugabamo quite well. He was a young man from Kigezi district in the west, who worked two or three *kitalla* jobs a day for Bernardo Gizaza. He, too, had to wait around the village for his wages so that he could return home. This was his first spell of work in Buganda and he had found the experience rather bruising. He had started the previous year by working on a building site in Kampala, but discovered he could not live in the city on the wages he was being paid. He felt he fared better in the countryside, for Gizaza provided him with food and a place to sleep. Balugabamo said that he had no friends in Bugerere, apart from two Ruandan labourers who shared a room with him. He was aware of the hostility of the villagers and found it best to keep out of their way as much as possible. When he had a shilling to spare he would go to Kangulu-mira, buy a Pepsi Cola or a Fanta, and sit in the bar listening to pop music. When I asked him if he thought he would return to Bugerere he told me guardedly that he bore no grudge against Gizaza, and that in any case the opportunities for earning money at home in Kigezi were even worse than in Bugerere.

The schism between settlers and labourers was clearly evident in the day-to-day life of Kamira. The 'porter' was always made con-spicuous by his tatty clothes, and the sight of a particularly ragged specimen strutting insouciantly through the village would evoke peals of malicious laughter. Men like Ngulabanga wore their rags like a uniform; he assured me that at home he had clothes every bit as smart as those of his Ganda employer, but what was the point of bringing them to a place like Bugerere? Who cared whether he dressed well or badly? In Kamira the labourers had no status to dress up to, and they took a certain pleasure in swaggering around the village in their scruffy apparel. Of course, this did not endear them to established villagers, one of whom told me that he no longer allowed his porters to live on his homestead: 'They are dirty and the sight of them around my house makes me sick.' In fact, everyone wore old clothes for farmwork, and among the coffee trees and matoke stems it was often hard to distinguish between employer and employee. Settlers were often reluctant to let me take photographs of them at work, saying that they did not want to 'look like a porter'. In exchange for a little co-operation in making a pictorial record of daily life in the village, I took numerous formal family protraits, all of them posed by the paterfamilias. I suppose that many of them still hang in the parlours of Kamira, presenting to the world at large a straight-backed image of the family in its Sunday best.

The labourers were also distinguished by their use of language. Whereas settlers would use the elaborate Ganda greetings when they met each other, most of the porters could not be bothered to come to grips with the niceties of the lingua franca, and preferred the brisk

Swahili salute '*jambo!*' Many of the things which had become associated with the labourers' way of life in Bugerere were disparaged by
the villagers. The thumb-piano was an example; this instrument
appears all over Africa and consists of narrow strips of metal pinned
to a wooden sounding-box. It is about the size of a small book, and
the player holds it between the palms of his hands, plucking the keys
with his thumbs. I was entertained by Ngulabanga and his com-
panions one evening to adroit and melodious music on the thumb-
piano. Joseph looked askance when I applauded them enthusiastically,
and on our way home remarked that although it was pretty enough it
was hardly *real* music. Sometime later he brought me a friend who
was apparently a virtuoso of the *endingidde*, the Ganda one-string
fiddle. As the musician scratched and scraped I had to restrain myself from making invidious comparisons with the artistry and charm
of the thumb-piano repertoire.

Just as the settlers in all their tribal diversity gained some coherence by regarding themselves as socially distinct from the ragged
brigade of porters, so too did the labourers have a sense of solidarity
which subsumed the variety of tribal identities among them. They
often made it evident that the concerns of the villagers were not their
concerns. As we walked through Kamira one morning, Joseph and I
came on one of the established settlers talking in a state of great
agitation to a group of his neighbours. We greeted him and asked him
what the trouble was. He pointed towards the front of his house, and
with some difficulty we identified the cause of his concern: a
suspicious-looking handful of crushed leaves. Who, he demanded,
waving his hands at the houses round about, was threatening him
with sorcery? While his neighbours stood tut-tutting sympathetically
at a safe distance, a labourer sauntered over to the 'magic' with his
hands in his pockets, kicked the leaves out of the compound and
scattered them in the undergrowth. He received his master's gratitude with a smile and a shrug, as if to say that such things were of no
concern to him. If such incidents drew attention to the labourer's
detachment from the affairs of the community, they also suggested
ways in which he might, if he wished, prey on the villager's fears and
insecurities.

Although the younger labourers tended to regard their visits to
Buganda as a kind of adventure, and bore their inferior status with a
kind of cheeky cynicism, there was no doubt that many of them

suffered great physical and emotional hardship. Those who could not, for one reason or another, return home to a community in which they were not despised, were particularly vulnerable. Kangulumira was haunted by a strange figure whose only possessions appeared to be a pair of ragged shorts, a large fragment of plate glass and a piece of rag. Holding the glass in the crook of his arm he would polish it for hours on end, exclaiming from time to time at his reflection. People laughed at these lost men whose identity had slipped away, and who had found somewhere inside themselves a mechanical, dreamlike way of existing. So long as they were not violent they were tolerated, and were given food now and then. One morning at Amos's I opened the door and met the empty gaze of one of these madmen, crouching on the dusty earth outside. Behind him, in another world, Mr Musoke's children circled and sang in the sunshine. He remained there for three days, very still and staring into my room. Nobody tried to move him and I was advised by Amos not to approach too close. He was soon surrounded by scraps of food which people had tossed to him, and I put a bowl of water beside him. I remember feeling surprised that someone could stay so still for so long without apparently excreting.

The more I learned about the predicament of the labourer in Bugerere, the more my mind went back to Claudien Kabuguma, the young Ruandan aristocrat who had visited me at Ntenjeru. He had the double misfortune of being a refugee, and being classed, by virtue of his nationality, as nothing better than an agricultural labourer. His stylish French and polished manners cut no ice with the Bugerere farmers. Although the resilience of youth was on his side, there was no doubt that he was overwhelmed by feelings of alienation. In Kitimbwa I met another young man whose circumstances were very similar to those of Claudien, but who had cracked under the strain of his new life in Bugerere. When I returned to Edinburgh with piles of field notes and no clear idea of how I should begin the process of writing-up, I took the story of this madman and made it the subject of my first published article on Bugerere.* Because I was unable to discover his real identity I borrowed part of Claudien's name and called him 'Kabu'.

Kabu danced into Kitimbwa one moonlit night and sat in the

* 'Kabu the Madman', *New Society*, vol. 8, no. 213, October 1966, pp. 640–3.

middle of the town, hooting and singing in a strange language. Several people, myself included, turned out to see what was going on. We found a tall, scraggy young man with hollow cheeks, dressed in the remains of a pair of shorts and a length of dirty dress material. When it was established that he was either drunk or mad, everyone went back to bed. Next day I found him sitting near one of the shops making passes at people coming and going with two long pieces of cane. His madness took the form of a kind of gleeful aggression which taxed the patience of the people he accosted. On one occasion he knocked over a bicycle in a manner which prompted its owner to hoist it above his head and hurl it at Kabu. A little later he knocked over the board on which a group of men were playing *mweso*, and earned himself a punch and a kick. Eventually a number of people complained to Nsubuga, the chief, who summoned the police. When the police Land Rover arrived two days later Kabu took flight, and the sergeant in charge refused to give chase. That evening Kabu was still with us.

Quite early he sought me out, pestering me continually for drinks and cigarettes in an elaborate mime-language. He sat for long periods on my doorstep, grimacing and hooting to attract my attention. He seemed to have singled out Nsubuga and myself for this treatment, maybe because he felt that we were best placed to help him. He ate very little, and when given anything by a villager he would antagonise them by taking a small bite, pulling a face and then treading on the food. However he was also accused of stealing food at night. His cadaverous and wall-eyed appearance attracted a good deal of attention, and earned him some respect among the younger children of Kitimbwa.

With Joseph's assistance I set to work, trying to find out who he was and what had happened to him. I discovered that he was a Tutsi aristocrat, like Claudien, who had been obliged to flee Ruanda during the civil war there. Eventually he found work with a prosperous Ganda farmer in Bugerere. Joseph talked to his master, who said he found Kabu sullen and withdrawn but a good enough worker. His account of the onset of Kabu's madness was colourful. Apparently Mukasa, the farmer, had three dogs which, according to the Ganda *lubaale* cult of ancestral spirits, had been possessed by three of his ancestors. One of these animals was particularly troublesome, killing chickens and stealing food. It would have amounted to patricide for

Kabu at Kitimbwa

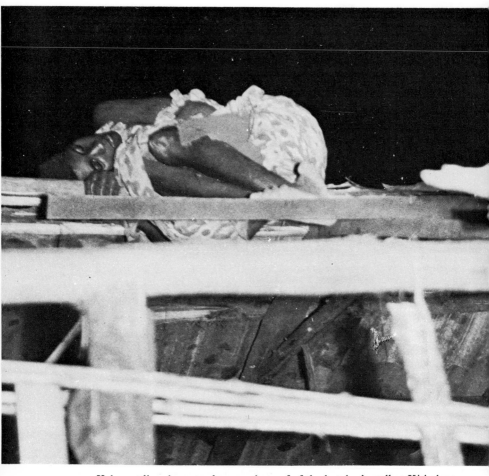

Kabu settling down to sleep on the roof of the butcher's stall at Kitimbwa

Mukasa to despatch the dog himself, but one day he declared in vexation that he would give ten shillings to anyone who got rid of it. Kabu heard this, and cut the animal's throat. The group of people who gathered around were awed; flustered, Mukasa denied having commissioned the execution, and as the discussion became more animated, Kabu became quite literally madder and madder. For the bystanders the explanation for his behaviour was simple: the delinquent spirit had found a new vehicle.

Kabu took refuge in his hut and threw stones at anyone who came near. After a couple of days he ran out and thrashed some little boys who were teasing him. Mukasa told him to leave, but Kabu was not prepared to go without the wages which were due to him. When Mukasa gave him the money he tore it up and stamped it into the mud, shouting over and over again that it was 'useless'. Mukasa then gave him a basket of food and an old pair of trousers and told him to go away, suggesting that a change of environment might shake off the spirit. There was no doubt that Kabu's departure, in the company of the troublesome ancestor, was a great relief.

After making a nuisance of himself in several villages, Kabu eventually turned up in Kitimbwa. His exhibitionism became worse, and one evening he climbed onto the roof of the butcher's stall and danced about, pulling at the tin sheets. Angry people gathered round, throwing sticks and stones at him. Apparently unconcerned he settled down on the roof to sleep. Two men got long sticks and began to prod him, but he only giggled like a child. I intervened and enticed him down with a cigarette, which I knew he could not resist. He was tied up roughly and taken to Nsubuga's house. The chief said angrily that he would take him in the morning to the police and have him thrown into jail. At this, Kabu seemed to sober a little and protested, in Luganda for the first time, that he had meant no harm and only wanted somewhere to sleep. Nsubuga untied him and he curled up quietly in a corner. I felt sure that his behaviour was an elaborate plea for help, and while trying to make arrangements to have him taken to hospital I watched the reactions of the local people to his antics. One day I tried to pierce what I thought might be only a veneer of madness; while he was grimacing at my doorway I suddenly dropped to my knees and grimaced back. He was clearly taken by surprise and rose slowly to his feet. I then smiled at him conspiratorially and passed him a cigarette. I said to him in Luganda: 'I know how you feel, but I have to work now, so please leave me for a bit.' He smiled faintly and strolled away puffing at his cigarette. I did not see him again until the following afternoon.

After about two weeks his antics changed. His clothes seemed to be disintegrating fast and occasionally he would stand with his genitals exposed, making something like a gesture of despair. As an act of self-vilification this was as shocking to a Muganda as it might have been to an English gentleman. Finally, one night Kabu stripped completely and wandered around the village wailing and beating himself. A group of men picked up his rags and covered him, and one of them, Bakisula the witch-doctor, took him to his house.

I was of course intrigued by this development, particularly when Kabu emerged two days later apparently calmed and wearing a new white kanzu. I went round to see Bakisula to try and wheedle out of him what had happened. Bakisula was inscrutable about all his professional business and, although quite amicable, he was not very forthcoming about Kabu. He told me he had fed him and bought him the kanzu; when I expressed surprise at this generosity, he asked me if I would feel happy wandering about naked. He said that he had persuaded Kabu to talk, and he filled in for me parts of the story I have related. I asked if he had managed to evict the malevolent spirit, and he replied that Kabu was not possessed, and never had been. Surprised, I asked if this meant he was not really mad. Bakisula shrugged, and said that he seemed *nnaku*, weary and dejected. He thought that Kabu's boss had been unsympathetic, and embarked on a lengthy peroration about the way some farmers maltreated their labourers. Sympathy, he explained, was what Kabu needed most. I pointed out that other people had found it impossible to communicate with Kabu. Bakisula shook his head and said: 'We talked a lot.' I left, with a new respect for Bakisula's talents, not just as a philanthropist but as a medical practitioner with an undoubted gift for psychotherapy.

Shortly afterwards the police Land Rover returned, and on this occasion Bakisula and Nsubuga made sure Kabu was on it when it left. As was so often the case, for me the story ended there. I tried to find out what happened to him, but like Claudien and the other misfits who came to my door, he seemed to disappear without trace.

10 Obote *versus* Mutesa

Among the immigrants to Bugerere I met many worldly-wise men. The ambitious, the literate and the wealthy read newspapers, listened to the radio and discussed international affairs with an enthusiasm which, in the case of a man like Amos, amounted to passion. When he sought me out in the evenings, brandishing a newspaper or party pamphlet, he was as much concerned to deliver his own opinions as to pursue explanations. I have no doubt that as a sparring partner he found me very flabby. As one who regarded the world as his oyster he seemed well aware that his own aspirations were intricately bound up with the activities of the political elite in Kampala, and with the relations between his own country and the world at large. A question like 'What does Queen Elizabeth actually *do*?' was not prompted by idle curiosity about the life and likings of Her Majesty, it was part of a wider argument which led him towards the conclusion that a businessman like himself might fare better under colonial government than under the existing pack of rascals.

Such curiosity was truly boundless and not always strictly pragmatic. There was, however, a sense in which the life and likings of Queen Elizabeth were construed as every bit as important as her formal constitutional functions. Amos's question was not simply about the British Monarchy, it was concerned with the actual incumbent of high office, for as every practical politician well knows the personality of the Emperor is as important as the throne he sits on. I was struck by the way in which the imagination of Amos and the others reached out into the world at large in direct and ingenuous ways. Their appraisal of great people simply as people who might have been neighbours made me realise how distant, impersonal and inaccessible the political heights were in my own thinking.

One afternoon, over a cup of tea at his house in Kamira, Musirimu Wamubireggwe confided to me that he admired President John

Kennedy and had been greatly upset by his assassination. He had
wanted to express his sympathy to Mrs Kennedy but no one could
give him her address. He felt sure that as a 'brother' (i.e. a white man)
of the President I would be able to help him send a letter and a small
gift to console the widow in her bereavement. This was one of a wide
variety of problems, often involving communication with the world
at large or with prior authority, in which I had been asked for assistance, so I said I would do my best. Two or three days later
Wamubireggwe arrived at my door with his letter and his gift: a large
crate packed with pineapples, oranges, bananas and a wide assortment
of other fruit and vegetables.

After careful thought I secretly ate and gave away to others the
contents of the crate. I then wrote to the United States Information
Service in Kampala, asking them to send me whatever photographs
and literature on the late President they might have. My next task
was to translate Wamubireggwe's letter, which he had composed and
written with Joseph's assistance:

It is with great honour that I address these few lines to the Lady, the
widow of John Kennedy.
I ask your pardon for not writing sooner to express my sympathy over
the loss of your husband.
First of all I write to say how sad I was over the death of Mr John
Kennedy, because he was such a young man to have reached the
highest ranks in political affairs. But even before he died he was known
in every country as a brave and famous man.
Mr Robertson has given me your address; he is a good man working
here to discover the ways of the Bugerere people. Through him I have
sent this present to you.

In fact, there was a lengthy paragraph at this point extolling the
many virtues of one Mr. A. R. Sunday, which modesty forbade me
to include in the translated version.

Now we all beg our Creator to keep you safe in this world after the sad
time you have had. I have nothing more to add, except that I should be
overjoyed to hear from you that the world was now a happier place for
you.
I am MUSIRIMU WAMUBIREGGWE, one who is unknown to you
but your friend by the grace of God.

With Joseph's help I established the approximate retail value of the
crate of food and pinned a couple of banknotes to the letter I had

Musirimu Wamubireggwe

composed to Senator Edward Kennedy, 'c/o the Capitol, Washington'. I explained the circumstances of the gift which, I suggested, could be regarded as a contribution to the Kennedy Memorial fund, asked him to pass Wamubireggwe's letter on to Mrs Kennedy, and rather anxiously suggested that some acknowledgement would be greatly appreciated. I posted the letter at Kangulumira and, with some misgivings, sat back to wait.

One morning a week or two later, Wamubireggwe came floating through the trees towards my door, whooping and waving a letter above his head. Next day I too received a letter of thanks from Mrs Kennedy on a handsome piece of black-edged cartridge paper, and in an envelope bearing her signature in lieu of a stamp. Wamubireggwe was deeply impressed and gratified, particularly when I was able to pass on to him a large package of material sent by the US Information Service. Everything was framed and hung up in his house, and the youngest of his children was taken aback to find himself renamed John F. Kennedy. I myself was a little bemused by my brief but effective term as American *chargé d'affaires* in Kamira.

New settlers from distant places, like Lario Sula of Budada, were too much concerned with the problems of coming to terms with their own immediate circumstances to be greatly excited by the problems of the wider world. Matters of day to day survival reduced the compass of Sula's economic concern to the welfare of his own household and its niche in the local community, and as a foreigner his political interest was limited to a tacit acceptance of the status quo. Between him on the one hand and Amos with his wide-ranging political interests on the other stood a man like Lubega, whose political arena was the village. As I have already explained, for the established settlers in Kamira making a new community was altogether too complex and too delicate a business to transact publicly and competitively. Their approach to village politics was deliberately low-keyed. Whatever private misgivings they may have had they were always quick to assert that Kamira *per se* was a happy place to live. True, the soil was less fertile than it had been ten years ago, and the weather had been unkind, but for them what was wrong in Kamira was pre-eminently what was wrong in Uganda and the world at large: low prices, high taxes and corrupt politicians. To come to grips with the *govumenti* and its iniquities one needed knowledge, experience, metropolitan contacts and wealth—all the things which were out of the ordinary man's reach.

Nevertheless, there were many keen students of the wider political world in Bugerere. Those who could read studied the half-dozen vernacular newspapers which circulated daily or weekly throughout the country. These would be read aloud to small groups of people in and around the towns and trading centres and, like the radio news broadcasts, would provoke animated discussion. The range of vernacular newspapers impressed me greatly. Buganda had a substantial literary and journalistic tradition, and on 1 September 1965 yet another daily paper appeared, called *Ssekanyolya* after the grey heron, a bird renowned in Ganda folklore. The principal English newspaper was the *Uganda Argus*, whose muted political commentaries reflected its expatriate management and its status as The National Newspaper.

One morning when I was still a newcomer to Bugerere I opened my copy of the *Argus* and was confronted with a glassy-eyed and morose photograph of myself. '*What is he doing in Bugerere?*' demanded the caption. I was rather shaken, but the attached paragraph explained quite affably what I actually *was* doing in Bugerere. Indeed, I had written it myself for a young man called David Kabogoza who worked as a part-time correspondent for the *Argus*. When I met him once in a Kayunga bar I remarked to him that I was spending much of my time trying to explain to people what my work entailed. He volunteered to send a short note about me to the paper, together with the photograph borrowed from my driving permit, and I reckoned that the publicity would do me no harm. I was less sure when I saw the caption which Kabogoza had devised, no doubt with good journalistic intentions. As it happened, the voice of the *Argus* had little impact in Bugerere. It was an English-language publication, preoccupied with metropolitan affairs. A murder in Kampala would receive extensive front-page coverage but items from the provinces were grouped together in a narrow column of small print on the centre pages. I used to call this 'the agony column' and it would look something like this:

Yesterday Suk raided Karamojong,
killed six herdsboys and stole
60 head of cattle.

★★

Budali Wanzira, a Mugisu of Monde
village, Kyaggwe, was strangled to
death by unknown people at night.

★★

Yesterday Karamojong raided Jie,
stole 50 head of cattle and killed
three herdsboys.

**

&c . . .

The most popular catch-phrase on Radio Uganda's pop-music request programmes was 'How's the world treating you?' The radio itself was, of course, the principal medium through which the citizens of Uganda discovered how the world was treating them. In September 1965, according to the first issue of *Ssekanyolya*, two radio channels (Red and Blue) broadcast programmes nationally and regionally (Midland, Northern and Western) from 6.30 a.m. until midnight. For the Kampala and Jinja areas a new television station broadcast three hours of programmes each evening, but this was soon to be extended to include morning and afternoon educational programmes. Radio Uganda broadcast news and specially prepared magazine programmes in *fifteen* different languages, including English and Hindustani; advertising and music took up most of the remaining time. Broadcasts from Nairobi were heard clearly in Uganda, and even the cheapest, government-subsidised transistor sets could pick up some of the many international stations which beamed entertainment and propaganda to East Africa. The General Overseas Service of the BBC (now the BBC World Service) was the most prominent of these; on 24 May 1966 it offered readers of the *Argus* twenty hours of programmes ranging from Gilbert and Sullivan to political profiles of Rhodesia and Malaysia. In the English winter months the sports programmes were particularly popular, as large numbers of Ugandans played the British football pools. The Voice of America provided lively competition, and I remember feeling outraged on many occasions when I was trying to pick up the morning news from London on my tiny radio, to hear a voice drawling in over Big Ben and the 'pips': 'This is the Voice of America Breakfast Show!'

Any evening one could hear with startling clarity the voice of Peking, relayed from Albania. Of all the external programmes this seemed most out of touch with what I understood to be the tastes of ordinary Ugandans. The two-hour broadcasts would consist of a reading of the news from an obviously committed point of view, extracts from the *People's Daily* editorial bristling with paper tigers and imperialist lackeys, and lengthy sequences of Chinese classical and revolutionary music. The South Africans also broadcast a lot of classical music, and had a distressing habit of playing three-quarters of each symphony or concerto. Moscow Radio devoted a good deal of time to dealing with listeners' correspondence; the queries from Uganda were so numerous and so politically pointed that I must confess that my suspicions as to their authenticity were often aroused.

After I had spent nearly a year in Bugerere I paid a visit to the Hon. David Kimaswa MP at the parliament building in Kampala. As we sat for a while in the visitors' gallery I was overwhelmed by contradictory feelings of *déjà vu* (my English constitutional perspective) and other-worldliness (my Bugerere perspective). Here was Westminster, replicated with curious differences of colour and language. At the centre sat the Speaker, a gowned and wigged Asian lawyer, and before him rested an enormous gleaming mace. The Members, mostly in dark suits, lounged on the opposed ranks of upholstered benches, interjecting 'shame!' and 'hear-hear' while a tall and very black northerner struggled through pages of a lengthy speech. The style was so very different from the rapid vernacular exchanges in the councils of local chiefs which I had seen at work in Bugerere. Some time previously Kimaswa had taken Amos to the visitors' gallery and it was plain that the rituals of parliamentary business had struck him as very odd. Over lunch in the Members' canteen, where the menu was an odd mixture of apple pie, curry and matoke, Kimaswa expatiated on the problems of his political role, which extended from the life of his constituency on Mount Elgon to the very rarified atmosphere of the National Assembly. He did not expect his constituents to understand the differences between these two worlds and was resigned to coping with the incompatibilities. At home in Bugisu it was known that he was an important link with the powers of government, but as such he was regarded more as an agent in the metropolis than a representative tied by the rules of parliamentary democracy and the strategies of a political party. His constituents would often seek him out in the capital with such problems as school entrance or the dilatoriness of the legal process. These visits usually had little bearing on his activities in the House and often involved the expenditure of much time and effort on his part. His visitors regarded him as their patron in Kampala and he was almost invariably obliged to pay their return fares.

Kimaswa had the reputation of attracting a good deal of government-sponsored development to his constituency. Such patronage was sadly lacking in Bugerere, and it seemed to me that political enthusiasts like Amos had genuine cause for grievance. Bugerere was the bread—or matoke—basket of Kampala and Jinja, and in terms of coffee and cotton production generated a large portion of the national wealth of Uganda. In return for this, and the graduated tax they were obliged to pay, the farmers of Bugerere could see little evidence of *govumenti* concern for their welfare.

For a population of more than one hundred thousand there was no hospital, although there was talk that one might be built at Kayunga or Kangulumira. The Agricultural Extension and Community Development officers were distributed so thinly as to be virtually invisible. The Agricultural officers would invest most of their energies on individual 'progressive farmers' in the hope that the success of these few might somehow fire the enthusiasm of others. In a similar way the energetic Community Development officer had concentrated all his efforts on one village near Kayunga, but was finding it impossible to communicate the joys of the Good Life to the hundreds of other communities in Bugerere. Government farm-improvement loans were directed towards those established farmers who could afford the collateral, which did little to help the newcomers who were struggling to make a living. The state primary schools were distributed extremely thinly and were poorly organised, leaving the way clear for innumerable shady private schools which preyed on the willingness of the settlers to invest in their children's future.

The main road into Bugerere was a superb, Italian-built highway, but inside the county the roads were so sporty that the East African Safari Rally was routed through Kayunga and Kangulumira. One afternoon each year the world came to Bugerere in the form of a string of Fords, Peugeots and Datsuns. Covered in dents and red dust they screamed through the towns at an incredible speed, blasting a passage through chickens, dogs and people. One afternoon while we were out looking for Big Farmers, Joseph and I bumped into a group of four white men, the first I had ever encountered off the beaten tracks. They told me they were surveying the lines of a new road which might one day run north to south through Bugerere. It was they who had been responsible for placing mysterious white crosses throughout the county.

These surveyors invited me to eat with them at their camp a few miles south of Kangulumira, a tiny expatriate enclave with a huge refrigerator crammed with beer and tinned food. I saw them several times during my remaining few weeks in Bugerere, and I found their company very strange; two of them were in their late 'teens and they all regarded their job as an adventure in the wilderness, whereas to me the landscape and people of Bugerere had become very familiar. Their dispassionate views on the mounting political crisis in Uganda were particularly striking, contrasting sharply with the enthusiastic comment and speculation I heard every day from Amos.

The immigrants to Bugerere could certainly be forgiven for finding the political world around them intractable and confusing. Amos was more assiduous than most in trying to come to grips with it, and in the evenings we would explore political issues to the limits of our shared vocabulary. Bugerere was part of the modern state of Uganda; this pleased him, as a modern and progressive man. Bugerere was also part of the traditional Kingdom of Buganda; he had chosen to come here as an immigrant so his subjection to the Kabaka's chiefs was fair enough. But was it fair that Buganda, unlike Bugisu or any other part of Uganda, should have its own more or less independent government? And why should Sir Edward Mutesa be both the Kabaka of Buganda and the President of Uganda? How could one man do these two jobs, and how could people say that the President was above party politics when it was very clear that one of the main parties, *Kabaka Yekka*, was promoting his interests?

Both of us agreed that Milton Obote, the Ugandan Prime Minister, was a crafty politician, and I suggested that he may have arranged the two incompatible jobs for Sir Edward simply to put him on the spot: sooner or later he would have to come down either on the side of Ugandan Unity or on the side of autonomy for Buganda. I reminded Amos that his own Democratic Party had formed the first government of the Independent Uganda, and that the astute Obote had come to power in August 1964 by forming an alliance between his Uganda People's Congress and Kabaka Yekka. It was now becoming evident that this *mariage de convenance* had not deflected Obote from his prime goal, to crack the power of the Buganda Kingdom.

The privileged position of Buganda put a man like Amos in a vexing position. As a Mugisu he was a Ugandan citizen, yet from the day he arrived in Bugerere it was made evident to him that he was first and foremost a citizen of Buganda. He held his land on the authority of the hierarchy of chiefs and his security as a settler was very much in their hands. He was entitled to elect a representative to the *Lukiiko*, the parliament of Buganda, but unlike the citizens of any other part of Uganda he could not elect a representative to the Ugandan parliament. This was done on his behalf by the Buganda Lukiiko. The Lukiiko was solidly *Kabaka Yekka*, the 'opposition' consisting of one UPC and three DP representatives, and, needless to say, the twenty-one MPs which the Lukiiko sent to the Uganda parliament were KY to a man. Amos felt, not without reason, that his enthusiasm for the DP was being frustrated by this constitutional trick. What was all this business about democracy, and the people having their say in government?

In particular, Milton Obote would have found a ready ally in Amos on the issue of whether the twenty Ganda Saza chiefs should be allowed to continue sitting, along with the elected representatives, in the Lukiiko. Surely it was not a sound constitutional principle for administrator-chiefs to take part in legislative processes? Amos felt that kow-towing to their authority as a settler in Bugerere was one thing, but what right did they have to represent his interests in the national political arena?

For Amos, and for many other immigrants in Bugerere, party membership was more an act of faith than a matter of participation in constitutional politics. The party language was revolutionary, with its call to 'overthrow' and 'seize power'. The parliamentary constituencies had very little to do with the all-important village, parish and gombolola boundaries (see Figure 1, page 18) and it is not surprising that they meant almost nothing, even to the longest established settlers. The constituencies had been drawn up very recently with the mathematics of democracy in mind, not in recognition of clearly defined patterns of local political sentiment. This meant that the Lukiiko representatives' sense of responsibility to the people was, to put it mildly, vague. Amos knew that the present system provided only the feeblest means of expressing the interests of the Bugerere people, and extracting from the government a fair share of the tax-payer's cake—schools, hospitals and so on. What little enthusiasm the government did express in the development of Bugerere was channelled through the hierarchy of chiefs. Visiting politicians did not waste their time arguing that their faction could work to improve the lot of a particular constituency; they demanded a much more personal kind of loyalty and declared or implied that benefits would accrue directly to those individuals who bought party cards.

When I asked the labourer David Balugabamo what his religion was, he promptly replied 'UPC'. He quickly acknowledged his error after further explanation, but his response was significant and in many respects apposite. Party politics in Uganda had in fact grown out of religious competition among the main proselytising churches. At the end of the last century the opposition between Catholic and Protestant was synonymous with the conflicting imperial interests of France and Britain. Subsequently, Catholic loyalties tended to coalesce within the Democratic Party, and Protestant loyalties within Milton Obote's Uganda People's Congress. Arising from the more primeval loyalty to the traditions of Buganda, Kabaka Yekka was something of the odd-party-out.

Although all the parties publicly disclaimed any religious bias, the fervour of party activities was very striking. 'Apostles' came from the capital to preach at public meetings, mainly about the iniquities of their opponents. Political images were painted boldly in black and white, never showing much detail. The gatherings were held together by rituals of slogan-shouting, the slogans themselves rarely amounting to more than the initials of the party: '*D.P.!*' These occasions had all the colour and excitement of a carnival, with hucksters doing a brisk trade in Coca-Cola, peanuts and party shirts, and I am sure that the most vocal participants lent their support at every party rally which came to town. The parties' appetite for recruits was voracious and even a labourer who was not a Ugandan citizen could be drawn into party activities, if only to strengthen the crowd at a public meeting. Religious enthusiasm is well-known as a concomitant of rapid social change, and it was tempting to see the success of the political parties in Bugerere as the new religious sects of a developing society.

The party's indiscriminate absorption of new recruits was in marked contrast to the process of settlement in a village like Kamira. If the party offered for a few shillings instant membership and a clear identity *vis à vis* members of other parties, incorporation within the village was a much more protracted affair, in which the distinctions between 'us' and 'them' ran along quite different lines. The settlers' feelings of security and hopes for the future were intricately bound up in the slow growth of new communities, whereas the parties offered nothing more substantial than an exciting sense of involvement. The incompatibility of village and party activities was clearly recognised. The towns bristled with party insignia and echoed to the chanting of party slogans, but these were rarely in evidence in the villages. One might, for example, have expected the leadership struggle in Budada to have taken on party colours, but this was evidently not the case; both Lubega and Dawakuta declared, with different degrees of enthusiasm, their support for Kabaka Yekka.

In Kamira, any overt demonstration of partisanship was regarded as the height of bad manners. To call someone's party loyalty to question within the village was considered dangerously provocative, and the occasional beer-party brawl could usually be traced to this kind of indiscretion. Sitting at Amos's house on the boundary between Kangulumira and Kamira I could actually witness the change from the political town to the non-political village: young men on their way home from a party meeting, flushed with a sense of participation, could be seen pulling off and rolling up their party shirts as they stepped across the village boundary. Even Amos shared this sense of propriety; I once heard him reprimand his storeman for challenging passers-by with the DP slogan. Such partisan behaviour was a little too close to home for comfort, nor was it particularly good for business.

I once asked Mubiru about this, and he remarked: 'The villages do not belong to the parties, they belong to the chiefs of Buganda.' Amos was obliged to agree that the parties had not done very much for the *Abanabugerere*, the people of Bugerere. I was interested to hear Amos identify himself in this way, for 'Abanabugerere' was a term which seemed to be gaining currency among the established settlers. It seemed to express common territorial interests beyond the level of the village community, a way of distinguishing 'us' from other people who had little or no sense of commitment to Bugerere, whether they were temporary labourers or government politicians. However, by calling themselves 'Abanabugerere' the settlers were inevitably associating themselves with a Saza of the Kingdom of Buganda, whose chief was officially designated 'the Mugerere'. Here again Amos was confronted with the ambiguity of national and local sentiments: when his political opinions were called to question over a pot of beer he could be a strident advocate of the Democratic Party point of view, but when his security and personal interests as a settler

Bonny Moses Sekasi reading from the *Uganda Argus* to a group of people at Kitimbwa, around the time when the political crisis in Uganda was coming to a head

in Bugerere were called to question, his alignment with the Kingdom of Buganda was inevitable.

As the political crisis in Uganda developed during the early months of 1966, this perplexing division of loyalties was put to the test. The growing antagonism between Dr Obote's government on the one hand, and the Kabaka's government on the other, was reflected in mounting political excitement in Bugerere. Matters came to a head with the President, Sir Edward Mutesa, and the Prime Minister, Dr Obote, accusing each other of acting *ultra vires*. A parliamentary squabble the previous year had turned into accusations of corruption in the armed forces and the highest echelons of government. Colonel Idi Amin, the Deputy Commander of the Uganda Army, was accused of benefiting heavily from gold and ivory stolen from the Congo. In February 1966 Daudi Ocheng, the Secretary General of Kabaka Yekka, accused Colonel Amin, Dr Obote and two other government ministers of peculating two and a half million shillings between them. Dr Obote ordered an independent commission of enquiry, but Ganda suspicions deepened when he left for a tour of the north of Uganda where Colonel Amin's troops were on manoeuvres. Alarmed by what he felt to be a threat to national security, Sir Edward Mutesa consulted the representatives of certain governments, including the United Kingdom. On his return from the north, Dr Obote expressed his sense of outrage, and on the 22 February he detained five of his own ministers (all of them southerners), and assumed personally the powers of government. Next day he appointed Colonel Amin Commander of the Army and the following day he suspended the 1962 Constitution, in which the 'special status' of Buganda had been assured. Even more drastic measures were to follow: on 2 March Dr Obote abolished the offices of President and Vice-President of Uganda, and in a broadcast explanation the following day he accused Sir Edward Mutesa of seeking military assistance from foreign powers and using the office of President to further the political ends of Buganda. Executive authority in Uganda was now vested in Dr Obote.

Sir Edward Mutesa's protests against these actions were endorsed by the Buganda Lukiiko, and in the Uganda parliament Mr Abu Mayanja MP filed a High Court complaint against Dr Obote. This did not deter Dr Obote from finally abrogating the 1962 Constitution and proposing another in which the powers and privileges of the

Ganda chiefly hierarchy were severely curtailed. The chiefs and Buganda government ministers were no longer entitled to collect certain land revenues, one of their major perks, and Saza chiefs were not allowed to sit with the elected representatives in the Lukiiko. Justifying these changes, Dr Obote declared: 'It is simply not possible to do what Buganda Lukiiko wants, it is simply not possible to do what Sir Edward wants.' Under pressure, the DP Opposition Members supported the new Constitution, which came into immediate effect in April 1966. The Buganda Lukiiko of course rejected the new Constitution. The Ganda Attorney General pointed out that, unlike the rest of Uganda, Buganda had had 'from time immemorial' a well-organised government, legislature and courts: 'We must fight to the end anybody who tries to snatch them away from us. And we shall die for the Kabaka and our land.'* Dr Obote could certainly have proposed more radical changes, but it seems that he was simply concerned to prime the fuse, stand back, and watch the Ganda state be blown to pieces. The Kabaka wrote a petition to the Secretary General of the United Nations, U Thant, which Dr Obote described as an act of sedition. At length, the Kabaka issued a bizarre ultimatum: since Buganda now regarded itself as outside the Constitution of Uganda, all the officers and institutions of Dr Obote's government should quit Buganda soil by 30 May 1966.

The final dénouement was triggered off early on Monday morning, 23 May, by the arrest of three Ganda Saza chiefs; their activities, according to Dr Obote, were 'known to be against peace and good government' and, furthermore, they had continued to take their seats in the Lukiiko. News of this was brought to the people waiting at Kangulumira by those most swift and efficient of newsagents, the taxi-drivers. By coincidence, I had arranged to meet the chairman of the Bugerere Kabaka Yekka that morning, and at ten o'clock I was still waiting for him. I was getting a little impatient, partly because he had already postponed our meeting twice. I sent Joseph into Kangulumira to make enquiries, and he returned with the dramatic news that Buganda was now at war. Understandably, the KY chairman had found more pressing business to attend to in Kayunga.

The taxi drivers reported that throughout Buganda people were setting up roadblocks and gathering weapons to defend themselves

* Report in the *Uganda Argus*, 27 April 1966.

against the Central Government forces. The sudden shift in the crisis from rhetoric to physical action took most of us by surprise. I think my own feelings were similar to those of many other people in and around Kangulumira. The prospect of a showdown was exciting, but no one could guess how long the trouble would last and how many lives were at stake. At the same time I felt it was a great opportunity to see a different and unexpected facet of life in Bugerere. I was supposed to leave for home in only two weeks and was already making arrangements for a big farewell party in Kamira. In retrospect, my stay in Bugerere had been eventful but not exactly thrilling. In February we had heard that Kwame Nkrumah had been overthrown in a police military coup d'état in Ghana, and in other African states there had been similar traumas of adjustment to independent statehood. When I got home I would be expected to give some first-hand account of the politics of the new Uganda. Until that Monday morning I felt I would have disappointingly little to say. All the same, now that the crisis had broken I was assailed by fears for the safety of my painstakingly-collected data. If I lost that, there would be little point in going home at all.

During the morning a large crowd gathered at Kangulumira, and with the tension of the previous weeks broken, a feeling of exhilaration prevailed. We were told that the Ganda ex-servicemen who had been resettled at Nazigo, some six miles to the north, had obeyed the call to arms and were manning a roadblock (see Map 1). I decided, against Joseph's better advice, to ride up the road towards Kayunga to see what was going on. As we approached Nazigo we met the European surveyors who were heading south at great speed in a loaded truck. They told me they were in the process of moving to a new camp at Galiraya in the extreme north of Bugerere, but had been turned back at the roadblock. They felt that the situation was getting out of control and proposed to escape from Bugerere by the southern road through the Mabira forest. Having had a vigorous reception at Nazigo they expressed doubts about my safety and offered to take me with them. I told them that for the moment I felt much safer staying in Kangulumira, and waved them goodbye.

At Nazigo, Joseph and I found that the road had been blocked by an overturned lorry and pieces of motor chassis. I propped the motor cycle at the side of the road and walked down to the group of men at the barricade. I knew several of them, and we exchanged greetings and news. They told me that they would not prevent me from continuing to Kayunga, but advised me to return to Kangulumira. When I got back to the motor cycle I turned round to take my first, and only, photograph of these events. Two policemen, who had presumably walked from Kayunga, were picking their way apprehensively through the barricade. I turned the camera slightly to see how the picket was reacting to this. Their attention seemed to be elsewhere. Through the viewfinder of the camera, rather like a spectator at a race meeting, I watched them running up the hill towards me.

I was knocked to the ground and the camera torn from my grip. With an unexpected show of authority, Joseph barked at my assailants and they stopped to look at him. He quickly explained that I had tried to take a picture of the two policemen, who had in the meantime melted into the undergrowth. Some of the men ran off in pursuit, while I stood gabbling apologies for my folly. My dented camera was handed back to me and with a grim warning I was allowed to return, chastened, to Kangulumira.

When we arrived back, we found the crowd in a state of excitement. The surveyors' heavily-loaded truck had aroused suspicion; they had disregarded a signal to stop but had been brought short by a tree which had been felled across the road at the south of the town. A man who had witnessed the incident told me that stones had been thrown, someone had opened the door of the truck, and the driver and one of the white men had been slashed with a panga or axe. Before worse could happen they had managed to drive off the road, round the tree, and escape south.

In the meantime a drum had been hung up outside one of the shops in the middle of the town, and the call-to-arms was being beaten out on it at regular intervals. People from the surrounding area were continuing to gather, some of them armed with sticks and spears, others looking decidedly apprehensive. Near midday someone came to tell me that the surveyors had just driven back through Kangulumira at high speed. No attempt had been made to molest them. Apparently there were three white men in the truck, and I wondered what had happened to the fourth member of their party. The possibility that he had been left at Nyize, to the south, prompted me to set out again on the motor cycle, ignoring Joseph's protests. At Nyize I met the gombolola chief from Kangulumira, who was even more concerned than I was and had driven south for the same reason. The people who had gathered at Nyize, collecting sticks and stones to defend themselves, could tell us little more than we already knew. Trees had been felled at regular intervals along the road through the forest, leaving the surveyors with no alternative but to make their way out of Bugerere via Kayunga.

When I got back to Kangulumira, Joseph was waiting for me with more news. Men, armed with sticks, stones and knives were piling into a large lorry, which had apparently been requisitioned from an Asian trader at Kayunga. They were off to strengthen the defences at Nazigo. The surveyors had apparently been caught up in a battle between the security forces and the people of Kayunga. While the men who remained at Kangulumira argued about how best to deploy themselves, a procession of women and children brought baskets of stones and dumped them in mounds around the centre of the town. It seemed to be the younger Baganda who were taking the initiative. A number of people I could identify as non-Ganda immigrants had obeyed the call to arms, but were hanging back looking apprehensive. I asked one of them why he had come to town, and he replied that the Kabaka had ordered him to do so. I asked him if he had brought a weapon, and he pointed to a rather flimsy stick propped up beside one of the shops: 'It is there if I should need it.' The news that the army had reached Kayunga sent many people creeping away— 'definitely not Baganda!' I was assured by a young man who was explaining to me, with flourishes of his panga, how he proposed to despatch Dr Obote and his entire army. At this time I too decided to creep off home for something to eat.

In the evening I walked back into Kangulumira and found a large watch-fire burning in the middle of the crossroads. The sight was awe-inspiring; the flames in the middle of the road seemed to symbolise dramatically the severence of Kangulumira from the outside world. The main road traffic was fundamental to the normal life of the town, and the fact that so many people passed through it each day made it very different from the more self-contained villages round about. Now that communications had been interrupted, the change was very striking. The firelight gave Kangulumira a feeling of closeness and intimacy, and for the first time it seemed to take on some of the qualities of a community. The town was strangely quiet; the bars were closed and shuttered, and overt party loyalties seemed to have evaporated. Now and then the people who had gathered round the fire would turn and peer into the darkness up the road towards Kayunga from where, sooner or later, the forces of the outside world would return. I met the gombolola chief, neatly suited and standing in the background. He had played no part in organising the defences of the town. 'The people have chosen,' he told me, 'now I can only watch and wait. I pray for no trouble.'

I walked home and tried to squeeze some news of the situation out of my transistor radio. None of the foreign stations had anything to say, and the Radio Uganda newscaster spoke blandly about Mr Ian Smith, a new Opposition Party in Kenya and Mr Wilson's declaration of a State of Emergency in Britain, following a seven-day seamen's strike. It was nearly a week before I heard what had happened in Kampala that day. Dr Obote had described the Kabaka's ultimatum to quit Buganda as an act of treason, and had accused Sir Edward and the Ganda Prime Minister of inciting the people to violence. Fifty were arrested by the security forces at the Presidential Lodge at Makindye, and throughout Buganda people had been obstructing roads and marshalling defences. In the evening Dr Obote declared a state of emergency in Buganda and imposed a dawn-to-dusk curfew.

Next morning Joseph arrived early to tell me the news. There had indeed been a big battle at Kayunga, and the surveyors had been killed. The UPC offices in Kangulumira had been ransacked and burned, and the party officials had fled. The ex-servicemen had strengthened the fortifications at Nazigo and so far the army had made no attempt to dislodge them. It was clear that I would have to stay put in Kangulumira, at least until this impasse was broken. I felt that the real trouble might begin a week hence with the deadline of the Kabaka's ultimatum to Dr Obote, but in fact the army was already, at that moment, launching an attack on the Lubiri palace.

I walked with Joseph into town, partly because I felt it was safer to keep myself evident and to offer some assurance that I was as concerned as anyone. The feeling of isolation had made people tense and Joseph told me that rumours were rife. Two people had been murdered during the night and it seemed that some opportunity was being taken of the crisis to settle old scores. Someone asked me if and when I proposed to use my gun. After much anxious enquiry I traced this rumour to the fact that Joseph often carried my camera tripod slung over his shoulder in a canvas case. The atmosphere of tension was increased by the persistent throb of the war drum, beating like an agitated heart in the middle of the town. Joseph and I stood a while watching the drummer, who held a cigarette clamped between his teeth as he hammered out the call to arms. At close quarters the sound became hypnotic; suddenly—I cannot remember how or why —the sticks were in my hands. Perhaps I am the only European to have called the people to arms on a Ganda war drum.

During the morning the foreman of the surveyors' work gang bicycled into town and sought me out. He was understandably alarmed, and as a stranger to Bugerere was concerned about his own safety. He wanted news of his employers, and we told him as much as we knew. Joseph took him in hand, gave him a meal and warned him against trying to make his way north. He suggested it might be best to return to Nyize and lie low until the trouble was over. We later heard that he had made his way out of Bugerere through the Mabira forest on foot, and had reached Jinja safely. Several people in Kangulumira expressed to me their concern about the death of my 'brothers', the surveyors. The crowd at Kayunga would automatically have assumed that, as white men, they were agents of the Central Government. They suggested darkly that, had I only recently arrived in Bugerere myself, a similar misjudgement might also have been made about me. I took some comfort from this assurance that I had crossed the pale, but in fact my reception in the town throughout the crisis was always warm and concerned. During the morning most of the shopkeepers were evacuating their stock and possessions, and carrying them out into the safety of the villages. There was no food for sale, but one of the traders I had got to know well, Mr Silvesteri, sent me a parcel of food. Some people who had no wish to be involved in the eventual confrontation with the army were moving their families out to stay with village friends, and the ferry some five miles away across the Nile to Busoga was doing a roaring trade. Fares were apparently grossly inflated and at one stage an overloaded boat capsized sweeping several people down the river to their deaths.

That evening I heard the first radio news of the uprising from Kenya, the BBC and South Africa. Radio Uganda continued to have little or nothing to say about events at home, although the capital had had a day of disorder and bloodshed. At ten in the morning the paramilitary Special Force surrounded the Kabaka's palace but met with unexpectedly strong resistance from the royal bodyguard. After two

hours the battle was washed out by heavy rain, during which the
Kabaka made his escape. As the Special Force had suffered many
casualties, army reinforcements were called in. By 3.00 p.m. troops
occupied the palace grounds and were setting fire to outbuildings. At
6.00 p.m. the army used artillery and bombs to blast its way into the
palace itself, and the remainder of the bodyguard, which had covered
the westward flight of the Kabaka, was massacred.

At seven in the evening, Amos arrived home unexpectedly. Before
the weekend he had left on a short visit to Bugisu and we had all
assumed that he would stay there until the trouble was over. However, when he had heard that white men had been killed in Bugerere
he had feared for my safety and had set out at once for home. He had
spent the day picking his way through the forest from Jinja, a
twenty-five mile hike which I would certainly not have chosen to
make myself. His family and I were pleased and relieved to see him,
and I was very touched that he should have shown such concern.

I settled down to write an account of the day's events, but at
9.30 there was a knock at my door. A small deputation from Kangulumira led by Mr Silvesteri had come to advise me about my personal
safety. 'The people are mad now,' I was told, and the town was full of
wild rumours. Some people were afraid that I knew too much, and
were suggesting that I should be taken prisoner. Mr Silvesteri dis-
counted this and said that my present action seemed sensible; I
should neither attempt to hide nor attempt to leave Bugerere. I made
it as clear as I could that I would avoid doing or saying anything
which might bring trouble to anyone in Kangulumira. We parted
company with warm assurances of mutual trust, but I was left with an
uncomfortable feeling that I was now in some kind of limbo between
the people on the one hand and the government on the other.

Next day, Wednesday 25 May, there was not much news and little
activity. Overnight the war drum had disappeared and an uneasy
silence had settled over Kangulumira. Rumours were rife, and the
fluctuating moods of optimism and pessimism brought stories of
victories and massacres. Reports that the Kabaka had been killed
spread a feeling of gloom; some argued that there was no longer much
point in trying to hold out against the government forces, but the
resolve of others was strengthened: 'The King is dead, long live the
King!' The lengthy vigil at the crossroads was certainly preying on
people's nerves. Someone confided to me that Joseph was arousing

suspicions, perhaps because he was being a little too assiduous in collecting scraps of news for me, or because he had spent some time with the surveyors' foreman. I laughed this off, but later in the day Joseph himself came to me in some distress: his room had been broken into and his belongings turned upside down. He also told me he was worried about his family who lived not far from Kayunga, so we agreed that it would be sensible for him to make his way north on foot through the villages.

During the day I noticed an interesting change in my own role. My assiduous attention to the international news broadcasts in English had turned me into a purveyor rather than a consumer of news. I was able to report that communications to and from Kampala had been cut and that the army was still strenuously engaged in the Buganda countryside. I explained about the curfew, which prompted some people to take a defiant delight in staying out in the streets all night. Most heartening was the news from London that the Kabaka was not dead but had escaped to the western borders of Uganda. The cool, equable voice of the BBC announcer and the chimes of Big Ben set me thinking about home and the probable anxiety of my parents and friends. To divert myself I picked up an old Sunday newspaper colour supplement but the feelings of remoteness which this engendered deepened my sense of gloom. Contemplating the fragility of civil order I decided grimly that Britain was a fools' paradise, but to arrest the downward spiral I polished off the remains of a bottle of whisky and retired to bed.

Next morning I decided that I should prepare myself for what might be an awkward jump across the gap between Kangulumira and the Ugandan authorities. I was packing my field notes into a steel box which sat comfortably on the carrier of the motor cycle, when Abudu breezed in to make lunch. I had not seen him for a couple of days, but now he assured me that things were returning to normal. He took a bowl of groundnuts and sat shelling them in the sunshine. As usual, he chattered while he worked and I half-listened to him while I organised my papers. 'Ah, danger!' he shouted melodramatically, and I laughed. A minute later I looked outside, and Abudu had vanished. I stepped out into the sunshine and heard the unmistakable sound of gunfire.

Men, women and children were running madly out of Kangulumira and down in the direction of the river. A woman with a child on her back scrambled out of the maize patch in front of me and ran past, yellow with fear. As she raced through Amos's back yard she turned and screamed at me '*Run!*' Another volley of shots rang out, alarmingly close. I turned to go back into the house and found myself facing five soldiers. I raised my hands above my head, while in the background people continued to pour down the hill. 'Where is the gombolola chief?' one of the soldiers demanded, in English. I said I did not know. 'Which is the chief's house?' I explained that I was a newcomer and was greatly alarmed by what was happening. If they could report that I was alive and well, I should be very grateful. They shouted to me to keep clear, and three of them went off towards the gombolola headquarters, one pushed his way into the maize patch and the fifth strode into Kamira with his rifle at the ready. As I turned back into the house I suddenly saw the whites of Amos's eyes. He was about twenty feet up a tree, and perched on a lower branch was the gombolola chief. I went into the house and lit the Primus stove to make a cup of tea. The doorway darkened and I looked round to see one of the soldiers peering in. 'Where are the people?' he asked. I told him that they had all run away. 'So this is where you stay,' he remarked. I nodded. He made a face and stomped off.

For half an hour I had Kangulumira to myself, then gradually people began to re-emerge. Fear slowly gave way to relief and laughter, as everyone told everyone else what had happened to them. We heard that the first batch of soldiers had driven up in a taxi and taken the town by surprise. They were followed by an army lorry and by soldiers beating their way along the periphery of the road. Apparently they had fired into the air and no-one had been hurt, although the gombolola chief's house had been smashed to pieces. Augustine's shop had been broken into and looted, no one knew by whom. The 'Kangulumira Crossroads' bar had also been smashed up. The soldiers had all driven away back towards Kayunga and that, we all assumed was that. The feeling of relief turned into jubilation; Obote's army had been repulsed! Sticks and spears began to reappear and something of the mood of Monday morning returned. I went home for something to eat.

Suddenly the noise in the town was cut dead by a sharp volley of gunfire. I heard the roar of a heavy vehicle driving into Kangulumira. Once again a torrent of people poured out of the town, down the hill towards the Nile. Bullets whined alarmingly through the trees, so I sat down on the doorstep, not knowing quite what to do. Suddenly a shot smacked into the front of Amos's house and a piece of cement dropped to the ground beside me. I went inside and sat down, my legs shaking.

After half an hour the rain came down in thick grey curtains, and all I could hear was the roar of the downpour on the roof. In the evening, watery red sunlight broke over a silent and almost deserted Kangulumira. I walked cautiously through the mud towards town. At the gombolola headquarters a group of men were carrying away the body of Benalikaki, the parish chief of the Nyize area. His kanzu was stained with orange mud and dark red blood. He had confronted the soldiers, apparently unarmed, and had been gunned down. I looked into the gombolola chief's house; windows and family pictures on the walls were shattered, plaster had been gouged out of the walls and light switches smashed. Clearly the soldiers were enraged that they had been unable to find the chief, and had returned to the town determined to teach the people a lesson. They had tried to persuade a woman to talk by pulling her ears until they ripped.

I still do not know how many people were killed in Kangulumira that afternoon, but I myself knew of four. Amos found a young man about my own age lying among the coffee trees near the house, with a bullet through his back. Nor do I know what became of the gombolola chief, although Amos assured me later that he had escaped. Subsequently I was told that the army considered Kangulumira to be the hard core of resistance in Bugerere. Men from the town were blamed for organising the mob which had confronted the Special Force at Kayunga, attacked the police station and killed the surveyors. The chief was supposed to have had a hand in this, but later I sought to assure the authorities that I believed this was not the case. It was clear to me that, in so far as resistance had been organised at all, it was the party activists and not the chiefs who had taken the initiative.

That evening Mubiru called, and with Amos we had a sombre discussion of this violent turn of events. We wondered if the army would return; it seemed to us that all the fight had been beaten out of Kangulumira, the resistance had evaporated and the isolation was broken. Did that mean that the road to Kampala was now clear? I explained that I was anxious to get a message to my parents, and that to do this I would have to put myself in the hands of the Ugandan authorities. Amos suggested that I should pretend to be a Catholic priest and ride the motor cycle boldly all the way to the capital. Both the army and the Ganda militants would surely allow me to pass unmolested. He reminded me that priests on motor cycles were a very familiar sight, and that I myself had often been mistaken for a 'father'. I could think of no better plan, so while we continued to discuss the crisis I tried to make myself a dog-collar out of a piece of white cardboard.

Now that Kangulumira had been tamed my thoughts turned, for the first time since Monday, to Kamira. I asked Mubiru for news and he replied, phlegmatically, that the village was 'still there'. It occurred to me that I had seen nothing of Gizaza, Mazaki, Bune and the others. Amos told me that Gizaza had gone ten days previously to Bugisu, and Mubiru told me that so far as he knew, everyone else was 'still there'. Some, himself and his family included, had run away from the gunfire, but he had no doubt that everyone would return home as soon as they could. Kamira was uncomfortably close to Kangulumira, but he seemed surprised by my suggestion that the security of the village might have been seriously threatened.

In the cold light of Friday morning my cardboard dog-collar looked very unconvincing. Kangulumira was almost deserted, but I was assured that the road to Kayunga was now clear. Leaving everything behind at Amos's house I set out northwards on the motor cycle. Along the way, houses were bolted and shuttered and the roadblock at Nazigo had been dismantled. I had very little petrol left, but I pressed on towards Kayunga. On the causeway side of the town there was evidence of Tuesday's battle; the shreds of a large plastic Mobil sign hung over a burned-out taxi, and stones and broken bottles still littered the road. As I rode slowly through Kayunga towards the police station I passed the overturned truck of the surveyors. Ahead of me I could see a military camp, so I propped up the motor cycle and walked forward, to the amusement of the sentries, with my hands above my head.

The police station had been taken over by the paramilitary Special Force, an elite organisation quite separate from the Uganda Army. I was received very kindly by the officer in charge, who declared that I should be 'retrieved' from Kangulumira. I explained to him what had happened the day before, and the delicacy of my own position. In the afternoon I made a painful return journey south in a Special

Force Land Rover bristling with armed men. What, I wondered in some distress, would my friends think of me? I explained to the lieutenant in charge that I had no wish to alarm the people, who had certainly not recovered from the army's vicious attack. He promised that he would be as quiet and as discreet as possible.

We arrived very swiftly outside Amos's house. Nampata, the woman who lived opposite, was caught standing in the middle of the road clutching a pot of water. I stepped out of the Land Rover and called to her. The pot slithered out of her hands and she ran towards me and pressed me to her ample bosom. Hoarsely, she begged the lieutenant not to shoot me. The soldiers laid all their weapons out of sight in the back of the truck and climbed out to stretch their legs. Amos, wide-eyed, came stumbling out of the house and I explained to him as quickly as I could what was happening. The lieutenant and one or two of his men were Bagisu, and they began chatting easily with Amos. While I loaded my trunk and field notes into the Land Rover some more people gathered, and to my great relief were able to see that nothing was seriously amiss. Nampata brought sweet bananas for the soldiers, while the lieutenant delivered a short lecture on the difference between the army and the Special Force. He had no difficulty in persuading the people that if they caught sight of an army man there was only one thing to do—run.

The soldiers were back in the truck, and as Amos and I tried to bid each other farewell the languages we shared deserted us. We clasped hands and jabbered at each other in English and Lugisu, then I clambered into the Land Rover beside the lieutenant before my upper lip betrayed me.

As we drove back through Kayunga, the lieutenant waved at the empty streets and remarked: 'The people have fled to the villages.' Only the Asian traders were in evidence, sitting in front of their closed shops as if to declare their neutrality and their readiness to recommence business. Near the police station I saw the unmistakable figure of Popatlal Savina, squatting on a bench outside his store in a white dhoti. Friday was pay day for the Special Force, and periodically he would rise to admit a small group of soldiers to the darkened interior of his shop.

In conversation that evening with the officer in charge I was able to piece together what had happened to the surveyors. Before the trouble began, Bob, their leader, had driven to Kampala. The others

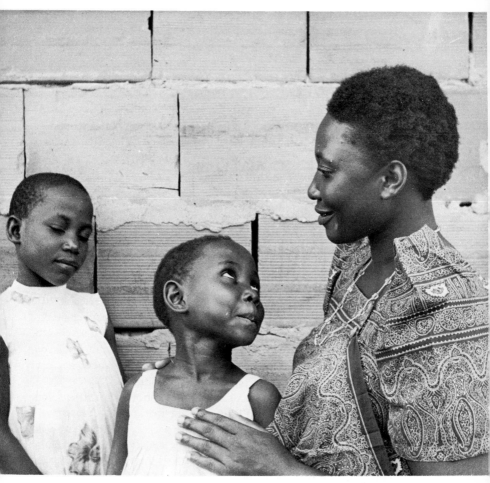

Nampata and her two daughters

were arranging to move camp to Galiraya when I met them on the road to Nazigo. Having been attacked at Kangulumira, and finding the road south blocked, they had headed back to Kayunga to look for medical aid. The clinic and the Saza headquarters at Ntenjeru were deserted, so they returned to seek refuge at the Kayunga police post. This was an unfortunate move, for an impassioned mob was at that moment closing in on the post. The police withdrew from the buildings, the surveyors returned to their truck and tried to drive through the approaching crowd. The vehicle was attacked and overturned; Tony Carter, aged 18, and David Jones, aged 19, were both killed, and Roy Morris was very severely injured. The arrival of the Special Force had been delayed by a pitched battle on the road into Kayunga, but by early on Tuesday afternoon order had been restored. The truck still lay where it had been overturned, and its contents had been thoroughly pillaged. Odds and ends lay trampled into the mud and a trunk, which had been opened raggedly like a sardine tin, stood on its side. I looked into the cab of the vehicle and at once wished that I had not done so. It seemed very difficult to imagine that the people I had been getting to know during more than a year in Bugerere could have been moved to such violence. I thought of Benalikaki, and could find no better justification for his death. Worst of all, I could find no assurance that I too, had I been caught up in the kind of fervour which had seized Kayunga that Tuesday morning, would not have been party to such acts of outrageous barbarity.

As I was about to return to the camp I noticed a sealed envelope lying in the grass. I picked it up and saw that it was addressed to a European living in Kenya. I put it in my pocket, intending to post it when I got back to Kampala. The night under canvas in Kayunga was very strange; I already felt that I had left Bugerere behind and was in transit back to the white urban world from which I came. In the morning my baggage was loaded again into the Land Rover and six soldiers climbed in on top. I rode sedately in front on the motor cycle all the way back to Kampala, the soldiers behind me on the alert for a possible ambush. The countryside seemed deserted and the heavy rain had brought out the coffee blossom, filling the air with fragrance. When my papers had been checked at the Special Force headquarters, we continued to the University.

My entry to Makerere was undoubtedly impressive. When he saw the Special Force Land Rover, the askari on duty at the gates dived into his box and slammed the door. As I thanked the lieutenant for his kindness and consideration the Institute Director, Ralph Tanner, emerged from his office to congratulate me calmly for my safe reappearance.

I am sure that during the next few days I dined out shamelessly on my experiences. As soon as I had sent my telegram home I was 'debriefed' by the Makerere Vice-Chancellor, and my return to the capital was politely acknowledged by the British High Commission. Amos and Joseph came to see me after several days, which gave me an opportunity to thank them properly for all they had done for me. I think that I was saved from the worst excesses of my own garrulity by an excursion to western Uganda during my last few days in the country. I went with one of the Institute Fellows, Simon Charsley, and I remember that we had to leave and enter Buganda in a military convoy but that we had the Queen Elizabeth game park virtually to ourselves. I was restrained and sobered by three other events which, even now, are painful to recall.

As I was sticking a stamp on the letter I had picked up at Kayunga I was seized by an irrational impulse to open it. I think it was as well I did so. The letter was from Tony Carter to a friend at home in Kenya, and I assume that he was carrying it in his shirt pocket at the time he was killed. Lying discarded in the grass, the envelope had been washed by the heavy rain, but inside, the sheets of paper were caked with dried blood. I burned the letter. In the week after my arrival in Kampala I went to see Roy Morris in Mulago hospital. He was able to speak to me for a few minutes but I was greatly shocked to find him so severely injured. He asked with concern how I had fared, but all I could say to him sounded sickeningly trivial. I left the hospital and his distraught parents feeling that I was very fortunate to have left Bugerere unscathed.

The third, and most chastening experience arose from a piece of personal stupidity. On the sunny Sunday morning a week after my return to Kampala one of the Fellows of the Institute invited me to join her for a picnic lunch on Namirembe hill, the site of one of Kampala's cathedrals. We had to drive past the foot of *Kabaka*

Anjagala, the avenue leading up to the Lubiri palace. My friend stopped her car and suggested that we might walk up the avenue to see what we could see. I argued against this, feeling that I had seen quite enough already, but she was determined to have a closer look. We agreed that we would walk about half way up the avenue to where a large tree had been felled across the road. There were no signs, no barriers, no sentries and nothing apart from what we already knew about Tuesday's battle to suggest that we should not proceed. We were very close to the tree when I saw a soldier rising from the ditch at the side of the road. I pulled my friend back and we turned to walk back to the car.

Several soldiers, who had been lying in wait, surrounded us and we were marched up to the palace gates. The corporal in charge made us stand against the wall and declared very aggressively that he intended to shoot us. I remember looking up into the clear blue sky and seeing the vultures turning slowly above the devastated palace. I could not believe that I should come to such a melodramatic end.

A sergeant appeared with pieces of rope to tie us up; flexing them in his hands he began to question us. His main concern seemed to be that we might be journalists and might have taken photographs of the palace area. At this time the government were anxious to disguise the fact that the battle at the palace had been hard and bloody. We were accused of being BBC reporters, a challenge which, even at the time, I found hard to take seriously. After some very bitter racial vituperation we were led back down the hill for an inspection of the contents of my friend's car. I remember that my greatest fear was that they might do something to her which would provoke me to some disastrous physical retaliation. However, their apparent purpose was only to frighten us, and in this they certainly succeeded. The film was pulled out of our cameras and exposed to the sun, and after we had written our names and addresses on the back of an envelope we were allowed to leave. There is no doubt that we were expected to go back and dissuade our inquisitive friends from making the same mistake, but we both agreed that we had no desire to talk about the incident. We returned to the Institute and sitting indoors tried, with dry mouths, to eat our picnic lunch.

On my return to Britain I spent a very pleasant summer in Cambridge reading about Uganda and discussing my work. Within a year

I had written a lengthy account of the Bugerere Big Farmers and had handed in my thesis. In 1967 I returned to Uganda to make a further short study of Big Farmers in Busoga District for the Cambridge African Studies Centre. For some reason which I cannot fully explain I could not bring myself to revisit Bugerere. This may have been something to do with the manner in which I had left it the previous year but in any case Buganda was still in a State of Emergency, which made it difficult to move around freely. Instead, I arranged to meet Joseph, Amos and some other friends in Kampala and Jinja, and from them I learned that Kamira and Budada were 'still there'. Although the rival political parties were no longer evident in the towns, things had more or less returned to normal.

The State of Emergency in Buganda was in fact extended at six monthly intervals until February 1971, shortly after General Amin's coup d'état. The letters I continued to receive assured me that my friends in Bugerere were 'still there', weathering the national political storms with great forbearance. During 1969 Dr Obote clamped down on the Democratic Party opposition, arresting its leader, Benedicto Kiwanuka, for writing a critical newspaper article. An attempt on Dr Obote's life in December provided a ready excuse for rounding up DP activists and turning Uganda into a one-party (UPC) state. By June 1970, sixty-six people were reportedly in detention under the terms of the nationwide State of Emergency which Dr Obote had declared after the assassination attempt.

On 25 January 1971, while Dr Obote was returning from a Commonwealth leaders' conference in Singapore, Major-General Idi Amin Dada seized power. He gave as his reasons the breakdown of law and order in Uganda, the recrudescence of tribalism, corruption and economic stagnation, and repressive taxation. The immediate reason for the coup was probably the pressure which Dr Obote had been bringing to bear on General Amin to respond to allegations that he was abusing his army command. In the brief honeymoon period which followed the coup, fifty of Dr Obote's detainees were released and Benedicto Kiwanuka was appointed Chief Justice. The State of Emergency and curfew were lifted, and Britain was among the first of the foreign governments to recognise the new regime. The previous November the Kabaka of Buganda, Sir Edward Mutesa, had died in London of alcoholic poisoning, and in February 1971 arrangements for the repatriation of his body and a state funeral were in hand. In a splendid 'act of reconciliation' with the Baganda, Mutesa was buried beside his ancestors in Kampala on 4 April. Shortly after this President Amin informed the optimistic Ganda leaders that re-establishment of the monarchy was out of the question.

After three months, the mood of enthusiasm began to evaporate. In March, President Amin suspended all political activities as 'a temporary measure' but promised an early return to civilian rule. Reports began to appear in the international press of mass killings and purges in the army. All 'reminders' of Dr Obote were removed from public places and a price put on the former President's head. General Amin accused Dr Obote of dividing and weakening the armed forces, and proudly announced that a rapid recruitment cam-paign had doubled the strength of the army and that large amounts of public money had been devoted to its re-equipment. In July an attempted coup d'état brought sharp reprisals and the prisons were once again filled with detainees. In August a military commission cleared General Amin of all accusations of misconduct dating back to charges of looting in 1965.

In 1972 the decline in civil order was rapid. President Amin's attempts to civilise his people included a decree banning mini-skirts and hot pants, and another demanding that the naked tribesmen of the north should wear trousers. While his capricious diplomacy amused the world, the General entertained Ugandans at home with a series of public executions. The British government was not at all amused when in September 1972 President Amin expelled the very large number of Ugandan Asians who held British passports. To the African citizens this was a popular move, and it released valuable business assets which the President could use to pay off his military and civilian supporters. By this and other means he has managed to survive several attempts on his life, 'invasions' from Tanzania appar-ently sponsored by the exiled Dr Obote, and sporadic attempted coups d'état.

Already a large number of prominent Ugandans had been liquid-ated, including the ill-fated Benedicto Kiwanuka. Towards the end of 1972 President Amin decreed that his soldiers should have the power to arrest without warrant any civilian. Next February he turned over the District administration of Uganda to his battalion com-manders, giving them the responsibility of appointing suitable sub-chiefs. In Kampala, thirty thousand people gathered to watch one of a series of public executions, designed to quell the rising tide of violent robbery. Dr Obote prudently ignored an invitation to return home unmolested, and instead addressed a letter to the African heads of state declaring that since he was ousted eighty to ninety thousand Ugandans had been killed. In June 1974 the International Commission of Jurists condemned the Amin regime for massive violations of human rights: 'By a series of decrees over-riding all constitutional safeguards and by a system of arbitrary repression operating outside any legal framework, there has been a total breakdown in the rule of law.' The report had been drawn up by Mr Niall Macdermott of Britain, and President Amin responded in a manner which was by now typical, threatening the lives and property of Britons in Uganda. However, he also appointed another Commission to discover why so many prominent people seemed to be disappearing.

In recent years I have heard very little from my friends in Bugerere. Amos was never a very good correspondent, but the last letter I received from Bonny Moses Sekasi in 1971 told me that William Lubega had been appointed Mutongole chief of Budada. I have been reluctant to write for I have been told that letters from Britain, a country which no longer has diplomatic relations with Uganda, may sometimes bring trouble to recipients. Of course, I often wonder if Kamira and Budada and all the people I met in Bugerere are 'still there'. I have no doubt that they are, for as immigrants they have learned a great deal about how to survive.

I also wonder whether Bugerere, as I experienced it, is 'still there' in the account which I have given in this book. Re-acquainting myself with Bugerere has certainly not simplified my views of it; indeed the account I gave of it ten years ago in my thesis is very much more clear-cut. For sure, social life will always remain much more complicated than our most elaborate descriptions and representations of it, but I have tried here to return to the detail of life in Bugerere and make evident the manner in which I personally discovered it.

Many of the people who talked to me in Bugerere did so because they wanted their children and grandchildren to have some understanding of their way of life. By reading my book, future educated generations would be able to learn something of the pioneering days.

For a stranger like myself this is a formidable commission, and I can only hope that I have represented the people of Bugerere in ways which they themselves would regard as both accurate and fair.

Dramatis Personae

This book is about a large number of different people. Although I have tried to make references to each of them sufficiently clear, the following list may be helpful in identifying people whose names appear more than once in the text. The part of their names by which I have referred to them is in italics, and they are arranged accordingly.

Abudu Gididu. Young Gisu immigrant who washed and cooked for me while I was living with Amos Natyera at Kamira.

Amos Natyera. Gisu immigrant to Kamira village in whose house I lived for eight months.

Raymond *Apthorpe*. Professor of Sociology at Makerere University; my research supervisor in Uganda.

Rainer *Arnhold*. Californian paediatrician working on child nutrition in Uganda; came to study the infants of Kamira and Budada villages.

Asinasi. Mother of *Amos* Natyera; 'mother' to me during my stay at Kamira.

Ayonge. Established settler in Budada village, from Lango District.

John *Bakisula*. Young immigrant from Busoga; the '*muganga*' or 'witch doctor' involved in the treatment of *Lubega's* sister (chapter eight) and *Kabu* (chapter nine).

Bakungulu. The people, many from the north of Bugerere, who followed the Ganda General Semei *Kakungulu*; their descendants, living in Bugerere and elsewhere.

David *Balugabamo*. Labourer in Kamira village; migrant from Kigezi District.

Benalikaki. A *muluka* (parish) chief from the Kangulumira area, killed during the disturbances in May 1966.

F. J. *Bennett*. Medical doctor with long experience of Uganda; visited me at Kitimbwa.

Israeli *Bune*. Sudanese immigrant, settled in Kamira village; successor to Gizaza as *Mutaka* (leader) of the village.

Caroline Hutton. Research Fellow at the East African Institute of Social Research.

Claudien Kabuguma. Young refugee from Ruanda, of the *tutsi* aristocratic caste, who visited me at Ntenjeru.

Paulo *Dawakuta*. Established Nyala settler in Budada village; uncle and arch-rival of William *Lubega*.

Bernardo *Gizaza*. The Mutaka (leader) of Kamira village; long-established Gisu settler (see chapter six).

Godfrey Binaisa. Young local government clerk who assisted me during my first month in Bugerere.

John. Kangulumira schoolteacher; very nearly became my assistant in Bugerere.

Joseph Kanene. My assistant throughout most of my stay in Bugerere.

Kabu. The madman who came to Kitimbwa; refugee of the aristocratic *tutsi* caste from Ruanda, working as a labourer in Bugerere (see chapter nine)

Kadada. The original settler in Budada village, now dead.

Kafifi. Very recent arrival in Kamira village, from Busoga District.

Kafuko. Young orphaned girl, born in Kamira (see the story of Kafuko and Mebulo, chapter six).

Semei *Kakungulu*. Ganda general who established control over Bugerere and made it part of the Kingdom of Buganda.

Kalimanzira. Ruandan labourer, involved in the story of Kafuko and Mebulo (chapter six).

Sam *Kasajja*. The *Askari* who guarded the rest house at Ntenjeru.

Kigate. Reclusive settler in Kamira village; from Ankole District.

Lameka *Kigozi*. The biggest farmer in Kamira village (see chapter nine).

The Hon. David *Kimaswa*. Democratic Party Member of Parliament for the Bugisu South constituency.

Benedicto *Kiwanuka*. Leader of the Democratic Party; first Prime Minister of Independent Uganda.

Issa *Kiwanuka*. Afro–Asian youth who visited me at Ntenjeru.

Kojjo Mupina. Chief of the Nyala people, ousted by *Namuyonjo* early in the nineteenth century (see chapter four).

William *Lubega*. Established Nyala settler in Budada village; my landlord at Kitimbwa.

Lukhoza. Long-established Nyala settler in Budada village.

George Willison *Luwano*. Newcomer to Budada village; one of the *Bakungulu* (q.v.); ostracised by the other villagers.

Luka *Manyala*. One of the first settlers in Kamira village; from Bugisu.

Simewo *Mazaki*. An established and popular settler in Kamira village; from Bugisu.

Mebulo. Young Ruandan labourer living in Kamira (see the story of Kafuko and Mebulo at the end of chapter six).

Mrs Amos Number One. My name for *Amos* Natyera's senior wife, *Nabusano.*

Mtesa (Speke's spelling). Mutesa I, the Kabaka, or King of Buganda, 1852–79.

Lameka *Mubiru.* A near neighbour of mine in Kamira village; prosperous Ganda farmer.

Joseph *Mukasa.* Established Ganda settler in Kamira village; cousin of Lameka *Kigozi.*

Kalisti Mukasa. Ganda settler in Kamira village, involved in court case (see chapter six).

George *Mukulu.* Sociology student at Makerere University who escorted me to Bugerere (see chapter two).

Mulengule. Established Gisu settler in Kamira village.

Erika *Musoke.* Village chief (*mutongole*) of Kamira.

Mr Musoke. Master of the primary school at Kangulumira.

Mutagasa. Established Nyala settler in Budada village.

Mutesa II. The last Kabaka (King) of Buganda, Sir Edward Mutesa; reigned 1939–66.

Nabusano. The senior wife of *Amos* Natyera; also referred to as *Mrs Amos Number One.*

Maria *Nampa.* Established woman settler in Kamira village; brewer and seller of beer.

Nampata. Woman who lived opposite *Amos* Natyera's house in Kangulumira.

Namuyonjo. Freebooting 'prince' who dominated the northern part of Bugerere in the early nineteenth century (see chapter four).

Mosa *Ngobi.* Immigrant to Kamira village from Busoga District; see the story of his arrival in chapter four.

Petero *Ngulabanga.* Labourer from Burundi, working in the Kangulumira area.

Martin Luther *Nsibiirwa.* A former Prime Minister of Buganda; absentee owner of a tract of *mailo* (freehold) land, part of which fell within the boundaries of Kamira village.

Edward *Nsubuga.* Chief (*mutongole*) of the group of villages which included Kitimbwa and Budada.

Apolo Milton *Obote.* Prime Minister of Uganda, 1963–66; President of Uganda, 1966–71.

Audrey *Richards.* Anthropologist and specialist on Buganda; rescued me from my financial plight, involved me in the 'Big Farmer' study and introduced me to Cambridge.

Esimafesi *Salongo.* Established and respected settler in Kamira village, from Busoga.

Popatlal *Savina.* Pioneer Asian trader in Kayunga.

Bonny Moses *Sekasi*. Young Ganda settler near Kitimbwa; staunch friend and adviser.

Sentongo. Nyala settler in Budada village.

Simon Musoke. Administrator of the East African Institute of Social Research at Kampala.

Martin *Southwold*. Anthropologist; specialist on Buganda.

Lario *Sula*. Sudanese immigrant to Budada village (see problems of farming and nutrition in chapter eight).

Sunday, usually *Mr Sunday*. The name by which I was generally known in Bugerere; pious-sounding rendering of Sandy, my first name.

Ralph *Tanner*. Director of the East African Institute of Social Research at Kampala.

Abudul *Tief*. Soga immigrant who washed and cooked for me during my stay in Kitimbwa.

Wamembi. Recent settler in Kamira village, from Bugisu.

Musirimu *Wamubireggwe*. Prosperous moslem who divided his time between Kamira village and home in Bukede District; much concerned about the welfare of Mrs Jacqueline Kennedy (see chapter ten).

Wasozi. Deputy to Erika *Musoke*, the village chief (*mutongole*) of Kamira.

Glossary

Names and terms in a variety of languages appear throughout this book, but the majority are in the Ganda language (*Luganda*), the lingua franca of the Bugerere immigrants. Like other Bantu languages, Luganda is highly inflected, and each class of nouns can take one of numerous prefixes, depending on grammatical context. The stem form is usually used in the text (e.g. 'Ganda'), but the following standard prefixed forms should be noted:

Mu—ganda (an individual Ganda person)
Ba—ganda (the personal plural)
Lu—ganda (the Ganda language)
Bu—ganda (the Ganda country)

The same set of prefixes are attached to other people, languages and places—for example: *Mu*soga, *Ba*nyoro, *Lu*gisu, *Bu*nyala.

As a rough guide to pronunciation of the Luganda words below, vowel sounds may be represented as follows:

a—as in 'far'
e—as in 'bay'
i—as in 'seek'
o—as in 'slow'
u—as in 'moon'

Syllables are stressed rather more evenly than in English.

Abanabugerere. The people of Bugerere; a collective identity which was gaining some currency.

Anyanya. Southern Sudanese guerillas, fighting against Northern Sudanese rule during the 1960s.

askari. Native policeman, usually applied to local government and private employees, and not to the Uganda Police Force.

Bulange. The parliament of the Kingdom of Buganda.

Bulondoganyi. Ganda name for what was formerly the southern part of Bugerere.

Bunyala. Ganda name for what was formerly the northern part of Bugerere.

Democratic Party (DP). The main opposition party in Uganda, led by Mr Benedicto Kiwanuka.

duka. Small shop.

gomasi. Long gown with tufted sleeves worn by Ganda women.

gombolola. An administrative sub-division of the Ganda Kingdom, usually translated as 'sub-county' (see Figure 1, page 18).

govumenti. Government; applied to land held in public trust by the government.

Hutu. The lower caste in Ruanda and Burundi.

imbalu. The circumcision rituals of the Gisu people.

jigger. A species of flea; the females burrow into the skin, usually on the feet, to lay their eggs.

Kabaka. Title of the King of Buganda; Sir Edward Mutesa II, the last Kabaka, ruled from 1939–66.

Kabaka Yekka (KY). 'The Kabaka, he alone'—name of the nationalist party in Buganda.

kanzu. Long nightshirt-like garment worn by Ganda men.

kitalla. A strip of land about 12 feet wide and of variable length, used to demarcate jobs for labourers in Buganda.

kitongole. An administrative sub-division of the Kingdom of Buganda, usually a *kyalo*, or village; the office held by the chief of this sub-division, who is called the *Mutongole* (see Figure 1).

kondo. Armed brigand.

kwashiorkor (Ghanaian word). Protein calorie malnutrition.

Luganda. The language of the Ganda people.

Lugisu. The language of the Gisu people of Mount Elgon, Eastern Uganda.

Lukiiko. Meeting place or council chamber; particularly the building where the Ganda parliament assembles.

Mailo. The Ganda freehold land tenure system established in 1900; called after the square *mile* units of the original allocation.

marwa. Millet beer.

Masaba. The Gisu name for their homeland at Mount Elgon, Eastern Uganda; otherwise called Bugisu.

matoke. The green banana staple food of Southern Uganda; usually eaten as a steamed pulp with something savoury like fish or ground-nut sauce.

mayembe. The black magic of Buganda; sorcery.

mbwa. Small black fly, *Simulium damnosum*, which used to infest the south of Bugerere.

mugagga (pl. *bagagga*). Ganda term for a rich man.

muganga. Luganda term for a magical specialist, translated here as 'witch doctor'.

muluka. An administrative sub-division of the Kingdom of Buganda, usually translated as 'parish' (see Figure 1).

mupakasi (pl. *bapakasi*). Labourer; usually translated as 'porter' in the English of East Africa.

murram. Hardened stony laterite used as road-surfacing material.

Mutaka (pl. *Bataka*). Ganda term for a clan head; used in Bugerere to describe a senior and established settler, and particularly the leader of a community (see chapter six).

Muzungu (pl. *Abazungu*). A European.

mweso. Ganda name for a board game of Arabic origin which is played in various forms throughout the world; otherwise known as Mankala.

nduulu. Whooping call, used as a distress signal in Buganda.

nkoko. Chicken; metaphor for the fee an official may collect, e.g. for issuing land. Another metaphor is *kanzu* (q.v.).

panga. East African name for a machete or cutlass, used by farmers throughout Africa.

pombe. A native beer, probably made from millet (see the prefatory quotation from Speke's *Journal*).

Saza. Administrative division of the Kingdom of Buganda, usually translated as 'county'. Bugerere is a Saza (see Figure 1).

Ssemaka. Ganda term for an established, property-owning family head.

talipa. Perch, fished from Lake Victoria and the Nile.

Tutsi. The ruling caste of Ruanda, overthrown in a bloody revolution in the early 1960s.

Uganda People's Congress (UPC). The ruling political party in Uganda, led by Dr Milton Obote.

waragi. White spirit, sometimes called 'Nubian gin'; distilled illicitly throughout Uganda, but now manufactured with a banana flavouring as the National Drink.

Select Bibliography

A. Political Development in Buganda and Uganda

David E. Apter, *The political Kingdom in Uganda: a study in bureaucratic nationalism*, Princeton University Press, 1961.
[A useful study of the years before Independence]

D. A. Low, *Buganda in Modern History*, Weidenfeld and Nicolson, London 1971.
[A survey from the early European contacts up to General Amin's coup d'état]

Ali A. Mazrui, *Soldiers and Kinsmen in Uganda: the making of a military ethnocracy*, Sage Publications, London 1975.
[An analysis of the Obote and the Amin regimes]

B. Buganda: Social and Political Background

L. P. Mair, *An African People in the Twentieth Century*, Routledge, London 1934.
[One of the earlier accounts of social organisation and patterns of social change]

John V. Taylor, *The Growth of the Church in Buganda: an attempt at understanding*, S.C.M. Press, London 1958.
[Notwithstanding its title, this book gives a vivid picture of rural life in Buganda]

L. A. Fallers (ed.) *The King's Men: leadership and status in Buganda on the eve of Independence*, E.A.I.S.R. and Oxford University Press, London 1964.
[A series of essays dealing with the economy, politics and social stratification in Buganda]

A. I. Richards, *The Changing Structure of a Ganda Village: Kisozi, 1892–1952*, E.A.I.S.R., Kampala 1966.
[Historical and anthropological account of a single Ganda village in Busiro County]

C. Migration, Change and Development

J. S. La Fontaine, *The Gisu of Uganda*, International African Institute, London 1959.
[Detailed ethnographic account of the Gisu people, many of whom have migrated to Bugerere]

A. I. Richards (ed.), *Economic Development and Tribal Change: a study of immigrant labour in Buganda*, Heffer and Sons, Cambridge 1954.

Caroline Hutton, *Reluctant Farmers? a study of unemployment and planned rural development in Uganda*, East African Publishing House, Nairobi 1973.
[Dealing with urban problems, settlement schemes and government planning, this book provides some excellent contrasts to the more spontaneous patterns of change and development I have described]

A. I. Richards, Ford Sturrock and Jean M Fortt (eds), *Subsistence to Commercial Farming in Present-day Buganda: an economic and anthropological study*, Cambridge University Press, 1973.
[The 'Big Farmers' study referred to in this book]

D. Fieldwork and the Anthropological Approach

John Beattie, *Understanding an African Kingdom: Bunyoro*, Holt, Rinehart and Winston, New York 1965.
[One of the very few candid accounts by a senior anthropologist of how he tackled fieldwork. Comparisons with my own experiences are interesting; Beattie worked in the Kingdom adjacent to Buganda *before* Independence]

Elinore Smith Bowen, *Return to Laughter: an anthropological novel*, Harper and Brothers, New York 1954.
[Using a *nom de plume*, this eminent anthropologist chose to describe her experiences of fieldwork in Nigeria in the style of a novel; very effective and amusing]

Colin Turnbull, *The Mountain People*, Jonathan Cape, London 1973.
[The famous Ik; a personal and profoundly pessimistic view of the problems of a small group of human flotsam in Northern Uganda. This book should be read and compared with *The Forest People*, an idyll by the same author]

A. L. Epstein (ed.), *The Craft of Social Anthropology*, Tavistock Publications, London 1967.
[A businesslike collection of essays about how anthropologists think they should set about finding things out]

Index

Principal references are in italics